THE AGE OF E-TAIL

Alex Birch, Philipp Gerbert and **Dirk Schneider**
OC&C and **The McKenna Group**

THE AGE OF

E-TAIL

conquering the new world
of **electronic shopping**

CAPSTONE

Copyright © Alex J. Birch, Philipp Gerbert and Dirk Schneider 2000

This book is based on *E-Shopping* by Dirk Schneider and Philipp Gerbert, © 1999 Gabler Verlag GmbH, Wiesbaden

The right of Alex Birch, Philipp Gerbert and Dirk Schneider to be identified as the authors of this work has been asserted in accordance with the Copyright, Designs and Patents Act 1988

First published 2000 by
Capstone Publishing Limited
Oxford Centre for Innovation
Mill Street
Oxford OX2 0JX
United Kingdom
http://www.capstone.co.uk

Capstone Publishing, Inc.
40 Commerce Park
Milford, CT 06460
USA
Contact: info@capstonepub.com

A catalogue records for this book are available from the British Library and the US Library of Congress
Library of Congress Card Number: 00-103176.

ISBN 1-84112-094-4

Typeset in Meridien by
Sparks Computer Solutions Ltd, Oxford, UK
http://www.sparks.co.uk
Printed and bound in the USA by
Sheridan Books, Ann Arbor, Michigan

This book is printed on acid-free paper

Substantial discounts on bulk quantities of Capstone books are available to corporations, professional associations and other organisations. If you are in the USA or Canada, phone the LPC Group, Attn: Special Sales Dept. for details at (1-800-626-4330) or fax (1-800-243-0138). Everywhere else, phone Capstone Publishing at +44-1865-811113 or fax +44-1865-240941.

Contents

Foreword

We live in changing times. How often have we heard that sentiment expressed? At the beginning of the new millennium what
stands out for those involved in business is an increase in the
pace of technology driven and enabled change. It is a dynamic
that is becoming evident in all consumer-driven industries.

Technology is already pervasive in our lives and touches us
as consumers and as business people. There is little in our lives
that is not touched in some way by information technology.
We live in a time where individual technologies are capable of
being knitted together at low cost, delivering functionality far
beyond what was envisaged as commercially possible only a
few years ago. The Internet and its associated technologies lie
at the root of these phenomena. Businesses and consumers
continue to embrace technology and with it more change, both

evolutionary and revolutionary. The 'Internet era' is about both the invention of new businesses and the radical reinvention of existing ones.

The 'Internet era' is well under way with well over 130 million people online. There are already examples of significant businesses that have misread its potential, the cost advantages and the pace of change it is bringing about. They underestimated the consumer's capacity and desire to adopt technology and to use it to interact and establish relationships with businesses, be it to extract better prices or higher levels of service.

We are witnessing the beginning of a new period in business–consumer relationships, where the technologically enabled consumer has begun to redress what has been a balance of power tipped strongly in favour of the business. As consumers we now live in an age of choice, and one in which the Internet now extends that choice into a truly global reach. We already see the effects of this choice in the rise of 'other' (or new and private label brands) as a major category in many consumer product areas. Electronic shopping will drive this even further, threatening the demise of even well-known brands. We also live in an age where instant gratification is a near reality in many areas of consumer purchasing. Gone are the days when one had to visit stores to browse for ideas and products. Increasingly, a vast array of goods and services are now a mouse click away.

Consumer behaviour is changing and bringing with it a transformation in the way businesses must think about customer groupings. Marketing has long sought to identify homogeneity within groups of potential customers and target segment focused marketing and advertising messages at these groups. But this discipline has been tied to and driven by the attributes of the physical world, while online consumers occupy an entirely different space. Behaviour and response in the two different environments do not necessarily coincide. In addition, the tools available to segment and target marketing have radically evolved, allowing marketing messages to be sent to individuals online in real time with instant and dynamic response, creating interactive, customized marketing campaigns for a segment of one.

In this era of choice, greater customer power, desire for instantaneous satisfaction, customised programs for individual customers and new capabilities in marketing, there is much for businesses to grasp. At a minimum, executives must understand the drivers behind these trends and identify those questions that they must answer for their own success.

The US leads the rest of the world in this area, but Europe is evolving rapidly. This book seeks, primarily for a European audience, to help in these tasks. Firstly it cogently identifies the forces that are shaping the redefinition of business – consumer interactions. It provides answers to the critical questions that businesses must address to be successful in serving the Internet customer, in the form of four steps to successful electronic shopping. Finally, it spells out a scenario along which the digital economy will evolve. It provides a basis for crafting a strategy for successful participation in the new era of business to consumer interaction.

The authors bring three complementary perspectives to their work. Philipp Gerbert has been working in Palo Alto with The McKenna Group creating Internet-based strategies for businesses, Alex Birch has been working in Europe with OC&C's media and content clients, while Dirk Schneider represents OC&C's European retail expertise.

They will challenge you to think; about brand relevance, about building customer loyalty, even about the true nature of 'product' and the sustainability of traditional economic models in some industry sectors. At the same time they will provide you with practical advice on how to succeed in the world of e-commerce.

Regis McKenna

Background

The Aim of the Book

Preamble: conquering the New World

Portugal, late fifteenth century – the spirit of discovery is in the air.

The confluence of three seafaring worlds, the Christian Mediterranean, the Arabian and the north Atlantic is spawning a host of new ideas. The diverse know-how of traders, academics and seafarers is brought together in Prince Henry the Navigator's famous school for shipbuilding and nautical science in Sagres on the Algarve coast of Portugal. A new type of ship, the three masted caravel, has been assembled using revolutionary new inventions. A central steering rudder and a flexible triangular sail enable sailors to steer a course against the wind, previously thought impossible. Compasses and astronomy from the Arab world allow the first sea charts to be drawn up, covering areas far outside coastal waters. Beyond the vast oceans lie enticing new lands.

A business goal soon crystallises: the sea passage to India. Pepper from the Malabar Coast, spices from the Moluccans and sea trade with China become the focal points for traders. Trade is firmly in the hands of merchants in the Mediterranean states, primarily the Venetians and Genoese, and the Arabs. But soon the race is on to circumnavigate Africa. Bartholemew Diaz successfully rounds the Cape of Good Hope in 1487/88. The sea route to India is traced out. This know-how gives the Portuguese a decisive lead that will eventually take Vasco da Gama to the coast of Malabar.

One man has a more original idea. An Italian, Christopher Columbus of Genoa, uses knowledge about the curvature of the earth, passed on from the Greeks to the Arabs, to plot a different path: sailing west to reach India. Turned down by the king of Portugal he receives money from the Spanish to carry out his plans.

Isaac Newton, creator of the Theory of Gravity, commented centuries later to his admirers: 'I could see so far because I was standing on the shoulders of giants.' In much the same way Columbus had his giants. He was an entrepreneur who climbed onto their shoulders and saw beyond his peers. Rather than joining the competition to circumnavigate Africa he struck out on a path of his own. Even from the shoulders of giants, however, Columbus could only guess at the New World he would find. His entrepreneurial spirit was to pay off, but in an unexpected way. The gold of the Americas replaced Indian spices and laid the foundations for the rise of the Spanish Empire.

As a result of the events begun on the, at the time, relatively unimportant Iberian peninsula, the world was conquered by the Europeans. In consequence the world has changed dramatically. But the direction of change could, however faintly, be discerned even at the end of the fifteenth century.

E-shopping: the giants are ready

Silicon Valley, end of the twentieth century: a new gold rush is buzzing.

The dramatic progress in the processing power of computers, also known as 'Moore's Law', the triumph of the PC and the networking of the world through the Internet is creating entirely new opportunities. At the start of the new millennium the sea passage to India is 'e-shopping'. Through the Internet the established customer relationships of all companies can suddenly be circumnavigated. Manufacturers, retailers and wholesalers today are as vulnerable as the Venetians, Genovese and Arabs of the late fifteenth century.

As a spawning ground for hi-tech industries Silicon Valley contains a fertile mix of relevant experience. The unique combination of technological know-how has produced amazing success stories. But the hi-tech industry has also shown how vulnerable market leaders are in a rapidly changing environment: every high school graduate in Palo Alto has understood that the economic threat is not to do your job poorly but to become irrelevant in what you are doing. Thus only one of the ten largest computer firms in 1985, IBM, is still in the top ten today.

Companies like Amazon.com and eBay have shown the way and enjoy a big lead. Amazon.com's customer databases are the modern equivalent of the charts of a Bartholomew Diaz – important tools that the others lack. Yet e-shopping initiatives are still risky and making no or at best very modest profits. Venture capital firms are nonetheless, like the Iberian monarchs before them, ready to finance such enterprises. They know that it is a race against time, any lead counts and the potential rewards are momentous.

The giants are ready – it is now up to companies to climb onto them and pursue the opportunities they spot. The race to circumnavigate the black continent is once again on and not yet decided. Hesitation is unpardonable because what were decades in the Middle Ages are now only months and days and an advantage of a few months can be crucial.

Joining the crowd is not, however, the only way to compete. Columbus showed us the way – in a radical upheaval completely new opportunities emerge. And the virtual world is much wider than the earth. It can accommodate more than one Columbus. We are just seeing the beginnings of the conquest of a New World of Shopping. We can, however, already see the revolution coming. And the early winners will reap fantastic rewards.

The aim of the book

This book is intended, just as in Henry the Navigator's nautical college, to bring together, analyse and further develop current knowledge to help entrepreneurial individuals and businesses make the right decisions in a period of upheaval.

First of all we are addressing the *entrepreneur* who is willing to grasp his opportunity. We describe the current state of play, the success factors and the techniques of e-shopping: the aids to circumnavigating Africa. We also consider future developments in e-shopping. Our hope is to be able to help entrepreneurs like Columbus emerge, adding their own ideas and producing new and original approaches.

We are also aiming at *manufacturers, retailers/wholesalers* and *media companies* with a strong traditional business. They are the Venetians, Genoese and Arabs of yesteryear, often bound up in traditional, multi-layered sales and marketing systems. We would like to help them craft a superior strategy for e-shopping. They can take part in the race, although their traditional strengths will prove of little use. They can oppose the onslaught, as the Arabs opposed the Portuguese at Mombasa – a defensive battle with only a delaying effect. Or they can look for new ways to put their current strengths to good use. Change in the face of adversity is often the route to survival. What would have become of the Portuguese dream if the Venetians and Arabs had, in spite of all their differences, reopened the old Pharaoh's canal that had been submerged for thousands of years? It could have enabled the journey by ship between the Mediterranean and the Red Sea several centuries before the French and the English.

We offer a perspective for *service and infrastructure providers*, who take part indirectly in e-shopping. The shipbuilders and maintainers of fortifications of Colombus' days are the infrastructure and logistics service providers of today. They need continually to evolve their own businesses and assess the prospects of their own customer base. Just as then, only those backing winners will grow.

Finally we have messages for *consumers*. They are the 'Indians' (American and Indian) of the New World of Shopping, who should at an early stage evaluate what the changes mean to them. Customers of the future can develop an 'attitude' and use the new players to their own advantage. They can, however, also fall into new dependencies – as Microsoft has demonstrated in another context with the lock-in to its Windows operating systems.

The authors

In the spring of 1999 a group of partners at OC&C Strategy Consultants had a heated discussion on the future of retailing, the birth of e-tailing and roles of the US and Europe in what is becoming a global marketplace. We saw the world from very different viewpoints:

◆ Philipp Gerbert lives in Palo Alto, the heart of Silicon Valley. His work focuses on convergence industries (telecommunications, computers, software, media) as well as creating Internet-based business systems for all industries. He examines e-shopping primarily from an attacker's point of view. He constantly receives how new business ideas on his desk which are ever-changing variations on the same basic theme: to use the Internet to lure customers away from established consumer goods and retailing concerns.

◆ Dirk Schneider lives in Germany and primarily advises clients in the European consumer-goods industry and retail. He observes how companies in the US have taken the opportunities and risks of e-tailing increasingly to their hearts. Whereas his clients in Europe often still seek advice on how to minimise its impact or even look for reassurance that they will be spared the ordeal.

◆ Alex Birch lives in the United Kindom and joins them by enriching their experience and targeting it to an Anglo-Saxon environment. He works with media and convergence-sector companies and retailers. Much of his work in the last few years has taken him to the US to deal with impact of the Internet and new media on companies' traditional business models and to help chart the routes to surviving and profiting from radical change.

We realised in the discussion that we had very different starting perspectives on how the future of retailing might evolve. We decided to write a book on e-tailing with relevance to Europe and the US. We want to inform a European audience, which seems in danger of lagging behind North America, and to urgently promote the aggressive adoption of the new possibilities which we see. At the same time, for an audience in North America, we want to provide both a review of and new thoughts about the routes to success, at home and abroad; for as we have said, the winners in the new race have not yet been determined.

Content and structure of the book

The book's twelve key themes give you an idea of its content:

1 *The future of shopping is online*
  E-shopping has reached a mass-market audience in the US and is set to conquer the world from there. For the established retailers and entrepreneurs the critical question is not which sector is ripe for Internet trading, but rather where has the game already been decided.
2 *Traditional physical assets are dead weight*
  Established companies must question the fundamentals of their business – otherwise an Internet start-up will do it for them. E-shopping is not about exploiting an additional sales channel, but about establishing a whole new business. Middlemen disappear, as do industry and sector boundaries. Established positions become obstacles on a path to the future. Traditional physical retail formats must restructure fundamentally to adapt to the new environment or perish.
3 *New players seizing power*
  New players are building up a lead in e-shopping. New com-

petitors are springing up everywhere, and competition is becoming increasingly intense. Portals and 'market makers' could hold the land rights for the next bonanza.

4 *Survival of the fastest*

The Internet has stimulated a new corporate Darwinism. Survival and winning become equivalent. Market leadership and the creation of successful new retail formats are critical. Cards for tomorrow's high-stakes poker game are being dealt today. Even brick-and-mortar players have to accept the Internet as the medium of the future and transform real world assets into – ideally entertainment-orientated – 'clicks and mortar' complements.

5 *Internet shops need new brands*

Traditional brands are yesterday's news: Internet brands have to be young, international and broad (i.e. able to encompass an as yet unknown spectrum of products). Superior brands are magnets to the Internet. The best players master the full repertoire of e-shopping promotion.

6 *Context makes the difference*

Internet stores have no chance if they are 'cloned' from the physical world or merely extended catalogues on the net. Product availability is no longer an issue, 'context' in the form of 'content', community' and 'commerce' drives the difference between success and failure. Convenience is also critical.

7 *Customer loyalty is most important but increasingly difficult to create*

The restless customer undermines an e-tailer's profitability. Winning loyalty is like entertainment; you must always offer more. Internet customers, however, demand personalised, rather than mass-marketed offers.

8 *Built-to-order offerings will upset traditional value chains*

There are hardly any limits to personalisation. Successful e-tailers will offer almost everything tailored individually to the customer.

9 *The Internet will pervade every communications device we use and more*

Connectivity is tomorrow's watchword. Televisions, 'smart phones' and other intelligent equipment capable of connection via the Internet will fuel the pace of change. Our 'net kids' will always be online and enjoy 24-hour access to information and artificial intelligence resources.

10 *Digitisable products will be free*
Digital products, for which the marginal cost of production and distribution is zero, will spark guerilla warfare waged by consumers unwilling to pay for them. Software, music, books and films will be first. Current legal frameworks will collapse. Risk takers can take their chances for reward now.

11 *Innovation will be driven from the duality of product and service*
The Internet is the ultimate self-service medium and will cut many service industries to the quick. The key concept here is 'duality', the complementary combination of products and services.

12 *Survival requires equity financing*
Traditional financial markets have a hard time with intangible company values. We offer a survival kit for the fast-changing Internet environment to every entrepreneur and investor. It teaches entrepreneurs the necessity of the many new uses for equity, and investors how to navigate through future turbulence.

These 12 themes give a flavour of the 12 chapters of our book. It is divided into three parts with four chapters in each. In the first part of the book we review the current market and competitive dynamics as we see them and introduce the most significant *strategies for the e-shopping age*. In the second part we walk through how to go about setting up a successful Internet business. It contains *four steps to e-shopping success*. In the third part we lay out the path ahead. We describe the infrastructure of the future, digital goods and services and the role of the capital market. This part provides a guide on the way *towards a digital economy*.

So that you can orient yourself when reading, our e-tail searchlight will illuminate the themes in each chapter.

A web site for the book – *www.theageofe-tail.com* – offers additional information and current developments. We hope it will also serve as an area for discussion.

We hope you enjoy your reading!

Alex Birch, Philipp Gerbert and Dirk Schneider

Introduction

The Net Imperative

In late August 1999 Merrill Lynch, one of America's leading investment houses, downgraded all retail sector shares. The justification: it expected an onslaught from online retailers in the 1999 Christmas season – cutting into both volumes and prices of 'brick-and-mortar' companies. Two days later Robert Nakasone, CEO of the once feared 'category killer' Toys-R-Us, earned the unwanted honour of becoming the first CEO of a major retailer to be ousted because he had not responded adequately to the attack of online aggressors.

Clearly, in the eyes of the shareholders e-shopping is starting to bite.

Is e-shopping going to affect retail only?

No! E-shopping affects all consumer businesses. Every company operating in a value chain that ends in a consumer will be affected. *Retailers* are clearly in the epicentre of e-shopping's earthquake, but *wholesalers* have to reinvent themselves too. Some are quickly learning to do 'packages of one' and to play a central role in e-shopping rather than being 'dis-intermediated'. Consumer goods *manufacturers* are trying to jump onto the Internet bandwagon, only to learn that the consumer does not appreciate their traditional product-centric approach. The *media companies*, with news and music at the forefront, are faced with consumers getting their product 'cost-free' in a digital format. These companies understand that they have to embrace the Internet and learn how to develop a profitable new business on it with revolutionary pricing models, or face certain extinction. Telecom players and Internet service providers are watching how their traditional infrastructure revenue is suddenly used as a loss leader in e-shopping and are rushing to get into the game themselves. Every kind of *service company*, starting with the most sophisticated financial services, is beginning to grasp that the Internet is the ultimate self-service medium and struggling to adjust their business model. Feel free to extend this list yourself: what do you think will happen to real estate? Or health? Or government?

Is the real e-commerce revolution in business-to-business?

No again! Obviously business-to-business is going to move 100% online, or can businesses interact effectively in any other way? The amazing phenomenon is not, how many business-to-business players have started to leverage the Internet, but rather, how many still have not. But Internet usage in itself is not a revolution. It is in the consumer space where companies have to reach millions of people that the true potential of the web emerges. The changes in economics of customer interaction are staggering. Perhaps we should relabel e-shopping: instead of 'business-to-consumer e-commerce', we should call it 'consumer-to-business e-commerce', which stresses the most fundamental change. Also, in the consumer area, do not underestimate the numbers. Almost all statistics leave important parts out: for example many don't want to mention the sex industry but it is big business. Others regard services as a separate thing, though not only are they the most affected, but the web is actually turning most product businesses into service businesses. Elsewhere statistics for goods such as cars and houses, for which the research is done online but the actual transaction occurs off-line, are often not included. Not to mention of course that statistics excel in showing you last year's numbers. Just ask any Internet start-up how relevant it considers those to be.

The real revolution is going to happen in the consumer space! It is here that the business systems have to change most dramatically and traditional assets can become completely worthless. Previously unthinkable models, combining 'high delivered value' (convenience, product range, service) with 'low price', not only become possible, but are expected. For example the built-to-order approach to personalise PCs or customise clothing, where the avoidance of time-perishable stock makes the economics work. We come back to this specifically as it applies to retailers in a moment.

Is e-shopping primarily a US phenomenon?

No again! But let us be more precise: The US enjoys a tremendous structural advantage for Internet players. It is the largest homogeneous market (there is no 'Common Market' online in Europe!), has by far the largest online consumer base today and the use of the web has penetrated everyday life in a much deeper way. In addition, Internet sales in the US receive a subsidy from the absence of sales tax. We believe that pure e-shopping players have to succeed in the US first, or they will simply be swallowed by their US counterparts later. But consumers in the rest of the world are embracing the web quickly. Interestingly some of the US advantages in online plays may be disadvantages when it comes to a combined online/off-line play. The point being that the sales tax regime actually forces companies into a pure online play, preventing most of the 'brick-and-mortar' players in the US developing consumer-friendly 'click-and-mortar' (i.e. combined online/off-line) concepts. In the rest of the world the current absence of dominant online players gives traditional companies a better chance of success-fully entering the Internet space.

Sadly, some of these perspectives have triggered the wrong conclusions in traditional companies all over the world. Many view the Internet as merely a sales channel and treat it as an add-on without fundamentally questioning their current business system. They are wrong! The 'Net Imperative' demands that the Internet be embraced as the central medium of the future and companies concentrate on developing truly comple-mentary off-line value (context and convenience, entertain-ment, customer acquisition and loyalty). Current asset bases should be aggressively transformed, built or divested accord-ingly. Strangely, in the US pure web players might actually be the first to develop a winning 'click-and-mortar' proposition – offline advertising is the first area to become dominated by them. The rest of the world has been infected by e-shopping, but hopefully in some respects it will leapfrog the development in the US.

Is e-shopping just a fad, driven by inflated valuations?

No again! Granted, most of the valuations of today's pure e-shop-ping players are outrageous and partially reflect the frustration of investors with the web strategies of established players. As a result, and for a variety of more intrinsic business reasons, every player in the Internet today must learn the art of equity financ-ing. An immediate consequence of the sky-high valuations is a glut of money, leading to a heavily subsidised, fiercely competitive online world. In particular price competition will be brutal, further enhanced by the ability of consumers to apply sophisticated, easy-to-use technology to optimise their shopping. This is bad news for the profitability of consumer businesses in the immediate future and the very survival of some players. It is, however, not an entirely unnatural phenomenon to occur in a fast changing environment. During the evolution of the earth, the Cambrian age was marked by the fastest rate of creation of new species, but also by the fastest rate of elimination of species. There were lots of dead ends. Staying aloof and preserving one's current form, however, is the surest way to extinction. Certainly the Cambrian age was not a 'fad', and likewise the Internet will not 'go away'.

Does customer inertia win time for traditional companies?

No again! Consumers are slow to change, but competitors become much faster to exploit any incremental shift. The record for building a so-called 'second generation' Internet company from scratch (to our knowledge held by Epinions) is down to twelve weeks. These 'instant companies' are fast to capitalise on even the slightest change in consumer preferences. Thus the time frames for established players to change keep shrinking dramatically.

Is it too late to experiment?

Finally an emphatic yes! Developing an e-shopping strategy without a thorough understanding of the current environment is criminal. You might just as well burn money!

This is what this book is all about. We try to give a comprehensive overview of the developments so far. And a practical guide on how to proceed. And a vision for the future to come. Strategy matters in these times of change and we cannot do it for you. But we can help.

We refrain from the temptation of becoming too US-centric. Certainly most of the lessons learned come from the US. But e-shopping is a world-wide phenomenon and the advice of this book should apply in any country. If anything we concentrate on Europe, which is the next continent to evolve and arguably the most interesting sample for the general business environment to come in other parts of the world, i.e. in Asia, Latin America and Africa.

We focus strongly on Internet plays only. 'E-shopping' is about getting the online consumer business right. We consider this to be the most important aspect. Most traditional companies fall into the trap of worrying about the way to combine e-shopping with their current assets before they fully grasp the Internet game. First you have to accept the 'net imperative' and truly understand the potential of the green field approach of a pure play serving your customers. Then – and only then – can you lean back and evaluate what to do with the current assets you might control and whether there is an interesting way to leverage them to complement the online business.

Part I

Strategies for the E-shopping Age

Our beliefs are simple.

The next age of shopping will be defined by electronic media. 'E-shopping', the sale of goods and services to consumers over the Internet, will, within the foreseeable future, not only be the most important growth market for consumer goods businesses, but will cause a revolution in all industries.

The future of shopping is online, driven by explosive demand for virtual shopping. Electronic shopping affects your business, whoever you are. All types of goods will, sooner or later, be affected by Internet trading. The issue is not which industries and categories are right to enter as e-shopping players, but where is it already too late to get in.

Established competitors – manufacturers, wholesalers and retailers – have very few advantages in Internet retailing or 'e-tailing'. Their *physical assets will become dead-weight* holding them back. Established companies have to think about shedding and reducing their dead-weight and taking today's business imperatives on board.

The main competitive battles in electronic shopping are not going to be between manufacturers and retailers, as they have been to date. The battles will be fought between established retailers and *new players*, who are appearing everywhere and making bold bids to seize market power. Markets are becoming increasingly competitive and the basis for lasting competitive advantage more transient. In the early stages of new market formation, market leaders can win grand prizes but lose them just as quickly.

Everyone competing in these new markets is in a race to get a foot into the customer's door. *Only the fastest will survive.* Any aspiring e-tailer has to learn from the lessons of the current e-tail leaders and use them to create their own leadership position, building creatively on others' experience to date.

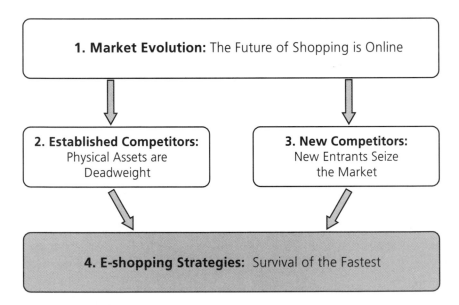

Fig. I.1   Summary of Part I.

Chapter 1

The Future of Shopping

is Online

In the US, e-shopping is causing a stir among established retailers as it represents an opportunity to create a 'format' which
was previously unthinkable, namely delivering high value, personalised product and service at low cost. Meanwhile in Europe, traditional shopping seems to be out and e-shopping may
be just the stimulus the market needs for growth. Since the
mid-90s in Europe there has been a gradual slowdown hitting
many retailers. Inflation-led growth can no longer be relied on
to move sales and profits up every year with reassuring certainty. In many sectors prices are stable in real terms, and in
some instances falling. Retailers are frustrated by restrictive
planning regulations in their quest to provide consumers with
larger-format stores offering greater product choice and availability. A limit on suitable space to open is a brake on growth.

Retailers, wholesalers, manufacturers and service providers, wherever you are! You can secure a future which includes valuable growth if you manage to set up innovative businesses in electronic shopping. If not you'll be hit hard. The future of shopping is online, with or without you.

E-tail searchlight illuminates Chapter 1

◆ *Retailing in the new millennium needs innovation*
In the US e-shopping represents a format revolution for retailers. In Europe it can re-invigorate the prospects of players in traditional consumer businesses operating in mature markets with low growth prospects.

◆ *E-tailing works – ask Amazon.com*
Amazon has proved that e-tailing creates growth in the market. But just copying Amazon.com won't help you.

◆ *The Internet is your chance for growth*
The World Wide Web is the fastest-growing medium of all time and, despite much apparent hype, the economic benefit it will bring is underestimated.

◆ *The US is way ahead – will Europe be colonised?*
The US is leading the e-tailing revolution. If they fail to act fast and decisively, Europeans will be colonised.

◆ *Electronic shopping affects everyone*
Your customers today are Internet shoppers tomorrow. Sooner or later every category will be affected by electronic shopping. In some areas it is already too late to get in.

◆ *Barriers to adoption are falling fast*
Barriers to online shopping are falling fast, spurred by recent developments.

◆ *E-tailing is your problem too!*
In some consumer goods categories, up to 50 per cent of sales will be Internet based. Take part, and eat your own lunch, or get used to having an ever smaller appetite.

Retailing in the new millennium needs innovation

As we have said, e-shopping is about change in all consumer industries, not just retail, but the logic of its potential in retail, particularly as it applies to buoyant markets, needs specific understanding.

The US has been the home of much retail innovation in the last 30 years. The ideas that US retailers have developed, with respect both to different shopping formats and to their supporting business models, have been successfully exported to many other parts of the globe. The discount store format of Wal-mart, the category-killing stores and warehouses of Toys 'R' Us and Home Depot, the warehouse club of Costco and the rebirth of the department store by the likes of Macy's, with store-in-store formats and other innovations, are all examples of evolution of retail formats. Isn't e-shopping merely another innovation along a path of progress?

We don't think so. It is much more than this. Lay aside the speed at which change is happening with this particular 'format' innovation, (which speed, by the way, is enabled by the fact that there are no physical stores to construct, staff and stock) and consider the business 'space' that e-shopping occupies with respect to retail formats. All the previous formats 'trade off' two essential dimensions: 'price' and 'delivered value' (see Fig. 1.1). 'Delivered value' can be considered as an aggregation of a number of factors including elements such as convenience, product range and service. Price is clear.

Until now, it has been intuitively (and obviously) the case that it is very difficult to exist in the extremes of this 'trade-off'. For example a 'high price' but 'low delivered value' position is not likely to be very successful with consumers! Conversely a 'low price' but 'high delivered value' position has been economically irrational (or at least very unattractive) to the retailer. Note that we said 'until now'. The Internet and e-shopping have changed this fundamentally. Many retailers still consider e-tailers to be discounters, delivering low service at low price. But they are fundamentally mistaken. Aggressive price discount-

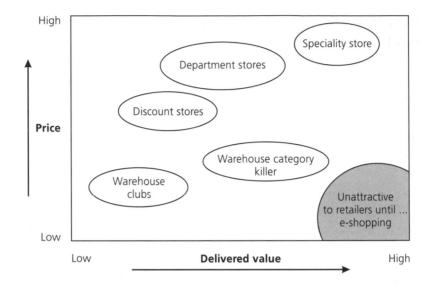

Fig. 1.1   Retail formats – 'the trade-off'.

ing by the pioneers should not lead you to equate them with the traditional discounters. What the Internet really does is to allow e-tailers to occupy a business space that was previously untenable, delivering high value at low cost (and price). This is the reason for the new gold rush fever. Those to stake their claim first can potentially dominate the space – given a number of other features of doing business on the Internet which we discuss elsewhere in the book.

Achieving dominance of a format has enormous value – but is also very challenging in this instance. As we have just said, it requires using new technology, new marketing skills and new business processes to make profit in what was previously a profit desert.

We believe that online shopping is of huge significance (in the US and elsewhere) as it will have knock on effects on most of the other retail formats we have described.

Just as Walmart and Home Depot are deemed responsible for the decimation of local neighbourhood stores in their respective categories, so online stores will have a profound effect on today's established formats. The effect is not a 'sledgehammer' blow of large market share loss to online shopping – although in a few specific categories this may happen. It is more subtle. E-shopping is beginning to re-segment retailers' customer bases in ways which they had not previously considered. In some cases the most attractive and profitable retail customers, those who are cash rich but time poor, are moving online.

E-shopping players are rather noisy stealth bombers flying through the traditional air defences of today's established retailers. You know they are coming, you can certainly hear their deafening PR noise, but you still can't pin down precisely where they are eating into existing customer bases. A seat in the plane is open to a number of potential pilots: e-tailers, manufacturers, wholesalers, entrepreneurs. Its targets are exactly those customers that 'big retail' cannot afford to lose, but may take time to realise they are losing. Irreparable damage can come swiftly.

In Europe the situation is even more serious. Firstly, there are hardly any European players at the forefront of e-shopping – and the expansion of US players can happen at the speed of light.

Secondly, Europe's traditional players are already operating in a stagnating market. We expand on this below. If you prefer to see the glass half full, then e-shopping is the new growth format that entrepreneurs have been waiting for!

The majority of European consumer goods businesses do not operate in attractive growth markets. Regardless of continuing economic development, manufacturers, retailers and service providers are preparing for very low or zero real growth in the new millennium.

A return to a period of rapid demand growth, mirroring the experience of the 1980s, allowing supplier profit margins to grow and covering up the structural weaknesses of retailers is just not going to happen in the mature markets of Western Europe. The truth is stark: retail markets are generally saturated and economic growth will stimulate demand in only a few niche areas.

There are a number of reasons that this lack of demand growth is structural and more likely to be permanent than transitory. *Demography*, for one, is changing. The population of the major European countries will start to decrease in the new millennium. At the same time, the advancing age of the population will cause a reduction in demand in many core categories. The last of the 'baby boomers' are now reaching middle age. In Europe, 16 per cent of the population is over 65 today and this is set to rise inexorably. The European Union projects that the over-65s could reach as much as 25 per cent of the population by 2020, with a third of these being over 80. The UK proportion of over-65s, currently at around 17 per cent today, will grow in line with this as will those over 80. In Germany, the largest and in this respect a reasonably representative nation, over-60s are projected to move up from 20 per cent of the population in 1990 to 30 per cent in 2020. Consumer demand patterns will be significantly altered. Older populations consume systematically less than 30–50-year-olds and across a very different mix of products and services.

Lack of demand growth is further exacerbated by a *real loss of buying power* in the economy, for people on middle incomes in particular. A period of low wage inflation has combined with a very significant structural shift from full- to part-time jobs in many sectors. Layer on to this much less certainty over job security now than existed in the '70s and '80s and the consequence is that the income situation becomes ever more uncertain. In the '90s these trends have already led to a reduction in personal disposable income (PDI) available for private consumption in a number of wage earning sectors. By 2005 the demographic trends identified earlier mean that Europe's working age population will begin to decline and buying power will begin to reduce in the economy. This will be exacerbated by a rising tax burden on those working, to fund those who have retired.

What is even more serious for retailers is that the *expenditure on consumer goods* for private consumption looks like being in long-term decline. In Germany, a powerhouse of consumer spending for many years, consumers spent 40 per cent of PDI in 1988 on short- and medium-term consumer goods like food, clothing and personal hygiene; ten years later it was only 32 per cent. In the UK the same has applied, although less dramatically, with a decline from 44 per cent to 40 per cent of PDI spend in these categories. Attractive market growth rates are not forecast for any one of these short- and medium-term categories. Other than personal computers and mobile phones, only leisure and health goods and services are expected to show slight growth. In the UK, real growth in consumer spending slowed from an annual average of over 5 per cent in 1985–1989 to less than 3 per cent in 1993–1997. In Germany, 'retailing' as a channel has been shrinking since 1992.

A further stake in the heart of consumer-led demand growth for traditional retailers is *consumer behaviour* that has changed in the '90s. Shopping no longer has the connotations of status associated with conspicuous consumption that it enjoyed world wide in the second half of the '80s. Shoppers who 'shop smart', not conspicuously, are on the increase. These consumers want to see more value for their money and they have less time and inclination to shop themselves. Fashion and its influence on consumer behaviour is changing too. In the 1980s much consumption was dictated by a number of very strong brands in specific categories on an almost global basis. In the 1990s and beyond, consumers are becoming more fragmented in their allegiance to specific brands. Better-informed consumers are becoming less loyal – to brands and to shops – as the fashion cycle speeds up.

How are traditional 'leading' companies in Europe reacting to these developments? *Consumer goods' manufacturers* are hardly offering innovation. In spite of constantly introducing new products, manufacturers are failing to raise the value of their products in the eyes of the consumer. The failure rate in new-product innovation speaks for itself. Leading brands are cannibalising their own sales with ever new variations, while third- and fourth-tier brands are becoming weaker and weaker. It all leaves the impression that the consumer goods industry is at its wit's end so far as innovation is concerned. Even experienced market leaders appear to be keen to drive top-line growth through frenzied sales promotion campaigns, rather than investing in innovations and the further strengthening of their brands.

European retailing is digging its own grave by constantly increasing selling space. In the '80s and '90s, retail sales areas in

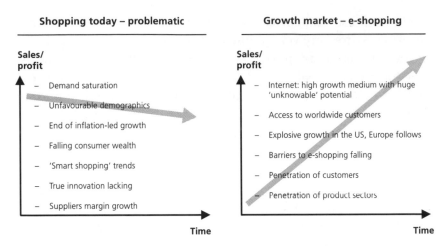

Shopping today – problematic

Sales/
profit

- Demand saturation
- Unfavourable demographics
- End of inflation-led growth
- Falling consumer wealth
- 'Smart shopping' trends
- True innovation lacking
- Suppliers margin growth

Time

Growth market – e-shopping

Sales/
profit

- Internet: high growth medium with huge 'unknowable' potential
- Access to worldwide customers
- Explosive growth in the US, Europe follows
- Barriers to e-shopping falling
- Penetration of customers
- Penetration of product sectors

Time

Fig. 1.2   The future of retail is online: European perspective.

the leading industrial countries in Europe more than doubled even though the population increased only slightly. Given a real reduction in demand, this rapidly turns into decreasing sales area productivity, followed by cost-cutting. The sector as a whole can't then discount and price-cut its way out of trouble. In the UK, in grocery retailing in particular, the arrival of the Walmart wolf, wearing the sheep's clothing of Asda, leaves very little room for other grocers to drive volume growth through price reduction. Everywhere in Europe consolidation is increasing. The grim reaper's diary for the new millennium is full of appointments with retailers in Europe.

The retail sector's dismal prospects are also being reflected in the personnel market, where retailers are becoming increasingly unattractive as prospective employers. Surveys of high-school graduates show that jobs in other industries are much preferred. The drastic action by Marks and Spencer, one of the UK's largest and most admired retailers, in 'terminating' many of its 1999 graduate trainees before they had started with the company, is a stark reminder of the bleak outlook for retail entering the new millennium. Across Europe, shopping at the end of the millennium is in a slough of depression. There are a few shining examples of pan-national innovation and growth, such as Ikea, who remain in the limelight, but most players are taking on the look of losers. The whole industry is fighting a rearguard action and is looking back fondly at the margins and growth rates of the past. Mega mergers are on the cards.

Electronic shopping works: ask Amazon.com

And then there was Amazon.com. We have no choice but to start a discussion of electronic shopping with Amazon.com: the mother of all Internet shops. Even though it was neither the first Internet retailer (or 'e-tailer' as we will now call them) nor was its original business model likely to be a success for the long term, it has proved two things:

◆ you can sell goods successfully over the Internet
◆ e-tailing can take significant market share from traditional retailers.

Amazon.com is the best-known electronic shopping brand in the world. It is the most visited virtual retailer and a benchmark in the retail industry for online success. As the largest Internet book-shop, Amazon has shown that the combination of a wide selection (more than 2.5 million titles, versus some 100,000 in a bookshop), low prices (justified by doing without a network of branches) and shopping comfort (simplicity of access, selection and ordering), can build huge sales volume on the web. They have shown how you build on success systematically, using in-novative customer loyalty and partner programmes.

Jeff Bezos, Amazon's founder has laid down what amount to three basic rules for his staff that capture the spirit of Ama-zon:

◆ *Be obsessed with your customers*
Concentrate on the whole experience the customer has with you, and constantly look to improve every detail of their interaction and your business processes.
◆ *Remember that the Internet is still in its infancy*
Always look for new opportunities and possibilities.

◆ *Satisfy each individual customer*
Dissatisfied customers don't influence five friends but 5,000 newsgroup readers.

Guided by these rules, Amazon.com has not only been a successful e-tailing pioneer, but remained at the forefront of development in this rapidly changing environment. Its success has been driven by a number of other important principles it has followed:

◆ *Strategic choice of types of goods*
Unlike Jason Olim, the music enthusiast who founded CDNow, Jeff Bezos made a specific rational choice for books as his target sector and then extended into related goods at the right time.
◆ *Systematic expansion to become a shopping hub*
Amazon now supplies CDs, videos, toys and electronics, greeting cards and auctions as well as books. It has interests in online pharmacy, grocery and pet shops and sporting goods, and enjoys a reputation that lends credibility to any sector it chooses to enter. In September 1999 it rein-

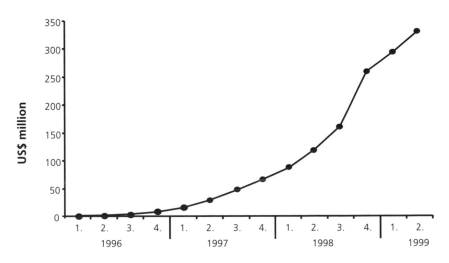

Fig. 1.3   Amazon's turnover growth.

forced its offer as a shopping destination with the creation of zShops. These allow third parties to create individual stores within the Amazon shopping space.

◆ *Formation of strategic partnerships*
Amazon has a clear policy of close co-operation with the other leading Internet companies like Yahoo, AOL and Dell.

◆ *Early internationalisation*
Amazon entered the most important European markets early in its corporate life.

◆ *Omnipresent advertising on the net*
Amazon has a hundred thousand advertising banners on the Internet, has built a network of ten thousand partners ('affiliates'), and is the leading advertiser on the net.

◆ *Excellent customer loyalty*
Amazon is acknowledged as leading the way in customer-relationship management on the web and more than 70% of sales are to repeat customers.

◆ *Creating value through investment*
Amazon has pursued a policy of rigorously investing for growth and long-term value.

Amazon has grown revenues at an astonishing annual rate and is aiming at a turnover for 1999 of around 1.5 billion dollars compared to a 1997 turnover of 150 million. The company is in a position to conquer large parts of the electronic shopping market. Investors appreciate this, even though, in some analysts' view, Amazon has a number of things to put right to fully justify its stock-market value.

Amazon has shown us how powerfully the new game can be played: how you can expand fast; how a great e-tailing brand can be extended, both geographically and into new categories; and how you can make it hard for latecomers to catch up. In spite of this proof that e-tailing does work, Amazon's success has also led many observers to a number of false conclusions, namely:

◆ e-tailing is constrained to packaged goods;
◆ copying Amazon is the best way forward;

◆ pure e-tailing is all about discounting and will never operate at a profit.

We will discuss why these are false conclusions later. For now,
let's reflect on the scale of the opportunity that the Internet
represents.

The Internet is your chance for growth

To understand e-tailing you first have to believe in the potential of the Internet as a medium. Luckily much has already been
written about this as a background to generating that belief, so
we will only recap the most important perspectives relatively
rapidly.

The world wide web is the fastest-growing medium of all
time. The telephone took 40 years to connect ten million users
to each other, the fax 20 and GSM standard mobile phone ten.
The web has connected 10 million users in only four years. By
the end of the millennium 200 million people world-wide will
be using the web. Most of them will live in North America and
the developed countries of Europe and Asia. These are markets
which currently represent more than 80 per cent of worldwide
consumer spending.

Perhaps you are already saturated with graphs turning up
everywhere showing the 'exponential' growth of the Internet.
Suffer us to add one more, just to clarify the fact that, in our
view, current projections for Internet users are only the tip of
the iceberg if one is to understand the economic benefit of the
web.

The lower part of the graph in Fig. 1.4 shows the known,
steeply rising number of Internet users. But the more interesting question is about the *economic benefits of the Internet*. We already know from other networked media, like the telephone,
that the functional utility of a communications medium grows
with the number of connections, i.e. with the square of the
number of subscribers. This is shown by the middle curve. But
that is by no means all. While the telephone only allows com-

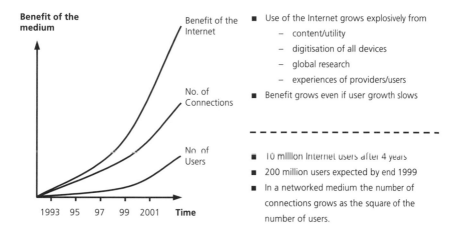

Fig. 1.4 Massive Internet growth.

munication between users, the Internet enables people to link to interactive communication media and personalised content. Constant new service offers, the increasing number of digitally enabled devices, the globalisation and rapidly accumulating experience of suppliers and users, all add to the value that the Internet can deliver to its users. The benefits of the Internet as a medium will increase *explosively* with the growing number of subscribers. The top curve in Fig. 1.4 makes this clear. Even when new-subscriber growth rates drop, economic benefits to users will continue to grow as the medium becomes more intensely used and as innovations for its use are made. Studies show that the uses made of the Internet become more varied the longer a subscriber has had Internet access.

In Chapter 9 'The Infrastructure of the Future', we describe in more detail some aspects of future Internet developments as we see them. We can only guess at the full potential of this extremely young medium today. We are strong believers that the market is underestimating the growth potential of the web. Remember that Alexander Graham Bell first thought that the telephone could be used to relay concerts – instead it has became a much more widely applicable and essential means of communication.

Given the economic benefits of the Internet as a tool for interaction and the economic motivations of companies it is highly likely, in our view, that interaction between companies ('Business-to-Business' or 'B2B') will rapidly shift to be almost 100 per cent Internet based. Embracing the Internet as an important, if not the most important, part of the future is relatively predictable in terms of a direction for a business engaged in B2B commerce.

E-tailing, engaging in 'Business-to-Consumer' (B2C) commerce, will also rise massively. There remain, however, many open questions about what are successful strategies for business-to-consumer e-commerce. It is these questions that we deal with in the book, attempting to provide a strategy handbook for actual or would-be e-tail practitioners.

The US is way ahead – will Europe be colonised?

Figure 1.5 shows the penetration of Internet usage in various countries.

The US has the highest number of Internet users and this US dominance of the Internet is supported by three factors:

◆ a high penetration rate (and relative accumulated experience of users);
◆ a high absolute number of users and the resultant 'network multiplier' effect which has already established the web as a valued tool in American business and society;
◆ the fact that there are no time-dependent usage fees in the US, allowing users to accumulate experience at a low fixed cost.

These factors combine to give the US total dominance on the Internet, to the extent that, for example, around *90 per cent of all loading processes on web-sites is done from the US.*

Let's take an everyday example that demonstrates the very significant differences between the US and Europe. In Europe if one wants directions to a company, one usually gets these by

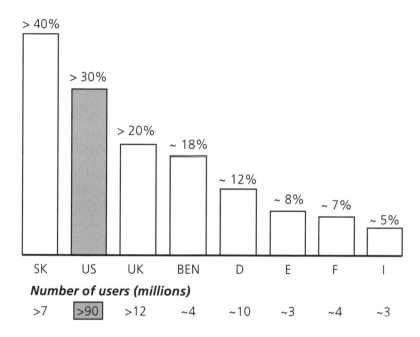

Fig. 1.5 International comparison of Internet penetration.
(Source: Benchmark Group, VUA, IDC, Forrester, journaldunet,
OC&C-Analysis.)

phone or fax, or one looks at a map. In Silicon Valley one turns
to an ever-present desktop or laptop PC, clicks on the (permanently connected) Internet browser and either downloads a
'directions' diagram from the company's web-site or searches
for it with Yahoo maps and if necessary prints it out. This example may seem banal, but it shows the fundamental differences in attitudes to using the Internet as an everyday tool.

The reasons for the US's lead are generally well recognised.
Firstly the Internet originated there. US companies and organisations led the Internet movement and the US has been the
birthplace of most Internet-related industries. In the consumer
area, the practice of not paying for local calls provided an ideal
basis to encourage the rapid adoption of the Internet into private households. The relatively low cost of personal computers
has also contributed to high take-up rates.

Europe is trying to catch up quickly, but prevailing conditions are not so favourable. Internet access costs are, with the potential exception of the UK, still high. Despite economic union, the European market is fundamentally more fragmented than the US domestic market, with many more systemic barriers to Internet adoption. These include language differences, more proprietary PC operating systems, multiple technical communications protocols, significant national differences in the quality of communications infrastructure and wider differences in user behaviour and propensity to adopt new technologies.

Judging the climate for e-tailing in Europe

Given these observations about Internet take up rates, the environment for e-tailers varies widely across Europe. In the spring of 1999 we carried out a comparative study of European countries with our international colleagues at OC&C. We considered a number of criteria to judge the e-tailing potential for various countries in Europe: the spread of PCs and Internet penetration; Internet access costs; users' disposable income; the number of 'Internet-ready' suppliers, and other criteria. The rankings are as follows:

- ◆ *very good*
  United Kingdom
- ◆ *good*
  Scandinavia
  the Netherlands
  Ireland
- ◆ *satisfactory*
  Germany
  Switzerland
  Austria
  Belgium/Luxembourg
- ◆ *adequate*
  France
  Italy

◆ *poor*
remaining countries.

The UK looks set to follow the US development curve fastest and already demonstrates a booming user *and* supplier market in electronic shopping. The recent success of Freeserve, stimulating the provision of so-called 'free' Internet connection (of which more later), has been an important catalyst for growth. Scandinavia, the Netherlands and Ireland already have good conditions for rapid growth in electronic shopping and e-tailing because of the high penetration of online households and the high number of English-speaking users. English-language websites actually have the most use and acceptance in these countries.

German-speaking areas have been behind until now, as have French-speaking Belgium and Luxembourg, but Germany offers good development opportunities for the future. Growth was hindered by prohibitively high Internet access costs, although these came down significantly in 1999. As a consequence Internet penetration in Germany should at least double from 10 to 20 per cent in the course of 1999.

France is strongly underdeveloped in Internet terms, probably due to the high user acceptance of Minitel, a proprietary communication system. Italy has been a slow starter in Internet development because of the low private use of PCs, and a perceived low-quality fixed-line telephone infrastructure. Both countries could, however, catch up quickly. The operators of Minitel announced in June 1999 that they intended to migrate the service to the Internet. If they succeed in equipping French households quickly with an Internet-capable Minitel, then France would, at a stroke, overtake even the UK in terms of Internet penetration. Italy's starting position could be underestimated too. In the early 1990s Italy was forecast as being one of the slowest-growing European markets for mobile telephony. In fact it has emerged as one of the fastest, partially driven by the fact that a mobile phone has become a must-have 'fashion' accessory while traffic congestion, unreliable public transport and habit spur continuous 'rescheduling' of meetings. Similar drivers could trigger rapid growth in e-shopping. The remaining European countries have, so far, played no real part in e-shopping and e-tailing.

Overall, opportunities for rapid development are most favourable in north and central Europe. Every European company interested in e-tailing should consider how it gets to the forefront of these markets. Be aware, however, that in terms of finding a market which is in aggregate equivalent in scale to that of the US one needs to include the whole of central and southern Europe. Unfortunately there is no trace of a 'common market' on the Internet – very few European sites have significance outside their home markets. Pure European Internet players, i.e. companies with no existing assets outside the web, will have to develop the lion's share of their customer base and early e-tailing experience in the US – otherwise their best hope is to be acquired by a fast-growing US equivalent. This is a challenge but not an impossible one. German Internet start-up Tiss, a supplier of 'grey market' airline tickets, has demonstrated success in doing just this.

A word about other countries. The strength of the 'big three' economic groups is just as influential on the Internet as it is in the world economy. North America, Europe and the developed countries in Asia will do the huge majority of Internet business. In comparison with Europe, prevailing conditions in Asia are much tougher. Let us take Japan as the dominant player. In the early days, the Internet there was in English because Japanese characters were difficult to reproduce. This excluded most of the Japanese population as potential users, and is only now beginning to change. Internet access costs are at least as high as in Europe. In the B2B arena, the Japanese traditionally place much more value on personal contacts in business than business people in Europe and the US, potentially slowing adoption of Internet tools in this sector. In B2C commerce, the e-tailing heartland, local infrastructure elements (PCs, telecommunications) are not as well developed as in North America. There are also complexities in Japan related to fulfilment which go beyond those present in Europe. Complicated multi-layered sales and marketing channels put a brake on active Internet trading. Finally there is a large amount of locally tailored and locally customised software in both business and individual use which creates difficulties for e-commerce at a desktop level. Overall the conditions for e-tailing in Japan are less favourable than in Europe.

A final word on country readiness needs to note that a number of governments have recognised the importance of the Internet as a factor in a nation's economic competitiveness. Canada and Finland have demonstrated foresight on this front. Many countries, like Czechoslovakia, New Zealand and India are aggressively investing in the spread of Internet skills, knowing that it is vitally important; at least in establishing the next generation of knowledge-based companies. E-tailing globally is going to gain further momentum from this encouragement at the national policy level.

Will Europe be colonised?

In the US the success of e-tailing is clear. Christmas 1998 was a mass-market 'E-Christmas'. VISA announced that in the fourth quarter of 1998 eight per cent of credit-card sales for the US retail trade came from Internet transactions. This trend has been sustained in following quarters.

The growth of e-tailing in the US continues to drive a dynamic supplier sector. Telecommunications companies, software houses, advertising agencies, logistics experts and credit-card companies are all poised with offers to support e-tailers. US players are using their rapidly accumulating experience to develop their electronic formats and their customer-management skills. Developments in the US, and observation of what has driven winners and losers, are increasingly important reference points for management decisions in Europe. At the same time, the Americans are coming to Europe. US e-tailers, and associated suppliers are already opening for business in Europe.

You won't be surprised, given the observations above, to find that by far and away the largest electronic-shopping volumes are forecast for the US. Figure 1.6 gives a summary of

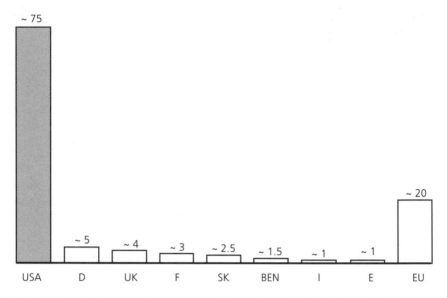

Fig. 1.6   An international comparison of e-tail sales in 2002 (figures in $US billion). (Source: Benchmark Group, VUA, IDC, Forrester, journaldunet, OC&C-Analysis.)

e-shopping sales for 2002 by country, based on forecasts drawn up by the various relevant market-research houses (Forrester, Jupiter, Datamonitor, Yankee Group). These predict a value of around $80 billion in e-tail sales for the US.

Europe is forecast to generate only some $21 billion in total. The critical thing with these forecasts is that they essentially imply total domination by US e-tailers, even in European sales. If proven right, these forecasters are effectively predicting that the majority of European e-tail sales will be generated by US-based businesses, either with operating subsidiaries in Europe or with local fulfilment capability. It implies a rough time for aspiring European e-tailers in many categories.

'The Europeans must go online in a big way this year, otherwise they will be overwhelmed by US suppliers like Amazon.com or eBay. That will be a rude awakening for the Old Continent.' This is Scott McNealy, Head of Sun Microsystems, expressing his views in a magazine interview in June 1999. We believe that bold plays by European companies can counteract the potential domination of e-tailing by US players. However, winning in Europe will not simply be a question of copying American models; the pace of change is too fast for that. Columbus was never going to reach India before the Portuguese sailing via Africa, so he set out west instead. This book is intended to provide you with the necessary know-how and tools to help you develop an original e-shopping strategy.

Electronic shopping affects everyone

The effects of e-tailing will be felt in all customer segments and across all categories of goods and service. The degree of impact will differ in many instances, but ultimately we, and all our purchases, will be touched in some way by the web. Internet users are rapidly becoming more representative of the general population than early Internet adopters were. 'Net-heads' were initially young, male and technically orientated. Increasingly we are all 'net-savvy' but those with the highest propensity to use the net still represent a more attractive customer group. Internet shoppers today have a significantly higher-than-average income and a higher-than-average level of education. They are both better off and more loyal customers. In the US about two-thirds of those actively using the Internet to shop are over 40, and almost as many women as men shop over the net. With the growing number of households online, the demography of Internet shoppers will increasingly approach the population average. One thing is certain for retailers – today's customers are tomorrow's e-shoppers.

E-shopping is going to affect all categories of goods. Accepted as being at the top of the list are personal computers, software, music, books and travel tickets. These categories currently make up almost 80 per cent of what is e-tailed. Some commentators regard these as the only products that can be sold in volume over the Internet. We don't share that view. The e-tailing boom is not limited to these categories. Experience in the US now indicates that clothes, lifestyle goods, gifts and cars are the next growth markets on the web. Suppliers

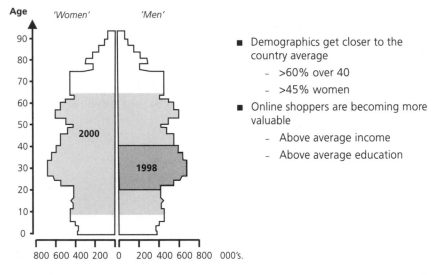

Fig. 1.7   Everyone's an e-shopper: electronic shopping penetrates all customer groups.

are recording rapid growth in Internet orders for event tickets, toys, cosmetics, health products and garden articles. Today in the US you can find, and buy, almost anything you want over the Internet. The only safe assumption is that ultimately *every category will be e-tailed*.

You should not regard the current sequencing of what categories have taken off fastest as reflecting a similar sequencing in terms of suitability for e-tail. Firstly, relatively standardised products were easy to sell over the Internet because customers had few uncertainties about them. It was also the case that these products had relatively high value and profit for their size – for example books, CDs and PCs – which makes shipping them economic. It is clear that other categories are catching up rapidly. The most dramatic growth will be in goods which can be digitised, like software or, in future, music, travel tickets and even books. Sale and delivery over the Internet will become the standard retail channel. We discuss the particular nature of digitisable goods in more detail in Chapter 10. The far-sighted have already reached this conclusion. 'Egghead', one of the largest US software retailers, very early on abandoned its physical branches and now supplies products only over the Internet. Services, especially financial services, and even information-based government services, are in a state of flux. We discuss the future for services in Chapter 11.

In other categories, like food and everyday goods, e-tail may only penetrate a small part of the customer base. However, a change in a small part of the customer base's behaviour can still represent big changes. Swedish supermarket Konsum, based in Stockholm, announced in February 1999 that more than 12 per cent of its sales had been ordered over the Internet. In Switzerland, Le Shop has established itself as a successful Internet supermarket. The most important factors in its success are believed to be:

- a concentration on families as the target group (with high average sales per order);
- a fully featured distribution and logistics infrastructure (using owned warehouses, delivering on a seven-days-a-week basis);
- an efficient cold chain for the delivery of fresh and chilled goods;
- the close co-operation of a number of strong partners (e.g. Nestlé, Schweizer Post, Swiss Telecom).

Le Shop, which went through a relatively long ramping-up phase, has now shown that food, a relatively difficult category, can be successfully e-tailed. Swiss market-leader Migros, observing Le Shop's success, has followed suit and set up an efficient Internet shop. In the UK the success of supermarket chain Tesco's home-shopping service, Tesco Direct, has spurred once sceptical rival J Sainsbury into launching a similar service. The biggest gamble in the groccery sector is currently taking place in the US. Here WebVan, a well-funded 'e-food' start-up, has commissioned warehouses at a cost of $1 billion – demonstrating storming confidence in future growth.

Food e-tailing is an area where, although the percentage of the category e-tailed is low, the size of the category makes for some substantial business opportunities. In the USA in 1998 food consumed at home was worth around $500 billion. Even at modest e-tail penetration of one per cent this is a sizeable opportunity. As most supermarkets demonstrate, there are many non-food categories which are purchased in the same basket. If these are added, an additional $200 billion of sales is available and e-tail penetrations may be higher here. This is perhaps the perspective which WebVan is taking (along with its powerful venture capital backers).

As we said earlier, the new e-tail formats are in their infancy with many still being tested, along with their supporting business models. This explains why online grocer Peapod, founded in 1989, is struggling to reach $100 million in revenues ten years later with a stock price 50% off its IPO peak, while WebVan, founded in early 1999, attracted a reputed $400 million of venture funding to launch itself into this market place.

In the US a 'consensus forecast', constructed from predictions that we have seen, suggests the following broad perspective at a category level: e-tail penetration will be above ten per cent by 2002 in today's most Internet active categories, namely software, books, music, PCs, travel tickets. With goods that already represent efficient e-tail ranges, electronic shopping will achieve a market share of between one and ten per cent. Some significant categories will still have Internet sales of less than one per cent. These may include food, do-it-yourself goods and furniture, because they are often supplied locally and/or because of the complexity of their range. As a general rule, products and categories which are particularly suitable for e-tailing are those which:

- have a high built-in *quality standard*, i.e. those which do not have to be physically checked by the customer when they are making the decision to buy (e.g. music and many strongly branded goods);
- are *context intensive*, i.e. need explaining and where ancillary information is valued (e.g. travel and health products);
- have a high *potential for reduced transaction costs*, i.e. e-tailing allows significantly cheaper sales and distribution costs than in the physical world (e.g. clothing and software);

◆ can use *customer feedback* to enhance and tailor the product for the customer (e.g. computers and cars);

◆ have a high profit potential per 'cube' (if being shipped).

This does not mean that categories not fulfilling all these conditions are unsuitable for electronic shopping. With the introduction of e-tailing the rules of the game in many industries is going to change. Internet shops will find new ways to help and stimulate the consumer to buy things electronically. It is worth remembering that we are in the infancy of a new retail format. Physical world retailers have had 30–40 years to hone their formats to sell their products in optimal fashion. Most e-tailers have not yet had 30 months! We talk more about e-tail formats in the second part of our book and how physical world retail practices can be combined with e-tail ones to great effect; for example, how the quality of a range of textiles for sale over the Internet can be assured by sending out physical samples. E-tailers will find ways of offering more information, more effectively and with more excitement over the Internet. Direct-to-home logistics capabilities, as well as digital-transfer technologies, are constantly evolving to lower-cost positions. Industries are changing their business processes, particularly relating to how they capture information and integrate it with their manufacturing processes, to offer products tailored to the individual.

Categories of goods which today we perceive as being difficult to e-tail will not be in the future. Let's consider upholstered furniture: at first glance a category which is not very suitable for e-tailing. Customers want to see patterns, feel material textures, sit on the merchandise etc. However, once they have decided what it is they want, it becomes clear that they can't take the model in the shop; they have to wait weeks for manufacture; the piece is damaged on delivery and then retailer and manufacturer dispute whose fault it was. At the same time it is expensive when compared with 'flatpack' options. Look beneath the surface of the business processes of retailer and manufacturer to understand what drives the cost and complexities in retailing in this category. You soon find a situation in which efficient and effective communication of information, avoiding bottlenecks and dead-ends, can significantly speed up and reduce the cost of the whole system. These benefits can be passed to the customer in the form of faster and better service: furniture becomes an e-tail-friendly category because e-tailing can give the customer enormous benefits. Although there are players already addressing this market (e.g. furniture.com) their offering is still a far cry from an efficient, customized, built-to-order process.

Constructing a summary for the potential development of e-tailing in categories by country around the world, the picture given in Fig. 1.8 emerges.

Let us dwell a little on this summary picture. We are often asked which products are ripe for e-tailing in Europe. Illustrations like Fig. 1.8 are often interpreted to suggest that entering book e-tailing in southern Europe is likely to be among the lowest risk options. This is the wrong interpretation.

The question is not in which areas is e-tailing possible, but where is it already too late to get in!

We discuss later in the book how simple it is for the successful e-tailer to expand geographically. The Internet has globalised retailing at a stroke. It is too late to try to start e-

State of development by sector	Country	US, Canada	North and mid-Europe (D, UK, etc.)	Other countries (F, I, etc.)
High	– Computers – Software – Travel – Books – Music	Electronic shopping mandatory for survival. Market leaders partially established.		
Medium	– Clothes – 'Lifestyle' – Toys – Drugstore/ cosmetics		Market established, no leader in place, followers with much freedom	
Low	– Food – Electricals – Furniture – DIY/gardening – Other		Opportunity for market leadership	

Fig. 1.8   E-tailing opportunities by category and country.

tailing books in Germany and the UK. Even a company as large as German publishing giant Bertelsmann is finding it hard to compete with Amazon.com, who only made a serious entry into Europe in late 1998. Bertelsmann and its partners have had to invest almost $500 million in the Internet book trade, and estimated recently that they were still two years behind Amazon.

How much fun do you think you would have entering the Internet book market now? Who knows, perhaps you might survive – but not create any value. Consider furniture or bicycles instead. If you really are keen on music or books, get into electronic distribution, for example Internet music delivery or electronic books, which we discuss later.

In this context, keep in mind what Royal P. Farros, CEO of the Internet print shop iPrint, said:

In 1995 I was driving down Highway 101 on the San Francisco Peninsula and was passing by Bay Meadows Race Track. On their digital billboard, they were advertising, http:// www.RaceTrack.com. Literally, I almost pulled to a stop on the freeway and just stared. All I could think was 'Geez ... if these guys are going online, then everybody's gonna go online.' That's when I knew it made business sense to put a print shop on the Web.

(Source: *Striking it rich.com*, J. Easton, New York, 1998.)

Royal P. Farros was clearly not the only curious driver, and the race track not the only billboard. 1995 was the year of the phenomenal stock market debut of Netscape; one in which many Americans recognised the business potential of the Internet and most of today's leading e-shopping companies were founded. Thus the leading American suppliers in well-known categories have a four-year start.

Does this mean Europe is doomed to follow, rather than lead? Not necessarily. E-tailing offers enormous scope for creative business initiatives. There will always be successful newcomers who find a gap in a market or a niche to serve. No-one predicted the early success of Internet retailers like Garden

Escape with garden equipment or Virtual Vineyards with wine. The Internet offers an opportunity even for the most exotic products. Coffee manufacturer Kona Kava, in search of new markets, had to close its unprofitable physical retail outlet on Hawaii, but rapidly developed as a niche supplier into the North American market by retailing over the Internet.

The barriers are coming down fast

Let's be honest: until now in most of Europe there have been serious obstacles to electronic shopping. But four major barriers to growth will rapidly disappear in the coming years:

- *The spread of private Internet connections* is increasing. Currently the number of households connected to the Internet is increasing by over 50 per cent a year. In a few years, the majority of private PCs will have an Internet connection. The Internet will soon reach more than half of the shopping population. A 99 per cent reach for the medium is a potential reality with the advent of the TV as an Internet access method. Set-top boxes, making it possible to have Internet access through your domestic television set, are already available today. Regardless of the exact technical solutions, interactive Internet shopping through the TV will be possible for almost every household in Europe in a few years. As the Internet reaches a mass-market audience, so e-tailers will benefit from the effects of scale reducing their operating cost positions, and further increase the attractiveness of their offer to customers.
- *Ease of use and speed* will constantly improve. Internet technology is still in its infancy with many web-sites too slow and anything but shopper-friendly. Developments are rapidly being made, however. Leading e-tailers are becoming aware of the need for speed. Using both raw investment in servers and network capacity, as well as sophisticated third-party traffic management providers, they are optimising their networks so that even today's technological slow-

coaches (those with analogue telephone connections) still have reasonable access speeds in spite of huge increases in Internet traffic. In future, broad-band technology is likely to be rapidly taken up by consumers and will greatly increase the transfer speeds and capacity for most of the population in five to ten years.

◆ *Data security* used to be the most frequently used excuse for not shopping on the Internet. To counter this, common security standards have been set up. Banks, credit-card companies and telecommunications suppliers are pursuing a clear push strategy to promote online sales. New payment systems, such as 'Electronic Wallets', which manage customer data centrally have already been tested and can offer security to both customers and suppliers. In the US people embraced the use of credit cards on the web in 1998.

◆ Q*uality of the e-tailer's offer* until recently did not represent a broadly based, customer-winning proposition, as most e-tailers did not have very much experience of the medium. The failure of early, simplistic 'virtual malls' is a reminder of this. The strength of e-tailers' offers is now growing rapidly. In a few years we will reflect on today's e-tailer sites as a driver of a top-of-the-range car today looks at the models of the 1920s and 1930s. Content and design of the web pages will be more and more polished and put together to provide a shopping experience, rather than a simple gateway to a transaction. New approaches to customer loyalty will mean growing satisfaction among Internet shoppers.

In Chapter 9 we discuss the technologies and innovations that are going to encourage the growth of electronic shopping in the next few years in more detail.

E-tailing is your challenge too!

Most e-tailers, even in the US, are operating at a loss. However, a few select market leaders have exceeded the break-even point. Operating cash flow is positive, but profits are not apparent because these e-tailers are investing massively – in new customers, new ranges and new technology. Amazon is a case in point here, with a steadfast belief in the need to invest in securing an unassailable lead over the competition.

The capital markets are giving Internet stocks very high market values. Ask yourself which company has more value: yours or an e-shopping one? And what would happen if you decide you want to, or need to, buy one of these 'small' Internet shops? Instead, most of the highly rated Internet brands are themselves on a corporate shopping spree, announcing new acquisitions in quick succession. We explain the importance of understanding the capital markets peculiar interpretation of Internet stocks, and its importance for development, in more detail in Chapter 12.

Overall the effects of the Internet on consumer-goods businesses are going to be significant. For the year 2010, several – clearly highly speculative – forecasts tell us that 10–50 per cent of consumer goods sales will be made over the Internet, dependent on which category of goods.

In many instances the growth of electronic shopping is going to be at the expense of traditional retailers. In stagnating markets this creates fierce competition between companies not active in e-shopping. If you are not eating at the Internet table, get used to having a smaller appetite.

The great challenge for today's established companies is to participate successfully as e-tailers in the future. Even if today's revenues seem small, remember that the hand to play in the future is being dealt now. This book should help you. You will realise that the answer is not simply about setting up a new sales and marketing channel within the framework of an existing business. Anybody who thinks that will fail. E-tailing is about establishing a new business that demands new strategies, new capabilities and reintroducing oneself to the most important actor in all of this – the customer.

E-tail searchlight on web-sites for Chapter 1

- ◆ Amazon   www.amazon.com
- ◆ Forrester Research   www.forrester.com
- ◆ Datamonitor   www.datamonitor.com
- ◆ Yankee Group   www.yankeegroup.com
- ◆ Egghead   www.egghead.com
- ◆ Le Shop   www.le-shop.ch
- ◆ Migros   www.migros-shop.ch
- ◆ Furniture.com   www.furniture.com
- ◆ Webvan   www.webvan.com
- ◆ iPrint   www.iprint.com
- ◆ Garden Escape   www.garden.com
- ◆ Virtual Vineyards   www.virtualvin.com
- ◆ Kona Kava   www.konakava.com

Chapter 2

Physical Assets are Dead-weight

Electronic shopping will radically rewrite the rules of competition in retailing. The traditional value-chain linking manufacturer, wholesaler and retailer will very soon be yesterday's model. But how will new types of competition impact those in the retail business chain, and, most crucially, who stands to win and lose? Many assume that manufacturers will benefit from direct sales by cutting out retailers. A subtler analysis of the situation recognises that it is *retailers* who should benefit in the age of electronic shopping. It may well not be today's entrenched retailers who will control the virtual stores, but the game is there to be won by new and old retailers alike. They must play by a new rulebook and adapt their propositions accordingly.

E-tail searchlight illuminates Chapter 2

◆ *Traditional industry boundaries are disappearing*
The boundaries between manufacturers, middlemen and retailers are being gradually eroded. Electronic shopping will accelerate this trend.

◆ *Today's middlemen are fighting to reinvent themselves*
Wholesalers, travelling salesmen, brokers and agents are most threatened by the Internet if they do not reinvent themselves.

◆ *Manufacturers have limited opportunities in direct sales*
The window of opportunity for consumer-goods manufacturers to leverage the Internet is closing. In spite of some early successes of built-to-order concepts, today's consumers have no sympathy for the product-centric position of most manufacturers. Instead the latter have to become as customer-centric as retailers.

◆ *Most established retailers are on a losing track*
Incumbents have been slow to react to the challenge of commerce over the Internet and, as a result, most of them are trailing far behind best practice in e-shopping.

◆ *There are fewer immediate synergies than one might think*
The strengths that established companies may have in the real world are of little help to them when it comes to competing in the virtual one.

◆ *Entrenched positions are a hindrance*
Traditional market leaders get caught in a variety of conflicts rather than creating online and offline synergies. Meanwhile, pure web players enjoy a huge freedom of action – and they may be the first to develop truly complementary offline offers.

Traditional industry boundaries are disappearing

The consumer-goods industry has traditionally been characterised by a value-chain connecting manufacturer, wholesaler
and retailer. In this view of the world, individual industries were
defined by their products e.g. clothing, cars, food. Although this
linear structure has been under threat for some time, it is wholly
obsolete when it comes to considering the dynamics governing
electronic shopping.

Concentration within the consumer goods and retail industries has in many cases eliminated wholesalers or at least reduced their importance. Wholesalers have to develop specific
strengths to survive: good examples of wholesalers evolving to
meet the challenges of Internet are those that were PC wholesalers now offering built-to-order services. Efficient logistics and
stock control are a prerequisite to competing in this way.

Internationalisation is creating new competitors such as
McDonald's or Ikea which do not adhere to national industrial
norms. Domestic companies are, to an ever greater extent, battling with both the context of new and 'foreign' business models.
An international study by OC&C Strategy Consultants showed
that in the retail trade in 1988, 20 companies world-wide could
be considered active on a truly international scale. These achieved
foreign sales of upwards of $33 billion. At the time of writing it is
estimated that by the year 2000 there will be more than 50 such
companies with revenues of more than $400 billion.

Vertical integration is blurring the one-time rigid distinction between manufacturers and retailers. At the forefront of
this development are retail food and grocery discounters like
Wal-Mart and Costco in the US and Aldi in Europe. They continue to increase their retail market share whilst effectively
controlling their own manufacturing functions. Meanwhile,
brand manufacturers have turned retailers through own stores
and factory outlet centres. When was the last time you tried to
classify a company like Nike? In this case, and in many others
like it, traditional retail activity categorisations don't work well.

The principles of efficient consumer response (ECR) and
category management tell us that manufacturers and retailers

should tailor the types of goods they supply to meet their customers' needs. This implies close involvement in manufacturing but many manufacturers are transferring their successful brand names onto products without necessarily being involved in their production. Textile retailers offer ranges of cosmetics and lifestyle items and specialists in electronic entertainment are entering the computer market.

Traditional activity chain thinking is fast becoming outdated in a number of other ways, and the advent of electronic shopping will speed this up. Virtual companies can become international companies with only a handful of employees; in this new arena, physical assets like modern production plants or long-term leases in good locations become dead-weight rather than the sources of competitive advantage. Consequently, building and maintaining networks with a number of different partners is crucial and becoming more so: the virtual company has the potential to be a hub for suppliers, customers, sales reps, service providers and even competitors. This interconnectivity will erode the boundaries between manufacturers and their sales channel.

Digression: basis for the Internet economy

Technologies are changing and raw economics are shaping our behaviour. The crucial question in this context is, what are the economic 'rules' governing electronic shopping? Here is a short summary of the most important foundations of the Internet economy:

◆ *Network effects*
   The Internet is above all a network – networking is both its means and its end. The benefits of a network increase with each new subscriber by more than the square of the number of new connections. This means that while high market investment yields minimal returns, this is offset against increasing marginal returns in the future

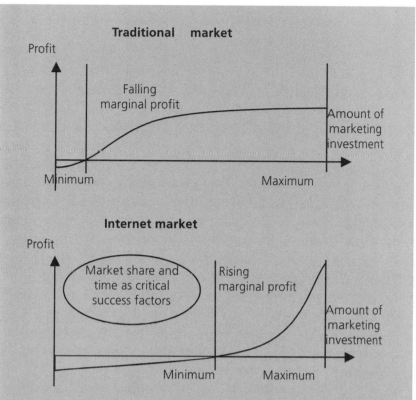

Fig. 2.1   Network effects favour market leaders.

(see Fig. 2.1). Gaining market share quickly is a key success factor, since network effects favour market-leaders and monopolies – look at Microsoft Windows! In other
words: 'The strong become stronger and the weak become weaker.' A few leading players profit. In the
Internet economy, 'net-effects' are often confused with
'scale-effects'. Scale-effects contribute towards strengthening the performance of leading players, but they do
not *per se* generate increasing returns. What is new to
the Internet economy is that digitisable products (software, music, information) can be reproduced at virtu-
ally zero marginal cost. In these areas, although they
may not be earning increasing returns, market leaders
are strengthened in their positions as they can generate

revenues from a cost structure that now includes a higher proportion of fixed costs.

The heavy emphasis on software and hardware standards relating to Internet applications has created a shared architecture that large numbers of net users adopt and support and which then becomes highly entrenched. This entrenchment actually benefits suppliers of software and equipment rather more than users, particularly if one manufacturer is dominant in a particular field. As examples, look at profits made by Intel in microchips or Cisco with Internet infrastructure.

It is important to consider this: 'net-effects' do not apply to most electronic shopping suppliers as, although their user numbers may grow, they neither increase interactions between customers nor do they create new standards that they can entrench.

◆ *Digitisation*
The founder of Intel, Geoffrey Moore, spelt out the basic law of digitisation; namely that every eighteen months the storage capacity of a silicon chip doubles. Consequently more applications and equipment are becoming faster, smaller and cheaper. The Internet connects digital equipment with communications standards and software so that innovations can now spread around the world in a matter of days. At the same time goods themselves are turning digital: software, books and newspapers have been at the forefront of a trend which is now extending from music recordings and photography into the travel industry. We use the whole of Chapter 10 to look at this more closely.

◆ *Globalisation*
We have been moving towards a global economy for at least two decades. The end of communism, capital markets operating at the international level, and continuing deregulation of industries from state ownership to private ownership are both drivers and indicators of

unprecedented economic convergence in the developed markets of Europe, Asia and North America. The Internet is a global medium. It can, in principle, be accessed by anybody and any institution anywhere in the whole world that possesses the minimum infrastructure. Use is not contingent on the geographical location of the user. The Internet intensifies and confirms the effects of globalisation by enabling a virtual economy in which country borders are all but obsolete. The gradual erosion of national sovereignty and governmental control of economies is part of the 'Internet effect'.

◆ *Transaction costs*
Coase's famous economic theory goes some way towards explaining why a few large companies are more efficient in the exchange of goods and commodities than thousands in a fragmented market. Search, information, negotiation, decision and transaction costs must be 'paid for' by all market subscribers, but are largely forgotten within a company. So the structure of an industry is fundamentally determined by its transaction costs. By efficiently bringing together suppliers and information seekers in real time, the Internet slashes such transaction costs, creating the stimulus to restructure industries. Intra-company communication and co-ordination costs also decrease proportionately (e.g. via intranet applications), but the impact is clearly less dramatic than that experienced at the aggregate market level. Since the Internet is an open system, ownership of specific access points to information is no longer necessary or relevant, which reduces the barriers to market entry. In this environment, small but strongly networked companies have an advantage over large, unwieldy or isolated counterparts. Put simply, businesses are finding new ways to transact and this is challenging traditional industry divisions and value chains all over the world.

Today's middlemen are fighting to reinvent themselves

Middlemen (wholesalers, reps, brokers, agents) are the hardest hit by electronic shopping. They fulfilled a number of functions in the traditional value-chain, such as information provision, financing, opening up markets, assembling requirements and logistics. The significance of these activities is being greatly reduced by the dynamics discussed above. For example, the lower the transaction costs in a given market, the lower the importance of middlemen operating within that market tends to be: the distribution of flight tickets or making a bank transfer cost less than a tenth of 'normal costs' when done via the Internet. It is not hard to understand why there is already very little scope for middlemen in industries like this.

The Internet throws the *raison d'être* of today's middlemen into question, because information can be transferred worldwide faster and more cost-effectively. It is becoming easier for highly concentrated suppliers (manufacturers) and buyers (retailers) to create markets and finance them themselves. It is a widely held view, therefore, that middlemen as we know them will completely disappear as a consequence of Internet development. This may be going too far, but it is no exaggeration to say that their roles will be greatly restricted unless they follow one of the two following strategies:

♦ Middlemen can survive by concentrating on a specific core-skill. Efficient logistics service providers or intermediaries offering an attractive aggregation of product ranges can be successful in the world of electronic shopping. The same applies to focused information service providers. In fact, the trend towards outsourcing is likely to ensure the survival of many service providers. Middlemen need to ask themselves searching questions about the cost/benefit of their services against Internet competition and not avoid 'downsizing' if it is appropriate.

♦ Alternatively middlemen can survive through forward integration. A look at the sectors that were first traded on the

Internet is informative: Ingram, one of the leading US computer wholesalers went into direct sales on the Internet at an early stage with *Buycomp.com*. This business boomed and Ingram changed its sales site's name to *Buy.com* enabling it to market other types of goods through this, now established, sales channel. So wholesalers can assume the role of both volume aggregator and retailer, while Internet technology makes this kind of forward integration possible and cost-effective.

In Chapter 3 we describe opportunities for new kinds of intermediaries. However, in their case the value-chain often turns out to be even shorter than that relied on by traditional middlemen.

Manufacturers have limited opportunities in direct sales

When enthusiasm for e-tailing first set in, many observers assumed that manufacturers would benefit from new opportunities in direct sales and would eliminate retailers. The argument went thus: the transaction costs of direct sales to individual customers are so low that the added expense of trading through a middleman would no longer be necessary or justified. But where are all these successful manufacturers who have become direct e-tailers? Although as a rule they were starting from the same point, the challenge of Internet selling has not been taken up by many established manufacturers. Most manufacturers are either wary of upsetting their retailers, or believe that direct sales are simply not their business. They have decided to avoid becoming embroiled in single unit delivery and stock logistics or contact with individual customers.

Established manufacturers are not prominent in most of the more developed areas of electronic shopping. In the music industry, the five big music labels at first disregarded trading on the Internet even though the MP3 standard threatened to undermine their whole business (see Chapter 10). In the bookselling industry in Europe, only Bertelsmann has moved rapidly to be at the e-tail forefront. Leading computer manufacturers like Compaq or IBM were late to move into direct sales, and then only when their hand was forced by increased competition from Dell. In the US market, still less than 10 per cent of all consumer-goods manufacturers offer their products over the Internet.

Part of this is, of course explained by the fact that a single manufacturer's assortment just does not cut ice with the customer. Unless you were a brand 'fiend' you would feel cheated to walk into a store with only one type of tennis racquet, or ski or only one manufacturer's toy. So *Tennisdirect.com*, for example, has more appeal than a single racquet manufacturer's site. None of the major racquet manufacturers sell direct on the web to date.

Another part of this is that single-manufacturer sites do not provide the opportunity to aggregate purchases in to a single 'basket' for shipping – so there is potentially a financial penalty in terms of paying to ship each good selected at a manufacturer's store individually. If a manufacturer's goods are more expensive, less frequently purchased items, this problem is potentially overcome, but customers may be less likely to commit to such a purchase. *Sony* represents an interesting example here, broad enough and strongly branded enough to draw customers, but extremely dependent on retailers in many of its product categories. It is playing a careful balancing game, so one can buy a Sony Vaio portable PC direct and audio 'accessories' but not a portable stereo.

On the other hand, the textiles and travel industries are often mentioned as successful examples where 'manufacturers' have become e-tailers. Clothing company *Levi's* was very quick to try and exploit its opportunities for direct sales. Conflict with the traditional sales channels broke out however, when Levi retailers wanted to market Levi's products on their own Internet web-sites. Levi's sought to prevent this but was not in a good position to do so. In contrast, integrated clothing brands like *The Gap*, *J. Crew* and *Abercrombie and Fitch* have a stronger position as e-tailers. Because the dividing line between these players as manufacturers and retailers in this part of the apparel industry is very fine, it is not really true to say that power has shifted to the manufacturers.

The *travel industry* is another case in point. Here, too, 'manufacturers', especially airlines like *American Airlines*, *Virgin Atlantic* and *easyJet* have seized the opportunity offered by the Internet. Although the question of who will control the future of virtual travel sales remains undecided, it appears that in this case the 'manufacturers' rather than the 'retailers' (the travel agents) hold all the aces. We see travel as an exception which has evolved out of a specific imbalance of power: the travel agency industry has always been relatively weak in comparison to airline companies and tour operators. Also, many travel agent chains actually belong to large travel companies. In this industry the manufacturer–retailer conflict has already been decided in favour of the manufacturer, even before the advent of electronic shopping. Add to this the consideration that travel agents' value creation is extremely low, and the fact that the products in question (i.e. travel tickets) can easily be transferred digitally, and it is not hard to understand the development.

Few of these factors apply in other areas – or, if they do, they do not converge so conclusively. As a result, manufacturers pursuing ambitious direct-sales strategies are few and far between in most sectors. As we have indicated, consumer feedback tells us that single-brand sites are unlikely to be successful, since most online shoppers seek and value a wide choice combined with the abundance of independent information that an Internet trader can offer. A (by definition) limited choice is the real reason that manufacturers have difficulty making great headway online. This is something which will become more significant as consumers become, quite literally, 'spoilt for choice'. Ultimately if manufacturers want to be successful on the Internet they must move closer to meeting consumer needs. This potentially means co-operating with competing manufacturers and offering a fuller range or becoming retailers themselves.

Most established retailers are on a losing track

So which retailers have been successful on the Internet so far? It is clear that newcomers like *Amazon*, *eBay*, *CDNow* and *eToys* have dominated the headlines, while many established retailers appear to downplay online selling. It is only as electronic shopping, at least in the US, has started to become a competitive weapon, that some major mainstream retailers like *Wal-Mart* and *Macy's* have been jolted into investing heavily in their own Internet shops.

Certain types of existing retailers or service providers are better equipped to go digital than their newcomer counterparts. The *mail order trade*, for example, operates under similar conditions to those imposed by the Internet so that business processes do not need to change dramatically when adapted to virtual selling: consumer logistics, handling payments and database systems have been a part of the mail-order trade for years. In Europe, large mail order firms, like *Quelle* and *Otto* in Germany, have generated significant Internet sales. In the US *Lands End* already does more than 10 per cent of its business on the net. The mail-order trade will continue to promote use of the Internet, as it represents both a very cost-effective way of ordering and huge opportunities to present products to customers creatively. Much of the mail-order trade will ultimately *transfer its whole business to the Internet*. They must take care not to stay too close to their former business and fail to recognise that the Internet is more than a more comfortable screen-text version of their catalogues. This may sound paradoxical. Try the following analogy: there are few Portuguese who speak excellent Spanish and vice versa *because* the languages are too similar: nobody bothers to learn them from scratch as they can get by with what they already know. The challenge is the same for mail-order players.

Why have *retailers* been so slow to take up the challenge of electronic shopping? Our comments and observations here particularly relate to Europe today (and the US a few years ago).

◆ Established market leaders *greatly underestimated the competitive lead that newcomers on the Internet could generate.* Considering themselves disadvantaged and the medium uncertain, many retailers decided to wait until others had developed the market. This defensive strategy is short-sighted, as electronic shopping has caught on and traditional retailers have found themselves in an even worse position to compete against specialist Internet businesses.

◆ Established retailers *were not flexible enough.* Lack of leadership and vision has been a key problem as top management remained completely unprepared and unconvinced about this new business arena. Institutional apathy was the result, so that instead of investing in Internet stores with uncertain sales futures, existing retailers preferred to continue operating within tried and tested parameters by opening new physical branches. In any case, retailers often lack the expertise and skills to set up and successfully operate an e-tailing site.

◆ Despite lack of evidence to this effect, the same retailing old guard has feared, in some areas, that actively pursuing Internet sales could lead to *cannibalisation of their existing business.* This widespread concern has fuelled the decision to eschew significant opportunities for growth by putting Internet selling onto the back burner.

◆ The scale of the problem is hidden. In markets in which electronic shopping is only making small inroads management attention is focused elsewhere. Managers have seen the tip of an iceberg but don't realise it.

There is little doubt in our minds that e-tailing and e-shopping will affect all industries and goods and even the most established of companies will be forced to adjust. Some will do so in good time, for others realisation will come late, and at a high cost. Remember: *'You can take part and lose – but if you do not take part, you've already lost.'*

There are fewer immediate synergies than one might think

Many observers are still of the opinion that established companies are sleeping giants, who need only to wake up in order to take e-tailing by storm. Indeed, it is easy to understand why anybody who views e-tailing as merely opening another sales channel is inclined to believe in the residual advantage of incumbent market leaders: they can benefit from synergies between their virtual and physical presence to an extent denied to pure Internet suppliers.

At first glance the synergy potential between doing business in the real and the virtual worlds seems high: the same company can sell the same products to the same customers at the same prices – simple. Established market leaders can expect synergistic advantage from the benefits of size (particularly in buying scale), knowledge of the market and their customers, or their financial strength. In this perspective, the Internet is both a new and cost-effective marketing tool for attracting new groups of customers, and a sales channel so full of potential that it is to be ignored at a retailer's peril.

A closer look at the success factors in e-tailing reveals that synergies between 'bricks' and 'clicks' are lower than anticipated, while the obstacles facing established companies are proportionately greater. The fact is that e-tailing is a completely different business. Retailer X provides an interesting case study on the nature of this difference. Until now, X's success has been built on the following factors:

- clear target-group profile
- outstanding locations
- attractive range
- competitive prices
- appealing shop layout
- progressive advertising
- disciplined sales staff
- superior stock-control system
- efficient processes and branch distribution.

Retailer X soon realised that, when it came to e-tailing, the foundations of its business had only limited relevance:

- X's brand no longer appeals to the *same target customer group*. It tends to be the case that the clearer the target customer is in the real world, the more of a hindrance it is in the virtual world. This may sound like a paradox at first, especially as the number of Internet users grows closer to the population average, but we show in Chapter 6 that, while established brands *sometimes* perform well on the net, new brands often perform the best.

- For retailer X, prime-site brick-and-mortar store locations are a key success factor but also constitute high barriers to entry. Of course on the Internet *all locations are (essentially) equal*. Store opening skills no longer count as much as they did. The Internet trader is everywhere and is open for business 24 hours a day, seven days a week. An American survey in the spring of 1999 confirmed the importance of the convenience factor. More than 40 per cent of online shopping is done between 9 pm and 9 am, and more than half of all purchases are made outside what were once considered 'standard' opening times. Good store locations are no longer an advantage when competing with e-tailers, and are a relatively low source of benefit for those moving onto the net.

- Successful retailers offer attractive ranges. However the average *e-tailer's range tends to be superior*. Our retailer X's range is limited by the available sales area in store. With the exception of flagship branches range is also often restricted according to locations. Meanwhile, provided he achieves efficient stock management, an e-tailer's range is practically unlimited. The complexity of a wide range can be simplified on the web with effective site layout. The ability to make intelligent selections from amongst a wide range of goods, building the assortment – a key prerequisite for traditional retailers – is a less relevant skill when it comes to the web. This fact obliterates one of the greatest advantages of 'real world experience': as newcomers start without a good knowledge of the range, a seasoned buyer's skills

Competitive advantages of a retailer in the real world ...		... and its use in the virtual world
Clear target group profile	⇒	Target group not necessarily identical
Outstanding locations	⇒	Locations insignificant
Attractive product range	⇒	Maximum width of Internet product range (ability to put together product range less important)
Competitive prices	⇒	Price advantage on the Internet less easy
Appealing shop layout	⇒	No advantage for Internet shop layout
Progressive advertising	⇒	Internet advertising different
Disciplined sales staff	⇒	Automation of the sales function on the Internet important *but* ...
Superior stock systems	⇒	Customer information systems on the Internet more important
Efficient processes	⇒	Business processes of the Internet shop different
Efficient branch distribution	⇒	End user logistics necessary

Fig. 2.2   Advantages of an established retailer in the virtual world.

are no longer crucial when setting up shop on the net. Meanwhile, the established retailer may be forced to provide a wider in-store range to match what is on the net, or even branch out into new types of goods – often not easy without staff retraining. Some high-street retailers may have the skill to use the knowledge gained from Internet selling to enhance their range in branches. This is, of course, an advantage to them but no disadvantage for the pure Internet competitor. In e-tailing, range architecture and other buying related skills are less important than marketing.

◆ The success of retailer X also lies in his purchasing power and in the favourable trade terms he can secure. Limiting himself to a certain range strengthens his negotiating position compared with a pure e-tailer. Having focused buying power and a well-known brand are the strongest potential attributes that an established company can have when entering e-tailing. But even this is no guarantee. As a rule you can assume that mail order, for example, is cheaper on the Internet and mail-order firms could offer better terms on Internet orders. However, it is very difficult to operate two pricing regimes. (So *Argos*, for example, maintains essentially the same prices on the web as in its home delivered catalogue.)

◆ The appealing shop layout of retailer X is an important sales generator. However, a bricks-and-mortar store-designer should never design an Internet store. So available *skills in store design are of less use*. That also applies to advertising. Your advertising campaigns and brochures can be as polished as you like: Internet advertising works differently. Conversely, promoting one's Internet shop in real world media is one of the greatest sources of synergy for the established company.

◆ One of retailer X's most challenging tasks is managing his *sales force*. A badly trained or underpaid shop assistant in New York or London can destroy a long-term customer relationship within a few minutes. Good advice and service are expected as standard, so that most retailers do not even consider good sales personnel as a real source of differentiation. An e-tailer need not worry about much of this: all that is needed is an efficient call centre offering ancillary advice and support to electronic shoppers. Even this will become less and less vital as *buying and selling become increasingly automated*. The virtual selling environment is less susceptible to human incompetence or error which renders it more predictable, and, in this respect, easier to manage. There are few advantages gained through having an experienced sales staff, because they are replaced as a source for customer feedback by the Internet.

◆ Successful retailer X has a superior stock-management system, whereas his online counterpart need only set up and maintain an adequate stock-management system. In fact, the importance of stock-control systems in retailing will diminish relative to the significance of *customer-information systems* (CIS). This is brought out if you look at sales forecasts for the software industry: customer information in almost all consumer-orientated companies, not just in retailing, is currently extremely limited. Software companies believe this to be a high growth area. E-tailers have to concentrate on CIS at the outset if they are to have any chance of success, which lends them a competitive edge *vis à vis* established rivals. Anyone who does not have a robust CIS cannot

hope to develop appropriate levels of consumer responsive-
ness – unless, that is, the retailer manages to use customer
data gathered via his web-site to improve his high street
offering.
◆ Retailer X has reached a high level of efficiency in terms of
distribution logistics, branch stocking or payment systems –
but few of these can be transferred to selling over the
Internet. Efficient branch distribution systems are redun-
dant as the e-tailer must get to grips with *consumer logistics*.
Most *internal processes* must be recreated to support electronic shopping.

Summary

When entering e-tailing, the established retailer has some apparent advantages but an Internet-focused trader has significantly more space for development. That said, an established
retailer does have potential sources of advantage in his regular
business, for example by intelligently linking the Internet with
his branches. But, at the end of the day we do not believe traditional retailers have an inherent competitive advantage over
pure Internet e-tailers.

Entrenched positions are a hindrance

It gets even worse. Established companies have many *disadvantages* when they get into electronic shopping. These operate
on three levels:

◆ conflict with existing sales networks
◆ ties to current assets
◆ rearguard actions from management.

Many companies shy away from *conflict with their sales staff* as
they discover that their sales force has little enthusiasm for
electronic shopping initiatives. Clearly an Internet store threat-

ens to take sales away from existing branches, so disturbing local firm or branch loyalties. Furthermore, setting up an expensive new sales system (an uncertain investment against limited short-term returns) effectively uses money that could be used for overdue expansion of sites or refitting. These are the conundrums with which management in the retail trade must grapple. While such concerns are nearly always driven by the spectre of cannibalisation there are ways to avoid this problem – by making Internet activity a huge success. *American Airlines* and *Hertz*, for example, have been able to expand their customer loyalty programmes considerably via the Internet. Mail-order companies like *Land's End* or *L.L.Bean* are overjoyed when a customer swaps to the Internet, because this type of customer contact is cheaper, more informative and has more chance of revenue creation. So don't listen to scare stories about cannibalisation. If you don't go into e-tailing, your competitors will.

Manufacturers are less frightened of cannibalisation than they are of conflict with their existing sales channels. No one wants to risk a reduction of their core business for what would at first be small additional revenues on the Internet. But to date, to our knowledge no successful brand manufacturer has been blacklisted because of their direct sales activities on the net. There are, admittedly, additional complications for manufacturers, such as Levi's, because retailers can also offer the same brand over the Internet. In some cases the Internet will be used to force greater co-operation between manufacturers and retailers. The American automobile industry is an emerging example of this.

Another obstacle for established companies is their *ties to existing business assets*. Far from translating into virtual advantages, existing assets can actually obstruct progress into electronic trading. Long-term agreements with preferred suppliers could be a hindrance. For example, if a retailer has long-term contracts for cheap own-brand product in categories that are unlikely to be bought online. There is an enormous temptation for an established business to rely on its existing resources to sustain its Internet business in the same way as it does its network of outlets, even though these may be ill-suited or irrelevant to electronic shopping.

A mature consumer business considering taking its business on line will often have to contend with a *management rearguard action*. They do not want to manage or believe explosive growth, but simply to maintain their position in their market. This attitude is fatal: if adopted by established managers, it not only leads to conflict with the growing e-tail area, but permeates the whole organisation. A siege mentality can quickly arise, whereby traditional business streams see themselves struggling in their market while the Internet store grows rich on their backs. Their fears are not entirely unfounded, if we believe the projected growth rates for electronic shopping, there is trouble coming for branch-based retail. Consider that normally about 10 per cent of any multi-branch retailer's portfolio are 'problem' branches, if the total demand in bricks-and-mortar trading goes down by 10 per cent, up to 40–50 per cent of the branch network can become problem branches. Retailers can become engrossed by restructuring their estate in an attempt to stem the tide of change, while missing out on the chance to participate in it.

So physical assets can become dead-weight in the fight for market share in the electronic arena. An important step to-

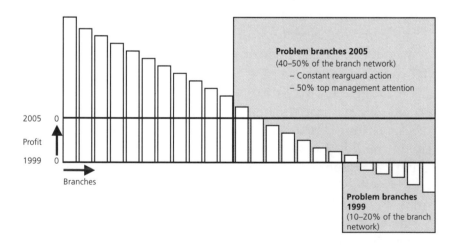

Fig. 2.3 Effects of a reduction in demand on the branch portfolio.

wards benefiting from the *inevitable rise of the Internet* is to break free from entrenched attitudes: the question should not be how to use the Internet to grow existing business, but how to use existing business to develop an Internet presence. That perspective is the one to grasp from day one!

This much should be clear by now: the most important dimension of competition in e-tailing is not the vertical competition between manufacturers and retailers, but the conflict of established companies with the new players who are seizing power.

E-tail searchlight on web-sites for Chapter 2

◆ Buy.com	www.buy.com
◆ Dell	www.dell.com
◆ Tennisdirect	www.tennisdirect.com
◆ Levi's	www.levis.com
◆ The Gap	www.gap.com
◆ J. Crew	www.jcrew.com
◆ A&F	www.abercrombie.com
◆ Sony	www.Sony.com
◆ American Airlines	www.aa.com
◆ easyJet	www.easyjet.com
◆ Virgin Atlantic	www.virginatlantic.com
◆ Wal-Mart	www.wal-mart.com
◆ Macy's	www.macys.com
◆ Argos	www.argos.co.uk

Chapter 3

New Players are
Seizing Power

The competitive landscape in electronic shopping is beginning to form. New players are seizing power. In this chapter we discuss the most important competitive struggles in the e-tail sector. In one dimension the dynamics of the power play between established suppliers and upstart e-tailers is critical. Moreover, consumer-goods manufacturers and retailers are fighting with newcomers for strategic positions in 'convergence industries' (computers, software, telecommunications, media, entertainment). Meanwhile the potential power of emerging 'portals' and the opportunities for 'market-makers' creates heated debate. Battle lines are being drawn and redrawn as previous enemies collaborate, partners fall out and everyone seeks the holy grail of market share and authoritative web presence.

E-tail searchlight illuminates Chapter 3

◆ *New competitors appear from everywhere*
So far, new players have generally taken the lead in most e-shopping segments. Competition is coming from a multitude of new formats: Internet stores, theme-related shopping centres, auction houses, intelligent agents, search engines, Internet service providers and virtual communities.

◆ *Competitive pressure is increasing*
E-shopping is rapidly developing. Every player is penetrating related categories and businesses. New battlefields appear as consumer goods companies and retailers suddenly face competition with companies coming out of telecoms, media, software and other areas.

◆ *Opportunities for new intermediaries are abundant*
Traditional middlemen are being replaced. New kinds of web-sites are evolving into comprehensive market places. A new generation of services, specific to the Internet, are being offered by innovative intermediaries.

◆ *Market-leaders win big, but can lose their leads quickly*
Market-leadership positions can be rapidly built on the Internet – but also more easily attacked and lost than in traditional retailing.

◆ *'Portal power' is growing*
Almost every successful e-tailer is trying to become a 'portal'. Successful evolution from e-tailer to portal will continue to be a strategic priority.

◆ *The 'market maker' remains elusive*
Visions of a few global markets in certain categories, controlled by single market makers remain a pipe dream. Electronic markets are already too developed to allow for control by a single company.

New competitors appear from everywhere

Large consumer goods companies have spent decades building strong brand names and established positions with consumers. They have considerable financial muscle to apply to attractive new business areas. In spite of this it has mainly been new players who have made the running in e-shopping. A short review of leading Internet players makes it clear that so far newcomers have the upper hand in most categories. There are a few exceptions, such as the fashion sector, but even in these areas there are also many innovative newcomers. It is only in industries in which e-shopping is already well developed that established companies have woken up and are trying to make up ground with aggressive Internet offers. The importance of newcomers is equally evident in the US and Europe.

We don't think that for established companies it is a question of merely waking up to the Internet – it's not that simple. But then again we don't think established companies have completely missed the boat – yet! It is worth taking a closer look at the different competitors in e-shopping.

For those readers who do not yet know their way around e-tailing and e-shopping country well, we recap the most important types of players. Generally competitors can be divided into groups depending on whether they:

- sell products to consumers
- arrange transactions
- facilitate market entry.

Although the boundaries between the categories are becoming more and more blurred, the framework is helpful for a discussion of competition in e-shopping in general. It shows what opportunities and risks there are for the various types of players.

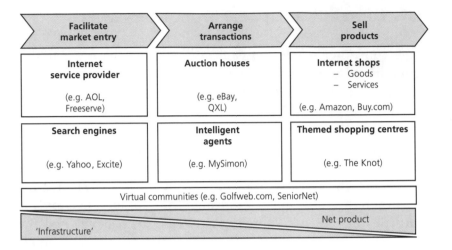

Fig. 3.1 Competition in e-shopping.

Internet stores

Internet stores are the most obvious participants in e-tailing. They sell goods direct to the customer and are therefore directly comparable to a high street retailer or mail-order company. As e-tailers Dell and Amazon.com can be regarded as prototypes for successful Internet stores. Texas-based Dell was successful as a direct seller before taking to the Internet. It was considered a value for money, efficient provider mainly because it had a 'built-to-order' production capability from day-one. Customer's got their own individual PC in a few days and at a low price. Dell was an early Internet adopter and the rest is, as they say, history. But this was only true as regards its core PC business, dominated by business customers. In spring 1999 Dell announced the creation of an online electronic superstore with over 30,000 consumer oriented items available. As *Gigabuys.com*, the company has opened a new, more strongly consumer-orientated computer shop, supplying hardware, software and services. The interesting development here is that Dell has taken its Internet business in a direction where its integrated production capability does not directly support its Internet position. A number of manufacturers who go into e-tailing will likely meet the same challenge, as a wide assortment is a key part of an attractive offer. In some categories single brands suffice, but in others, consumers want choice which a single manufacturer cannot meet. Dell has not excluded the possibility that sometime in the future production and retailing may separate to achieve maximum value for the company. An e-tailing store front which developed rapidly because of the close process integration of manufacturing and selling may now be able to abandon the roots of its success.

Virtual shopping centres

As well as individual Internet stores, there have been many attempts to create virtual shopping malls, copying the physical world 'mall' or 'shopping centre' model. Early examples of universal e-tailing centres, such as German company Otto's *Shopping24*, were largely failures, because merely copying the physical world offered no additional value to the Internet user over the original.

Without an independent theme and without integration of the various shop systems, such as payment processes, Internet malls are not very attractive. An ambitious start-up, *Shoppinggate*, intends to avoid these problems with a set of themed regional malls covered by a single basket for purchases. Innovative theme-related shopping centres on the Internet can be very successful. A well-established example is *The Knot*, a site offering goods and services around weddings. Such formats cannot be rendered in the physical world and therefore offer a particularly interesting service. The Knot has been such a success in the US that it has spawned a number of UK clones; among them startup *Confetti.co.uk* and Moss Bros' intended offer 'Ourbigday'. Successful theme-related shopping centres obtain a significant amount of their income from negotiation and advertising fees for other shops.

Virtual Vineyards is a more traditional theme-related website, the best-known wine and delicatessen trader on the Internet. Virtual Vineyards gathered its own Internet community around it very early; gourmets whose needs did not stop at

Screenshot: The Knot.

wine. It offers customers good wines, but also spirits, delicatessen products and gifts. The shop was originally aimed at gourmets, but it has appealed more to interested non-connoisseurs.
Mirroring this, theme-related shopping centres have the opportunity to build up a wide group of profitable regular customers who are emotionally linked to the shopping site. To many
customers, Peter Granoff, the founder and 'Cork dork' of Virtual Vineyards, has become an important adviser.

Auction houses

In 1998 a new category of players emerged, the auction houses.
These divide into two types: firstly business-to-business auctions that auction stock and are therefore an instrument for
the Internet sales of manufacturers or retailers between one
another. Secondly, consumer-to-consumer auctions which have
established themselves as an electronic market place for private individuals and small trades people (e.g. *eBay* in the US

Case study of Alando

One of Europe's equivalents to eBay is Alando. A rapidly growing German auction house founded at the end of February 1999 by six young high-school graduates. Helped by 'business angels' they raised more than five million dollars.

Alando grew quickly. Within six weeks it had 10,000 registered members, by the summer of 1999 it was 50,000, expected to be more than 100,000 by the end of the year.

Alando has copied eBay's business system, being a pure middleman with minimal costs and few handling expenses. Transfer of goods and payment are arranged by the customers. In the first million successful auctions there were only 27 suspected frauds. As with eBay, when a transaction is concluded the buyer and seller assess each other and post their assessment giving other potential customers access to an accumulating transaction performance history. Suppliers are given stars after at least 100 faultless transactions. About 40 per cent of the goods offered are new, a quarter of customers provide digital photos with their offer. The average age of customers is early thirties and about 35 per cent of members are women.

For business suppliers, Alando is interesting in three respects. Smaller traders (e.g. stamps or antique dealers) can open up a new sales channel that is not dependent on location. Manufacturers can market goods by post without coming into conflict with their other sales channels. Large companies can advertise their products by sponsoring a highly frequented sector of the site.

eBay has continued as US market leader with volume mounting towards a billion hits a month but realised that it had to transfer its successful business model to Europe. In June 1999 eBay took a multi-million stake in Alando and the young founders became millionaires overnight.

Another publicly quoted European e-Bay clone is QXL. The name was chosen to sound like 'Quick to sell' – something that the venture-capital-backed founders were perhaps keen to do once eBay bought Alando.

and *QXL* in Europe). Private auctions are one of the most at-tractive market segments on the Internet. What is especially interesting about Internet auctions is that prior to their crea-tion, auctions had been a niche market. The Internet has made them mass-market, enlarged by active Internet suppliers.

eBay is both the most successful example of an auction house in the world, and recently the web's most visited shopping site. It has its own business system, acting like a broker. While mil-lions of members mutually deal in the various goods, eBay lim-its itself to organising the market place and auctioning. It already has such a volume of sellers and buyers that buying used goods is becoming a real value-for-money alternative to buying new. As such it represents new competition to e-tailers (and retail-ers). It also has the distinction in the US of accounting for more than 15 per cent of all the packages delivered by the US postal service! The company makes its money charging commission on sales and from advertising. Advertising income is above av-erage for this e-tailer because of the length of time its custom-ers spend at the site and the possibilities for reaching specific interest groups very easily. As a result eBay is one of the few e-tail businesses that is already profitable.

Intelligent agents

A new category of players in e-shopping is the 'intelligent agent'. These usually offer price comparison services, examin-ing offers from a number of shops for customers. Although hardly any of these web-sites are profit-making yet, they strike terror in the hearts of many suppliers because they threaten to bring about world-wide transparency of price. Agents such as *MySimon* or *Priceline* search the Internet for the cheapest offer available. Comparisons are possible on a world-wide basis and customers can switch to the most favourable supplier at the click of a mouse. Customer loyalty becomes paramount, which we discuss later. *Jango.com* is another product-finding service, owned by *Excite*, which aims to distinguish itself by finding the best prices on the web across a very wide set of categories.

Screenshot: MySimon.

Who'd have thought that you could compare prices for bowling shoes, from the comfort of your desktop? (Try it!) We look at the significance of intelligent agents more closely in Chapter 9.

Close to the space occupied by the intelligent agents are companies which intend to become a source of trusted recommendation based on more than just price. Brandwise.com and epinions.com operate this kind of service, offering recommendation from specialist editors, as well as the general public.

Search engines

Most Internet users still reach a specific web-site via a search engine, not because they know the Internet address. Yahoo, Lycos, Excite, Altavista or Infoseek all offer different types of search algorithms and classification indexes to help users around the Internet. Arguably today's most successful company that began life as a search engine is *Yahoo* (actually an indexing system but let's not be picky). For the truly non 'net-savvy' reader:

Yahoo's catalogue is split into subjects and offers visitors free information. Users enter a term and receives a list of 'hits'. Clicking the 'hit' links directly to the appropriate web-site.

The weakness of the search engines is that the customer rapidly disappears from the original search site. Yahoo's strength is that more than two thirds of visitors use not only its search engine capabilities but also its own services, such as its Stock Market ticker price 'teleprinter'. This increases the amount of time the customer is online within the site and raises advertising income and also the probability that the customer will be tempted by shopping offers. Making sites 'sticky' in this way is a key to business profitability. Yahoo's business model goes far beyond being a search engine, but search is still at the core of its success and its visitor frequency.

Internet Service Provider

Anyone who wants to surf the web privately needs an access service i.e. an Internet Service Provider (ISP) or an online service with Internet access like *AOL*. We should talk a little about AOL, the most successful service provider world wide. AOL is the most valuable Internet company of all. In spring 1999 it had a capitalisation of almost $160 billion. It has more than 15 million customers in the US and is clearly the market-leader in Internet access, especially for private customers. Strategic alliances, for example with Sun, and acquisitions such as of *Netscape* and *Compuserve* have reinforced its market position. It is investing heavily in wide-band technology and Internet TV. In Europe, where the company partners with *Bertelsmann*, AOL's position is somewhat weaker. In Germany (*T-Online*) and the UK (*Freeserve*) there are other leading ISP competitors.

Virtual communities

Virtual communities on the Internet are the equivalent of clubs in which like-minded people meet. On web-sites like *Geocities*,

Metropolis or *Tripod* private individuals can hire accommodation cheaply, chat with their neighbours, exchange experiences or do business. In the early days of the Internet there was much discussion of how consumers with similar interests could organise to combine their purchasing power and extract deals from e-tailers. *Mercata* is one such buyers' association. *Accompany Inc*, *NextTag.com* and *e.wanted* have all evolved to pursue similar notions. However, this new consumer power is taking time to emerge, as it is difficult to organise and successful organisers quickly discover their own commercial interests in keeping margins for themselves. Virtual communities offering access to a large homogenous target audience have their own vested interests given that they are in a position to negotiate with suppliers and build their own e-tailing business.

One of the best known virtual associations is *GolfWeb* offering the golfer any information he wants about the sport: playing tips, golf courses, tournament calendar, golfing trips, a golf magazine etc. *GolfWeb* has become a 19th hole for golfers. The 'ProShop' offers a huge selection of golfing equipment from clubs through bags and clothes to devotional articles and lithographs with views of famous golf courses. Also a success is *SeniorNet*, a virtual association for senior citizens which is an ideal marketing platform for financial services, health products, education offers. Its US success has spawned *vavo.com* in the UK. The success of SeniorNet has now spawned a new target group *JuniorNet*. Just as successful are *HorseNet*, the riding community on the Internet or *Gayforum*, a German association which recently went public on the Stock Market this year.

Particularly interesting is the proposition offered by *The Mountain Zone*, a virtual playground for skiers, mountaineers and mountain bikers which skilfully combines a number of virtual communities. Content can be used across a number of target groups and the number of potential members, and their loyalty to the community, is high as members can 'belong' to more than one interest.

Screenshot: MountainZone.

Competitive pressure is increasing

The boundaries between the various different competitors in e-shopping is blurring. Virtual Vineyards as a 'theme' related site actually has a great deal of an Internet store and a virtual community to it. Internet stores now offer auctions. Here *Dell* is a notable and recent auction entrant since July 1999. Golfweb.com is developing towards being a theme-related 'shopping hub'. Amazon.com is constantly extending its product range through acquisitions and it has almost become a 'purchasing centre' rather than an online store. Search engine players are branching into every possible Internet business – little wonder, as the basic search service is free. Internet Service Providers have online services that provide associations and web stores for the most varied interest groups. Although the boundaries are disappearing, there is some coherence in today's competitive landscape as it appears to us.

Would-be players in e-shopping need to understand current trends in competition:

◆ *The industry is developing fast*

The full set of e-shopping participants is definitely not yet established. New players continue to enter, while new acquisitions and strategic alliances are the order of the day. The competitive scene is highly dynamic. 'An Internet year lasts no longer than three months'.

◆ *Competitors attack related businesses*

Successful Internet stores are constantly extending their offer. Companies like Buy.com start with an intent to establish themselves in one product area and then rapidly make a name for themselves in another. Search engines and Internet service providers are becoming e-tailers as a business founded on a range of pure market-access services is not robust in the long term for many of them.

◆ *New competitive groupings emerge*

As e-shopping grows, consumer-goods manufacturers and retailers find themselves up against competitors such as computer firms (e.g. Ingram Micro), software houses (e.g. Microsoft), telecommunications firms (e.g. AT&T), media groups (e.g. Time Warner) and entertainment industry players (e.g. Disney). In these 'convergence industries', competition is unusually strong and conducted at a global level. The competitive landscape is constantly changing and there

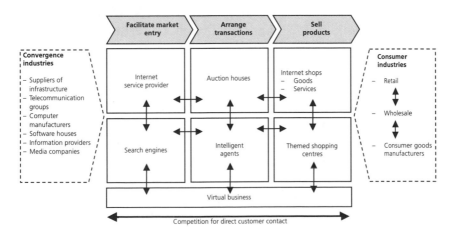

Fig. 3.2 Competitive dynamics in e-tailing.

are major heavyweights tussling here. In Europe a partnership between German media owner Bertelsmann and
Deutsche Telekom has united two giants. Anyone entering
in e-shopping is entering a dynamic, global, no-holds-barred
competitive business.

Everyone is fighting for direct customer contact, because only
a solid customer base creates an Internet business and only the
sale of products and services to those customers can ensure
future profitability.

Opportunities for new intermediaries are abundant

As well as the established players we have described there are
a large number of new middlemen or intermediaries, whose
business models depend on the growth of electronic shopping.
In Chapter 2 we described how former middlemen were fighting for their very survival. The disappearance of middlemen is
now termed *disintermediation*. Its effects are most felt where
goods are digital (for example software and information), but
will soon affect books, music, photos, videos, games and travel
ticketing too. Distribution of these goods on the Internet makes
the middleman a costly luxury today. *Real Networks* for example, sells pieces of music for downloading over the Internet and
has almost as many users as eBay and Amazon. In June 1999,
more than 175,000 customers a day were downloading Real's
players. Just to emphasise the abundance of opportunity, note
that Real Networks is not alone. *MP3.com*, *Riffage* and *Spinner*
are all lively competitors. We look in more detail at the peculiarities of digital goods for e-tailers in Chapter 10. Even in the
UK we can see the first moves toward disintermediation in the
package holiday market. Tour operator *Airtours* has recently
launched *Direct-Holidays* selling package holidays on the web,
promising to cut out (and pass on) agents' commissions. Business travellers are being targeted in the same way for low-cost
travel by BA subsidiary '*Go*'.

Other markets will be affected by a development which we term *transintermediation*, that is the replacement of offline middlemen by online specialists. Affected here are all types of broker businesses like real-estate and job agencies, even dating agencies. *SpringStreet* and *Realtor.com* are agents in the US for hundreds of thousands of apartments or houses respectively. There are dating agencies on many community web sites such as Europe's *PeopleUnited.com*. In Europe there are hundreds of Internet job search sites similar to that of *Monster Job*, which has more than 200,000 jobs listed. Banks have operated a similar sort of successful transintermediation with the result that in Europe, online bank *Consors* has become the fifth largest in Germany by capitalisation. The greatest challenge for former middlemen is to equal or exceed their original physical-world position on the Internet as well. Discount broker *Charles Schwab* is a clear success in this. The company is a market leader in both branch based and Internet business.

There are opportunities everywhere for new intermediaries. We term this trend *reintermediation*. Search engines, intelligent agents, recommendation service and auction houses are the first examples of new intermediaries. Of course they had their predecessors in the real world, but address books, price-comparison agencies and flea markets are no comparison with their counterparts on the Internet. All three categories are constantly developing. For example, *Ask.com* is a search engine which does not search for topic categories any more, but answers whole questions. In Chapter 9 we look at how intelligent agents are creating opportunities for pure price-based comparisons. New types of web-sites, such as Microsoft *CarPoint*, combine several intermediary functions and intend to become a comprehensive market place. CarPoint, as a market place for cars, combines negotiating for new cars, a used-car list, price lists and car tests as well as information on finance and insurance. It also carries news and editorial contributions about cars. In an area called 'My vehicle', targeted at the individual customer, a visitor can leave the details of his car so that he can be reminded about servicing dates and other relevant anniversaries. Most of these services have their predecessors in the real

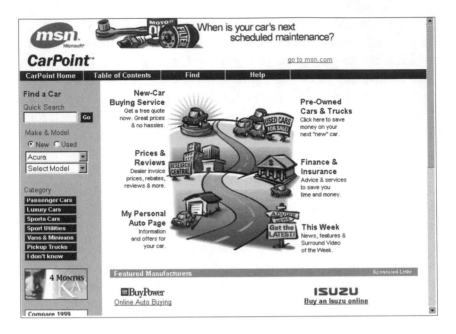

Screenshot: Carpoint.

world but the combination of services makes web-sites like CarPoint a new intermediary. In this way Microsoft is positioning to become a powerful player in the activity chain of the automobile industry and its related industries. It is building a commerce-centric car and motoring portal. In plain English: a place you can buy and sell a car and get other useful stuff too!

The interesting question in this space is what is the winning shape of such a portal (or 'vortal' – as it concentrates on a 'vertical' industry sector) in terms of proposition to the customer and business model. There are a number of alternatives to CarPoint. In the US *Autobytel*, *Car Max*, *GMBuypower* and *Carsdirect.com* are attacking a similar space. In Europe the UK's *Autotrader*, originally a print-based magazine serving buyers and sellers, is building such a portal. Other logical players include car-specific travel and support organisations such as the breakdown and recovery service companies. In the UK the Automobile Association and the Royal Automobile Club are the leaders – both of which have 'sold out' of their membership-based club status and been taken over by new, aggressive commercial

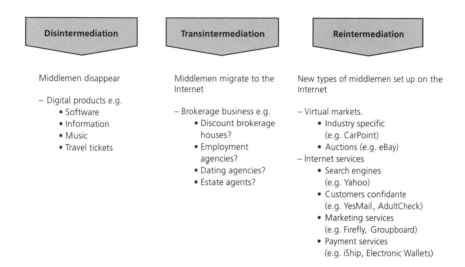

Fig. 3.3 Intermediaries in electronic shopping.

owners. Car hire companies such as Avis, Hertz and EuropCar could be logical participants here too, along with insurers such as Direct Line who recently purchased breakdown service Green Flag.

Finally there are new intermediaries whose services have developed only as a consequence of the Internet. 'Electronic Wallets' offer online shoppers the possibility of making all their payments on the Internet using a partner they trust. *AdultCheck* for example offers a service enabling web-sites to ensure they are free of minors. *YesMail* enables Internet customers to limit advertising e-mails to selected themes of their choice – and at the same time offers targeted direct marketing activities for companies. *Anonymizer* goes further and allows you to surf the net completely anonymously. *iShip* organises logistics for subscribers to Internet auctions. *Groupboard* provides the technology with which several Internet users can draw a picture at the same time. *Flashbase* offers web-hosted database tools. The Internet is constantly opening new opportunities for innovative service providers and intermediaries which e-tailers need to understand and exploit as they develop their 'offer' on the web.

Market leaders win but can lose their leads quickly

Successful competitors are proportionately more dangerous in e-shopping than in the real world, because they can evolve into market leaders much more quickly. Country borders, good locations, the difficulties of setting up an extensive branch network and legal limitations for sales area size have protected weak retailers from extinction. On the other hand, electronic shopping is global, not dependent on location and largely unregulated. Market leaders can develop quickly on the web, if they invest to do so or are simply faster than the rest. As CEO of Amazon.com, Jeff Bezos notes, 'The Internet has created an opportunity for companies to build brand names far more quickly than has been historically possible'. A likely consequence here is that there will be a further *concentration of suppliers*, because there can only be a few or even one market leader in each sector. For suppliers this is disturbing, Internet e-tailing of books, CDs and computers currently have uncomfortable parallels with the software industry. By this we mean that some electronic shopping markets are already beginning to look like monopolies or oligopolies.

Further concentration of retailer power means established suppliers are going to see serious changes in their competitive situation. Today most national consumer markets are controlled by a set of relatively concentrated suppliers. The global nature of some electronic shopping markets means that they may become dominated by a few global suppliers and a long 'tail' of niche suppliers. There will be dramatic shifts in market share among suppliers as they align with successful e-tailers, creating significant upsets for some established companies along the way.

Working against the possibility of further concentration is the fact that market-entry barriers for new suppliers are falling, aided by the Internet. There are some countervailing forces at work here. Before we all feel too sorry for the supplier base, reflect that market leading e-tailers are under threat too. First of all from the *other strong Internet brands attacking their category*.

Virtual retailers can extend their business without having to create new sales space. This is how Amazon, for example, entered the music business after their success with books. Within three months they had overtaken the then market leader CDNow. Ominously for some, Amazon is moving into the gifts and drugstore markets, positioning even more aggressively as a virtual 'shopping hub'.

The second danger for leading e-tailers are new players who win customers by creating innovative virtual formats. So the net's leading sports-goods retailers and the best health food store could be attacked by a successful Wellbeing shop. The leading toyshops and the largest suppliers of children's clothes could be put at risk by an innovative kids' shop, perhaps an extension of something like *Kidstuff.com*. Given this threat we can expect to see category-focused e-tailers assemble related web entities around them to act as competitive 'buffer zones' protecting and enhancing their core offer. eToys' acquisition of Babycenter.com may have been in part motivated by this thinking. The Internet makes it far easier to develop new formats tailored to the customer than ever before. The strongest market-entry barriers in e-shopping will be strong brands, but even these will offer no greater protection than in the physical world.

The critical dynamic in all of this is that the Internet is allowing a very fundamental re-segmentation of what have been long considered by physical-world retailers as well-established segments. Even the first generation of e-tailers are waiting to see if their virtual formats and propositions are appropriate to online consumer segments. Of course, many of the early leaders have 'hit' a good proportion of their possible targets with an appropriate format and have built large revenue streams already. They are doing their mightiest to make sure they continue to meet customers' needs and desires as they evolve. Evolution is the key theme here and why all is not lost for later entrants and niche players, just more difficult. We are at the beginning of a very rapid shake-up in shopping habits, preferences and, as a result, shopper segmentation. Our malls and high streets have evolved over the last 100 years, their virtual equivalents will do so in less than ten, meaning there is still much experimentation to be done. How do e-bookstore 'min-nows' such as *Fatbrain* and *Powell's* exist alongside Amazon? Because they very effectively serve a sub-segment of Amazon's potential customer base – for now!

'Portal' power is growing

To get Internet customers through the doors of online stores, search engines and Internet service providers are critical. In the early days of the net, and these are still early days for many users, the bewildering assortment of possible sites to visit, services to access etc. created a need for some tools to navigate around the net. The search engines and search indexes (Yahoo, Lycos, Altavista, Infoseek, Excite) provided the first signposts to what was where on the web. These became natural starting points for every web visit – until the user was familiar with where he wanted to go and typed the address directly, bypassing the search stage. To avoid this drop-off in users, and subsequent effects on their business model which was largely 'advertising' and 'click-through' revenue-driven; the search

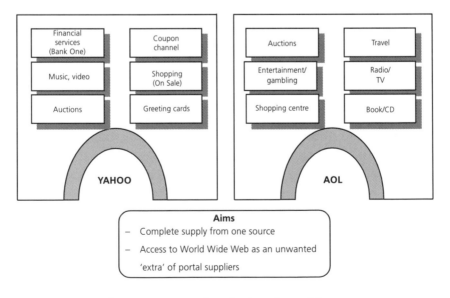

Fig. 3.4 Portals as access to 'closed' virtual worlds.

engines have added features and functions to keep surfers coming back to them and drive new revenue streams: information services; web pages; news; e-mail; evening shopping. The *Concise Oxford Dictionary* offers this definition of *portal*: 'a doorway or gate, especially a large and elaborate one', which quite nicely describes a significant part of what today's portals are.

Portals have great power as they channel their streams of visitors through the rows of hit lists, click through advertising or banners. The 'portal' model, holding a customer relationship, is so exciting that almost all major suppliers of products or services dream of becoming a portal and are queuing up to get into a 'partnership' with AOL. We don't want to go into a detailed analysis of the power of portals here, but a few comments are appropriate.

Portals can fall

Portals offer a free service that attracts visitors. If the service is not free to the visitor, portals can be vulnerable. For example AOL has long demanded a monthly user fee for its online services. It did not take long before someone thought that visitors to portals were so valuable for commercial suppliers that you could make the service free and still do good business. So Dixon's, the leading British electrical goods retailer, launched their own free online service 'Freeserve'. Within a matter of months Freeserve was the market leader in Internet-access provision and has made great strides in raising Internet penetration in Great Britain. Many suppliers have followed suit so that of the 300 or so ISPs in Britain now, around 200 offer a 'free' service. AOL have themselves launched a free service, carefully positioned under the Netscape Online brand. This example shows that AOL did not manage to set up high changeover costs with its customers, which would have prevented them going over to another supplier. The portal's latest efforts at reducing switching have been to allow personalisation so that a user returns to a 'tailored' rather than generic home page. But such measures are easily copied. Just as nobody would have thought of paying a fee for search engines, simple access services are doomed for the foreseeable future to be offered free. These examples show how vulnerable portals are. If a competitor makes an attractive offer, the changeover costs for the customer are small, even if all portals work feverishly to increase them.

The importance of mega-portals will reduce

The big electronic shopping suppliers like Amazon.com or Buy.com are building such strong brand names that they themselves are becoming portals, offering advertising and 'click through' space to other companies. As users become more familiar and established in their Internet habits, navigating via a search engine to make standard purchases becomes less relevant. For today's portals it is a race against time to establish more utility than just navigation as they are becoming less important in the eyes of users. This does not mean, however, that Yahoo or Lycos will disappear, they just have to change quickly. Yahoo has taken a great step here with the takeover of Broadcast.com, allowing the company to offer content and beginning to position as a 'channel' on the Internet much like a TV property. AOL is also determined to extend its offer with new content and service partnerships.

No portal, no e-shopping

Specialist portals focused on specific sectors and areas of interest, will grow significantly. Suppliers who want to become e-tail market leaders in their segment, have to think along the lines of portals. In current discussions with many clients, portal strategy plays a central role. Instead of an Internet store for men's clothes, it is a 'men's lifestyle portal'. Instead of perfume stores there will be a 'portal for the modern woman'. To achieve this, the relevant manufacturers and retailers will need new partners from completely different industries, (e.g. other manufacturers of related products; fashion magazines; leisure services etc.). There will be some 'themed' or specific customer group orientated portals that win significant mind share among consumers, as places in which they can take care of a group of, or all, their shopping needs over the Internet. The challenge for every would-be e-tailer is to become the 'gateway to the customer'. To do so they must co-operate with relevant partners. The ability to rapidly conclude link agreements, alliances and play in 'Business webs' will become key assets for success. In this space *Handbag.com*, a joint venture between *Boots* and the *Daily Telegraph*, is a good example of what we are describing.

The 'market-maker' remains elusive

Since e-shopping took off in the US, there has been a holy grail posited, which is to be a 'market maker'. By this we mean becoming the *de facto* controller of all the segments of electronic shopping through which nearly all transactions are made. For example, imagine that no one would give their credit card details on the net. In this case a 'Trust Centre' at which customers had an account might handle all their transactions. If this company also offered a superior search function, a personalised home page, an efficient price comparison service and more, then it could become the pivot and crux of world-wide electronic shopping. And by the way it would stand to make fabulous profits.

There is clearly potential for someone, without selling anything themselves, to take up such a decisive position as 'market maker' and these models are emerging in the business-to-business world. As such they would have to guarantee good access to consumers and build a secure, efficient market place. To ensure payment clearing and arrange logistics they would need market power to enforce standards among business partners. They would need both to have a position in the US, and to be active globally. Finally the 'market-maker' would have to be a neutral participant, offering no shopping ranges of their own.

There are candidates for the role: telecommunications companies like AT&T and British Telecom; financial services providers like Visa and Citibank who have set their sights on being a 'Trust Centre'. This could be expanded to being a 'market-maker'. IBM and Microsoft, and now AOL and Yahoo are following a 'market-maker' strategy. In our view Microsoft's failing is likely to be the distrust is has generated from 'partners' in its core computer applications software market. Meanwhile eBay is arguably on route to being a market-maker in consumer-to-consumer auctions.

The good news is that e-shopping is altogether too far developed and too fast moving for a single participant to build up a dominant market position and control the industry – but it does not mean that many won't at least try.

E-tail searchlight on web-sites for Chapter 3

- Dell   www.dell.com
- Gigabuys.com   www.gigabuys.com
- Shopping 24   www.shopping24.de
- The Knot   www.theknot.com
- Confetti   www.confetti.co.uk
- Ourbigday   www.ourbigday.co.uk
- Virtual Vineyards   www.wine.com
- eBay   www.ebay.com
- Alando   www.alando.de
- Qxl   www.qxl.com
- Acses   www.acses.com
- Priceline   www.priceline.com
- TISS   www.tiss.com
- Jango   www.jango.com
- Brandwise   www.brandwise.com
- ePinions   www.epinions.com
- Yahoo   www.yahoo.com
- AOL   www.aol.com
- T-Online   www.t-online.de
- Geocities   www.geocities.com
- Metropolis   www.metropolis.de
- Tripod   www.tripod.com
- Mercata   www.mercata.com
- Golfweb   www.golfweb.com
- SeniorNet   www.seniornet.com
- Vavo   www.vavo.com
- JuniorNet   www.juniornet.com
- HorseNet   www.horsenet.com
- The Mountain Zone   www.mountainzone.com
- Gayforum   www.gayforum.de
- Amazon   www.amazon.com
- Buy.com   www.buy.com
- Disney   www.disney.com
- Realnetworks   www.real.com

- Riffage   www.riffage.com
- Spinner   www.spinner.com
- Direct Holidays   www.direct-holidays.co.uk
- Go   www.go-fly.co.uk
- SpringStreet   www.springstreet.com
- Realtor   www.realtor.com
- PeopleUnited   www.people-united.de
- MonsterJob   www.monster.de
- Charles Schwab   www.schwab.com
- Ask.com   www.ask.com
- CarPoint   carpoint.msn.com
- Autobytel   www.autobytel.com
- Car Max   www.carmax.com
- GM Buypower   www.gmbuypower.com
- Carsdirect   www.carsdirect.com
- Autotrader   www.autotrader.co.uk
- Adult Check   www.adultcheck.com
- YesMail   www.yesmail.com
- Anonymizer   www.anonymizer.com
- iShip   www.iship.com
- Groupboard   www.groupboard.com
- Flashbase   www.flashbase.com
- Kidstuff   www.kidstuff.com
- Fatbrain   www.fatbrain.com
- Powell's books   www.powells.com
- Handbag   www.handbag.com

Chapter 4

Survival of the Fastest

What conclusions do we draw so far? The future of shopping is online. Like it or not, e-tailing is here to stay and is going to be big business. Established competitors have few advantages in the new world and physical infrastructure is at best deadweight. New competitors are emerging from many different fields as potential e-tailers and e-shopping service providers. Everyone is in a race to win a gateway to the customer. But only the fastest survive.

E-tail searchlight illuminates Chapter 4

◆ *Late comers are punished by the net*
Being faster and more flexible than the competition is the key to survival in e-tailing. Developing options for the long term means establishing a position now.

◆ *Become an authority in the customer's eyes!*
Being the authority, in the consumer's mind, in a specific sector is foundation for a long-term business. But there are no natural authorities – yet.

◆ *Follow a well-defined strategy!*
Plan to occupy an area that matches customers' needs. Differentiate. Think global from the outset. Don't do it all yourself – outsource and use partners. Co-operate with complementary players and even with the competition. Build a selective, truly complementary real-world presence with a focus on context/convenience, entertainment and loyalty creation.

◆ *Exploit opponents' weaknesses mercilessly!*
Find your competitors' weaknesses and pursue them. But 'if you can't beat them, join them!'

◆ *Arm yourself on equal terms with pure players to do battle on the net!*
Don't be constrained by physical-world thinking and organisational constructs when seeking Internet opportunities.

◆ *Take the long view!*
Concentrate on growth and cash-management rather than profit. There are good economic reasons for taking the long view.

◆ *Be courageous, act fast but think quicker*
Strategy and management in the Internet age has to be flexible. Aim high, structure the company to act rapidly and ensure that the company can think on its feet.

Latecomers are punished by the net

'Two men are out on safari. Suddenly they are spotted by a lion. One pulls off his walking boots and quickly puts on his trainers. The other says: 'You don't think that you can run faster than a lion with those do you?' To this the first replies: 'I don't have to be faster than the lion, just faster than you.'

A well-known joke but a good analogy for Internet competition. It's not a question of whether you want electronic shopping and e-tailing to happen or whether being an Internet player will be worth less in the long term than your current business. It's about being faster and more flexible than the competition in order to be able to survive. Darwinism rules in e-shopping and forces you to reconsider your competitiveness constantly. Rapid adaptation to a quickly changing environment will become the critical competitive edge. Until now 'strong' competitors have – as we have seen – not always had the best starting positions in e-shopping. Or in the words of Intel CEO Andy Grove: 'There are only two types of company today – the quick and the dead.'

Internet competition is tough and sometimes irrational. Latecomers are always trying to make up lost ground and do not shrink from suffering heavy initial losses to build sales. The fight between *Amazon* and *Barnes & Noble* shows how valuable the market leadership is. And how powerful market followers, who have recognised the dangers of Internet competition, are willing to invest heavily in improving their position.

The cards for a game of global poker are now being dealt. Actually, in some of the most developed US sectors they have already been dealt. Successful US firms will not wait long for expansion into Europe. If Europeans want to have a place at the table in the long term they must quickly establish their position and stop using the small, everyday excuses that many companies fall prey to:

- 'The US is different.'
- 'Our products are not suitable for the Internet.'
- 'Our customers won't buy over the Internet.'

- ◆ 'We are already widely represented.'
- ◆ 'We can wait until others have developed the market.'
- ◆ 'We have not yet found the right people to take us onto the Internet.'
- ◆ 'We'll make more if we focus on our traditional strengths.'
- ◆ 'You can't make money on the Internet.'
- ◆ ' .... ' *<Please complete yourself>*

Our advice is to start from first principles and give yourself a 'clean sheet'. Adopt an attacking stance on the Internet. Think how a newcomer from Silicon Valley would attack your market. You will very quickly find the opportunities which a well-planned entry into e-shopping could open up – and at the same time identify the threats to your existing business.

Become an authority in the customer's eyes

The most attractive long-term position in e-shopping is to own a gateway to the customer. This does not mean monopoly-based Internet access, but being linked with a specific shopping theme in the minds of a relevant segment of consumers. This can provide the basis for a sustainable Internet business. We saw in Chapters 2 and 3 that there is a rationale for almost anyone to take up such a position. It applies not only to existing manufacturers and retailers but also to newcomers, information providers and infrastructure providers.

For example, who might occupy a gateway to the fitness sector? It might be a sports-goods manufacturer (Nike, Reebok, Head). It could just as well be a manufacturer of fitness equipment, a fitness-club chain (*LivingWell, Holmes Place*), or a focused Internet offer (*BodyIsland*). Then again it could be the publisher of a specialist fitness magazine that might occupy the area. Even a travel operator of active holidays or the pharmaceutical industry could come in as a lateral entrant. Ultimately every company has the chance to address segments of the market. Those who take part in the race may have specific strengths and weaknesses, but no company is a natural favour-

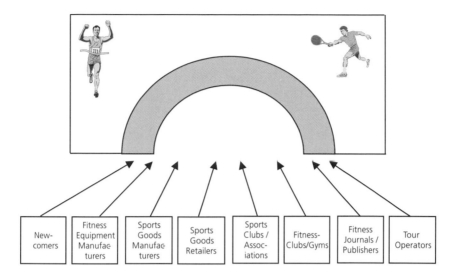

Fig. 4.1 The race to be the gateway to fitness customers.

ite. For each individual player, being the fastest to market means gaining a lead over the competition and shaping early users expectations and habits. As we said previously, e-shopping formats are rapidly evolving, if enough users become accustomed to a particular offer or format, it can become a *de facto* standard.

We have already emphasised explanations why market leadership is so important on the Internet and why 'fast imitators' rather than innovators will have problems establishing a profitable business model. Market leaders have learnt the following lessons.

Lessons from e-shopping leaders

- ◆ Follow a well-defined strategy.
  - – Target an attractive 'theme' and create a new business around it.
  - – Make yourself different.
  - – Think global from the outset.
  - – Use partners to help you grow more quickly.
  - – Co-operate with competitors if it increases your lead.
  - – Use your Internet initiative to integrate complementary business.

- Exploit your opponents' weaknesses.
- Arm yourself on equal terms with 'pure players' to do battle on the net.
- Take the long view. Concentrate on growth and cash management rather than profit.

We discuss these lessons further in the chapter. If you heed them, your chances of success as an e-shopping player are much higher.

Follow a well-defined strategy

Decide early on the right business area for your Internet store. Usually an e-tailer will want to be in the same market segments, with a similar proposition, as their established business. Emulating the physical world in the virtual world is a start but it is not enough, a new approach to the opportunity is what is needed.

Target an attractive 'theme' and create a new business around it!

Don't simply try to transfer an existing 'area of business' onto the Internet. Think about creating something new, that meets customer needs outstandingly well. Question yourself again and again about a suitable product range and the right target group to serve. Check how you compare with other ranges in the real world. E-tailers' ranges should be wider and deeper. There are opportunities for range extensions and new services, that will require 'carrying' new products. Internet stores specialising in a narrow range find life difficult currently because the total volume of Internet sales in almost all categories is still too small to represent a viable customer base. Decide whether you can or should attract the same target group on the Internet as in the physical world. If you do aim to attract the same target group do not assume that their buying behaviour is the same on the web.

An interesting example here is online groceries. Grocery chains have spent millions of dollars trying to segment their customers and understand their buying habits. Loyalty-card information is crunched and re-crunched, cluster analysis performed and groups of similar customers emerge whom the grocery's marketing bombards with in-store, or direct-mailed, or magazine-based offers and promotions. There is an industry built around interpreting grocery sales data to get at customers' buying habits and practices. When this industry was asked to advise major grocers in the UK about what online shopping habits might look like, it had some difficulty. For example one highly valuable (profitable) shopper segment comprises the 'weekly shoppers'. These are time-poor, cash-rich families who do their whole week's grocery buying in one go. You see them on a Saturday morning with cart(s) piled high at the checkout, probably with their children on board too. Purchases from almost every aisle fill their carts. Vegetables, fruit, fish, meat, frozen items, cereal, dog food, beer, wine, toilet paper, it's all in there.

From the retailers' perspective these are great customers. Their transaction/basket value is very high, they need relatively little 'checkout time' per dollar bought and their kids are great impulse purchasers, while mother and father allow each other a 'little luxury' here and there. They are very profitable and they come back week in, week out.

The bad news for big grocers is that online shopping is made for these types. They have the PC, have the inclination to save time and don't mind paying delivery charges. They may even use their favourite branded physical grocer as their online supplier. Fine so far, but then their purchase profile changes. Most of the basics are still bought but some disappear. The kids don't grab chocolate bars at the checkout, the parents don't trade luxuries ('you had this so I'll get that'). Wine is no longer bought because a virtual wine store is only a click away and its more fun to buy wine where they have great advice and information. Dog food now gets bought by the case via the 'pet portal' (see Chapter 6). Beer is bought from a specialist importer's site that offers some great Belgian, German and Czech beers not carried at the

chain store. Frozen-food buying has fallen: now there is a company on the net who delivers great home-made frozen pies and
fish in sauces to the door which are much tastier than the TV
dinners and other convenience frozen meals the family used to
buy (e.g. *The Pie Man*).

No analysis of how 'the weekly shoppers' behaved in store
would have predicted this – but some good creative thinking
about customer needs might have got you pretty close.

Some would-be e-tailers may start with a specific target-
group in their physical business, their issue is should they go
beyond this group on the Internet? Here it pays to take a look
at other offers in the physical world which are close to the original core. A needs-based analysis, from a customer perspective,
coupled with some boldness around brand appeal may reveal
an attractive business area that can be developed as the physical business migrates to the web.

Make yourself different!

Internet stores need to have some clear distinguishing features.

You remember shopping at the best physical stores, you should
do so with the best e-stores. For most e-tailers an offer based on
lowest price is not tenable long-term as price becomes more and
more transparent on the web. If you don't have a distinguishing
feature you are starting in the slow lane. Every potential customer of yours is potentially a customer of another web-site if all
you offer is low prices. Buy.com's '10percentoffamazon.com' is
annoying for Amazon, but would not, in our view, be the basis
for an independent site. There are many sources of differentiation and they vary from industry to industry.

Think global from the outset!

Don't be constrained by geography. If you are a retailer or supplier, set your Internet sights world-wide right from the outset,
even if it sounds and feels over the top. In a fight for global

market leadership, leaving any company with a similar business model in a position of strength will later come to an expensive and unavoidable confrontation. There is only one reason to copy an already dominant Internet store in a leading market, namely to speculate on being acquired at a high price. If you want to limit your e-shopping activities to a geographical region, make sure there are good reasons to do so from a customer point of view. In some areas there are opportunities for e-tail offers and ranges that appeal to specific regional groups. In these cases the trick is to transfer the business idea quickly from one region to another.

Use partners to help you grow more quickly!

Fall back on external service providers to organise your business processes for the Internet. You can outsource nearly all the functions of your e-store. Remember that your business model has to be rapidly scaleable, and this can be most easily done if you use specialists in logistics and web hosting rather than doing it yourself. We go into the special requirements for business processes and external partners in more detail in Chapter 8. Forming strategic alliances with suppliers and partners who can supply innovative products and services to your Internet customers should be the goal. Building a network of closely linked companies who are interested in your success can be a great benefit.

Co-operate with competitors if it increases your lead!

Be open to strategic partnerships with other suppliers if they increase your lead on the net. The alliance of Barnes & Noble with Bertelsmann or Amazon with Dell are good examples of how co-operation strengthens overall competitive position in a web business. If, as an e-tailer, you are forced into offering a wide product range because you are in competition with portals, service providers or other 'neutral' suppliers, then your

Internet store may need to offer your competitors products to maintain high traffic levels. Airlines' web stores sell competitors' flight tickets, otherwise they would have no chance against independent suppliers like Microsoft *Expedia* or *Travelocity*. Competition in their web stores follows different rules from the competition between the airlines more generally, where many will refuse to accept each other's tickets even if at a 'full fare' price. Compare this with *Mercedes-Benz* who supplies US visitors to its S-class web-site with BMW's and Jaguar's comparison data and test evaluations so that potential Mercedes buyers do not go anywhere else for this information.

Use your Internet intiatives to integrate complementary businesses

One of the biggest developments in the next few years in e-shopping will be creating stores that in one way or another link Internet presence with that in the real world. Although we regard the assets of traditional retailers as more of a problem than a solution for e-tailing, we do believe that online and offline presence can be used to mutually strengthen one another. These complementary formats are coming increasingly into focus for those players who are late into the game but aspire to be among the Internet leaders. We observe three main types of complementary formats:

1   context oriented
2   dialogue oriented
3   service and loyalty oriented.

A readily understandable *context-oriented complementary format* in the real world is the theme park. Here customers are drawn by the opportunity to totally immerse themselves and interact with a particular theme or interest area. *Legoland* in the UK exhorts you to exercise your imagination, but it is strongly oriented to imagining what you can do with Lego. A clearer example in the retail area is that of *REI*. This west coast US-based business positions itself as much as a specialist in outdoor leisure activities as a retailer of outdoor gear for those pursuits. REI seeks to get the very most out of its strength in both worlds. Its megastores include their own forests and climbing walls on which to test equipment and make shopping at the stores a unique experience. In the stores there are Internet kiosks to provide customers with access to information undisturbed via the REI web-site. The company aims to make its multichannel offer highly complementary.

By way of contrast, look at the typical book buyer in the US who buys typically on the web with Amazon and on the street with Barnes and Noble. The latter have built up a position online (at huge cost) but their synergy with their physical branches is almost nothing currently. Customers in their physical branches can only easily get sales information from sales assistants, while the online customer's access to information has almost no limit. Books bought online with Barnes and Noble cannot be exchanged or returned in store. Jeff Bezos, founder of Amazon.com, has often expressed the view that the greatest threat from traditional competitors will come from their ability to drive synergy between their online and offline stores. On the other hand, Amazon could establish megastores itself.

Dialogue-oriented formats are based on the assumption that electronic shopping is fast becoming part of normal life for almost everyone but that they do not want to spend their time at home on their PCs on their own! To combat this many e-shopping businesses will begin to include media and entertainment in their offer and some will begin to migrate their whole model to this basis. For example, one can imagine a restaurant concept based loosely around the Hard Rock Cafe style, but in which music can be downloaded from the net to your own table and you can have a meal with friends while going shopping on the net. The importance of social dialogue while shopping has been picked up by US mail order and Internet player *Lands End*. In an attempt to make online shopping more sociable they will launch an instant messaging service, connecting two specific shoppers who are online together. The service is intended to mimic the effect of going shopping with a friend and being able to chat about the purchases to be made. We can expect to see many more initiatives intended to make online shopping a sociable rather than solo activity, and more like leisure, less like doing chores.

Service and loyalty oriented formats arise from the co-ordination of customer service and/or customer loyalty schemes between the online and offline worlds. If successful they can drastically lower the cost of customer acquisition and retention and raise levels of customer satisfaction. Online stockbroker *Charles Schwab* is ready and able to serve its online customers through its branch network if they walk in off the street (more of this in Chapter 11). Department store *Debenhams* can now provide an excellent wedding list service to many more prospective brides and grooms and their guests than they could serve purely through their physical stores. Elsewhere, AOL has invested many millions of dollars in technology companies providing systems to support service to customer across multiple technology platforms and devices. The point here is that in the future you have to retain a customers loyalty with great serv-

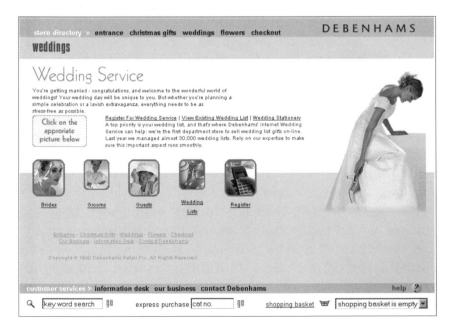

Screenshot: Debenhams Wedding Service

ice through a number of points of contact – be it the TV at home, the next generation mobile phone in hand, or via the journey support system in car.

Exploit your opponents' weaknesses

There is only one guideline for competing with other e-tailers who may be newcomers, manufacturers or retailers: attack their weaknesses!

Against *newcomers*, don't forget that they are usually companies which will not be perfectly organised. Take the customer's perspective and analyse the weaknesses in their web pages and service range when compared to your Internet store. Most founders of Internet shops will help you identify what they think their strong points are because they love reporting on their 'secrets for success'. Remember that a completely new company has to build up trust slowly amongst its consumers. Benchmark their range quality, and service performance and beat them at these measures. It will slow down their trust building. If you can acquire your way to a leadership position, do so. Clearly this rule predominantly applies to companies that are not yet quoted on a Stock Exchange, after which values may be too high to contemplate purchase.

If your main e-tail competitor is a *manufacturer*, he will usually have a strong brand, but no experience in direct customer contact. Identify where customers think the brand has weaknesses and focus on selling against these. Manufacturers may have a limited range to offer: exploit this, offer a significantly wider range of products in the same category. The strongest weapon against e-tailing manufacturers will be an ability to set up superior built-to-order facilities enabling customers to have made-to-measure products. Built-to-order ranges have serious consequences for manufacturers and may require a complete change in the activity chain of an industry. Established manufacturers may be unable to achieve this change, whereas newcomers can.

Retailers are the easiest to attack if they lack a strong retail brand and set up their Internet store like a branch or a mail-

Newcomers	Manufacturers	Retailers
– Discover the secret of success of other start ups – Take full advantage of weaknesses of small operators – Suppress the growth of newcomers – Drive towards acquisitions	– Take advantage of end user contact – Find out weaknesses in customers view – Offer broad range of products according to customer requirements – Develop built-to-order capabilities – Possibly enter strategic partnerships	– Take advantage of weak market position – Consciously differentiate the shopping experience from the real world – Establish strong own brands – Rely on superior customer relationship management – Possibly develop built-to-order capabilities

Fig. 4.2   Strategies for Internet competitors.

order catalogue. Many have a tendency to equip their store on the Internet just as they would their real sales 'floor' and with the same product ranges. Compete here by offering something extra, for example creating a virtual shopping experience which has little in common with a local shopping trip. If a retailer has a large proportion of own-brand products in his mix, again built-to-order ranges can be used to compete against them.

If you do not manage to beat the direct competition, then rule number 2 applies: 'If you can't beat them, join them!'

Arm yourself on equal terms with pure players to do battle on the net

Established companies can be successful on the net. But you may have to set aside the interests of many of your management team and make sure you have the appropriate weapons for your Internet initiative. A web store needs the same opportunities for development as an independent player would give it, with all the freedom in the world. Once again the *Internet imperative* applies here: Ask yourself how you use your present business to get leverage on the Internet and not how you can use the Internet for your present business. Failing this, the management team for your web initiative may put the idea into practice outside your company! 'Appropriate weapons' includes freedom to develop the Internet business quickly according to its specific needs, without having to make allowances for the established business. If the Internet store needs to source new ranges, new suppliers, new categories or even competitors' products, this has to be possible.

Always treat your e-shopping initiative as separate from your core business in the first instance. E-shopping activities have to be operated as an independent business unit which pursues new growth opportunities for the company. Ultimately it should be able to leverage the advantage that belonging to the company can offer, but let the division decide for itself which of the existing assets and ranges it would like to use. Internal services like EDP, advertising or accounts should have to compete with external service-providers to serve the e-shopping division. If there are real benefits between the traditional and the new business, it will automatically use internal services.

Strategic direction   **Organisational direction**

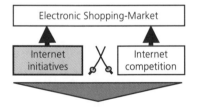   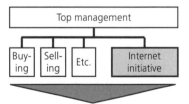

■ Alignment with direct competition

■ Quick decisions from flexibility

■ Development of the business according to own requirements

■ Freedom to utilise synergies with current business

■ Direct top management linkage

■ Best available personnel

■ Strict separation from core business

   – Independent growth through own resources

   – No submission to existing processes/systems

   – Internal services compete with external suppliers

Fig. 4.3 Appropriate weapons for Internet battles.

Electronic shopping requires *fast decision-making*, which may mean new processes. Speed is a key to success. Building an e-shopping business is likely to require a new management team who are allowed to develop their own business processes and practices. Choosing the right team is critical and you may want outside help in this area.

E-tailing and e-shopping must be on the CEO's agenda. Only the direct involvement of top management can ensure the rapid growth of a new business area and allow resolution of conflicts with the established parts of the businesses. Without good support from 'above' Internet initiatives come to grief.

Take the long view – concentrate on growth and cash management rather than profit

We assume by now we have convinced you that electronic shopping will happen, that you must get in quickly and that going in will demand serious changes in your business system. But, at the end of the day, what will happen if you set out on this adventure? The good news is that you can concentrate on growth and cash management because growth is the basis for economic success on the Internet while cash management ensures your survival as you become successful. We explain more closely in Chapter 12 why balance sheets and profit-and-loss accounts don't help much in this business. However, if you do need 'economic' reasons to go into e-tailing and e-shopping, we present the following eight arguments, any one of which should be enough to convince you:

◆ *Lower operating costs*
   Although e-shopping is not just about having a new cost-effective sales channel it is an important feature. Giving up sales floor area, no need for centralised stock or sales personnel, the fact that customers serve themselves, all represent a huge retail operating-cost saving. Mail-order businesses have not been in a position to push cost reduc-

tion to its full potential, because until now they have not had the Internet as a cheap information and transaction medium.

◆ *Permanent customer access*

E-shopping offers customers the opportunity to shop at home any time of the day or night. As more users begin to shop via the net, the greater the incentive to provide improved and varied access methods. This in turn reinforces usage and adoption including continuous wide-band access (see Chapter 9 for more on underlying technologies).

◆ *Customer feedback allows for built-to-order ranges*

Many products are heading towards being manufactured only when their requirements have been specified at order. With low costs and fast delivery, this becomes a superior competitive position – good for the customer and good for the supplier. The Internet is the ideal medium with which to implement such built-to-order ranges. We go into this further in Chapter 8.

◆ *Excellent customer-relations at low cost*

Many direct-marketing activities are only viable for e-tailers. Direct and individual marketing to customers through the web creates a cost-efficient platform for a whole range of new services in customer-relations management (CRM), as we describe in Chapter 7. Systems-investment costs for setting up Internet stores are relatively low given that the same systems would be required for CRM in the traditional business

◆ *Rapid-expansion opportunities*

E-shopping makes world-wide customer access possible at a stroke and it is easily scaled. For many companies it will be the first time they can expand geographically quickly but with low investment.

◆ *Customer relationships up for grabs*

As all players are starting afresh at a certain level, even established customer-and-supplier relationships are open to attack. Many contractual agreements do not apply explicitly to Internet trade and will sooner or later be circumvented – certainly when new players come into the picture.

◆ *New format opportunities*
  The Internet is creating many possibilities for new, innovative formats, which themselves may be entirely new sources
  of value for the e-tailer.
◆ *Help from the capital markets*
  The high values being achieved by quoted Internet companies act to minimise risk for entrepreneurs. The capital
  markets have a large appetite for risk in this area, often
  providing rewards today for what will be tomorrow's success. We go into the role of the capital market in more detail in Chapter 12. Even if there were a massive slump in
  Internet values, there would still be more capital available
  for investment than good opportunities to invest in.

So does this mean that you will automatically strike it rich when
you start an Internet offensive? No way. The only way to make
money on the web so far has been in one of two ways:

1 Set up as an internet infrastructure provider (Cisco, IBM).
2 IPO on the capital markets as a '.com' business.

Most e-shopping sites are heavily loss making, driven by two
things:

1 Heavy start-up and investment costs. (As we explain in
   Chapter 12 this shouldn't put you off!)
2 E-tailing business models are easy to copy and competitors
   are waging price wars to establish market share positions.
   (This should put you off!)

Let's examine the second of these more closely.
  More businesses are beginning to recognise the fundamental nature of the threat posed by the Internet to their traditional organisation. In reaction to this they set up a web-based
selling initiative as a new sales channel for their products. The
reality here is that in contrast to the real world, where physical
location has a part to play in the competitive structure of retail
industries, there are not going to be several thousand geographi-

cally dispersed stores with similar offers. Competition will develop which is unbelievably intense and not previously seen in the world of physical retailing. Unsuccessful companies, understanding the strategic importance of web success, will employ last-ditch strategies to try and carve out a position. The head of one e-tailing concern recently shared this with us: 'We have CDs at half the high street price. That doesn't cause us too much pain, as our market share is pretty small. But it hits the big guys right where it hurts.'

It's worth exploding another myth. Many Internet businesses believe that they can earn substantial money through advertising. Note that Internet advertising in the US was in excess of $2 billion in 1998 and so was larger than the whole of the outdoor display advertising market. But as part of this, search engines such as Yahoo and other 'hot' Internet site owners took unusually high premiums for their 'space' compared to TV and other traditional media. Click-through rates on web banner adverts have fallen from industry averages of 2% to around 0.5% and much advertising has shifted from simple banners to affiliate programmes, in which payment is effectively made only on success. So the marketing spend for web players is going up while income from advertising is becoming more uncertain.

That web advertising will continue to grow rapidly is by no means clear. It is different to TV advertising in many respects. For example, breaking into people's surfing time for an extended period is almost inconceivable without a significant reward to the customer for allowing this. Repeating adverts is relatively inefficient if no one has clicked on them in the first place. New advertising ideas are popping up every day but there is no escaping the fact that not all Internet businesses can live off advertising. At the end of the day, someone has to pay for the adverts to be placed. As an aside here, note that the total annual expenditure in US advertising is less than the value of the ten largest Internet players. So, important as advertising revenues are, they need to be only one part of a broader revenue stream for a successful Internet business.

So how do you make money then? Definitely not by simply copying earlier concepts (unless your clear intention is to offer them in an area that a leader has not got to yet and then sell out). You need to have an original idea, a different perspective. You need to implement it rapidly and begin to raise barriers to others copying you. The second part of the book describes how you can do this. E-shopping is going to lead to a major redistribution of value in many business systems. Market leaders will stand to make a fortune. Make sure you take part. Your mantra should be 'It's difficult to make money betting on the net, but it's more difficult to make money betting against it.'

Be courageous. Act fast but think quicker

The rapid pace of change in e-shopping has a particular effect on companies. Long-term competitive strategies, such as those propagated by Michael Porter, work only to a limited degree in the Internet economy. They do not deal well with network effects in fast-growing industries. Strategy studies have long shown that systematic strategy-planning does not explain the success of the best companies of the world. Management scientists like Mintzberg have proved that most spectacular successes in economic history are based not on brilliant plans, but on a succession of clever pragmatic decisions and the timely exploitation of opportunities. Strategic planning in the traditional sense is dead. In the Internet age plans have to be flexible. The success of companies in future will depend on how far they succeed in finding and holding the right business 'options' to exploit, and their choice of investment-timing in them in terms of making financial and human resources and management available to capitalise on them.

Exploiting a set of individual investment 'options' to be mutually productive and, when the opportunity arises, amalgamating them into new operating units, is the route to success. This is the secret of companies like General Electric, 3M and the successful venture-capital firms.

The sheer scale of forthcoming change to come may frighten you. Even more frightening is the fact that it is not just that a revolution is going on, but the pace of business change continues to rise. In the future you will have to execute change at a rate that is much faster than today. Many of today's managers will fail. But for many the 'creative destruction' of existing business structures and processes will create massive opportunities. Entrepreneurs will have the chance to win or lose everything and not just once in a lifetime.

More generally all those in employment will want to – and have to – keep changing and educating themselves if they want sustained economic success over a long period. Employees and management have to ensure that they maintain their value through constant learning. They cannot hope for a lucrative permanent job which makes limited demands on their intellect or time. The revolution is not under your control. You can look on change as a danger, a challenge or an opportunity. Your own perception is the only thing you can control. Do you look at the glass as 'half full' rather than 'half empty'? We are in favour of exercising corporate courage and taking up the challenge of e-tailing to exploit the massive opportunities of the future. This is the only way to create new businesses, new success and new value.

E-tail searchlight on web-sites for Chapter 4

- Amazon   www.amazon.com
- Barnes and Noble   www.barnesandnoble.com
- LivingWell   www.livingwell.co.uk
- Holmes Place   www.holmesplace.co.uk
- BodyIsland   www.bodyIsland.co.uk
- The Pie Man   www.thepieman.co.uk
- Travelocity   www.travelocity.com
- Expedia   www.expedia.com
- Mercedes Benz   www.mbusa.com
- Legoland   www.legoland.co.uk
- REI   www.rei.com
- Lands End   www.landsend.com
- Debenhams   www.debenhams.co.uk/weddings

Part II

Four Steps to E-shopping Success

If you have had technicians leading your Internet initiative until now, you have a problem. Forget technology, it's all about marketing. The customer has to be the focus of an e-tailer's attention and activities, not the technology.

Marketing strategies have to lead to differentiation on the Internet. At the same time, differentiation does not mean losing sight of costs. Low costs are a necessity. The trick is differentiation achieved at minimal additional cost. Overall you need creativity, not just the marketing manager's budget.

So what is there to do in e-tail marketing? *Follow the e-tailer's success spiral.* Four customer-focused steps drive success:

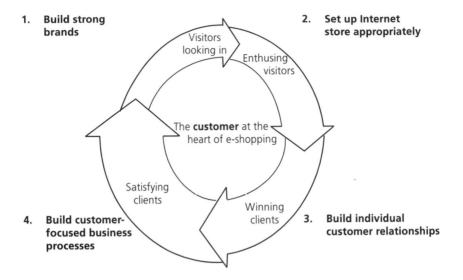

1. **Build strong brands**

2. **Set up Internet store appropriately**

4. **Build customer-focused business processes**

3. **Build individual customer relationships**

Visitors looking in

Enthusing visitors

The **customer** at the heart of e-shopping

Satisfying clients

Winning clients

Fig. II.1   The e-tailer's success spiral.

- ◆ *to attract visitors*, create superior brands;
- ◆ *to fire visitors with enthusiasm*, set Internet stores up appropriately;
- ◆ *to win customers*, build individual customer relations; and
- ◆ *to satisfy customers*, build customer-focused business processes.

We discuss these four steps in detail in the next four chapters, giving recommendations for each step so that your e-tail venture can climb the ladder of success. At the start of each chapter we introduce a core theme and discuss it as it relates to each step. These core themes are:

- ◆ e-tailers need new brands;
- ◆ context makes the difference;
- ◆ true customer loyalty to a site is becoming more important but more and more difficult to win; and
- ◆ built-to-order ranges will revolutionise industry value chains.

Chapter 5

Build Killer Brands

Strong brands are critical for success in consumer-goods businesses. Brands create a basis for trust between the company and the consumer. They provide consistent reference points for what to expect in a world with almost unlimited ranges to select from, and a torrent of marketing messages aimed at distracting our purchasing attention. Manufacturers of product brands such as Coca-Cola, Nivea or Pampers have been investing for decades in the integrity of their brands and have created almost unassailable leadership in their respective market sectors. Retailers such as Wal-Mart, Tesco and Ikea and successful service-providers such as McDonald's have established strong brands beyond specific products. Successful brands require continuous investment, but are rewarded with a price and/or volume advantage over their competition. The same is true for e-tail brands, but the dynamics of brand creation and maintenance are much more intensely concentrated. Days not decades are when e-tail brands are built.

E-tail searchlight illuminates Chapter 5

◆ *E-tailers need new brands*
New environments, new segments and new international partnerships need new brands to be relevant, and to emphasise new propositions. Established retail brands should be used for e-tailing only when the distance to the market leader is already huge or benefits of using a physical world brand are very clear.
◆ *Protect your brand!*
Domain-name registrations are currently very limited. Anyone not protecting their brand fully is guilty of e-tail negligence.
◆ *Practise real-time marketing!*
Internet marketing is characterised by the intensity of its customer interaction and its efficiency in targeting very specific customer groups. There is a whole new set of marketing possibilities to discover.
◆ *Promote, promote, promote!*
 - Level 1: On your web-site
 - Level 2: On other commercial web-sites
 - Level 3: Within Internet communities
 - Level 4: Beyond the net.

E-tailers need new brands

Strong brands are critical for e-tailers. The virtual world offers the consumer an incalculably large universe of product ranges to choose from, with potentially hundreds of thousands of Internet stores all over the world, but paradoxically few single streets full of stores to walk down and simply find one's way around. Similarly there is no hustle and bustle and no obstacle to a customer leaving one store and jumping instantly into another one at any time. The stores and product ranges that many Internet brands present cannot be touched and can only be experienced electronically. The basic reason for creating a relationship with consumers is to a large extent to instil confidence in the performance ability and integrity of the supplier. Only strong brand names create this confidence across a broad customer-base which in turn provides the volume for suppliers to reinvest in product quality and delivery performance. So in the virtual world strong brands will be even more successful than their weaker counterparts.

Choosing the right brand name is a critical decision for e-tailers. As we have seen, new Internet brands appear to be leading the game online. These new brands themselves have had to become well known and build up trust and customer preference on the web. Firms like *Amazon.com* or *eBay* are now well regarded in the US and in the rest of the world. But how strong a brand is 'Amazon'? Well, firstly, US market leader in the physical book trade, *Barnes and Noble*, has had to make an estimated billion dollar cumulative investment together with partner Bertelsmann to catch up, and they are not there yet. Secondly, after Amazon went into the music business in spring 1998, it took only three months to become market leader in this segment in spite of having a poorer range than competitors *CDNow* or *MusicBoulevard*.

So, should one always use a new brand for an Internet initiative? Well, weighed against the apparent ease of online brand creation is the fact that established brands can be transferred to virtual world customers and so bring loyal customers with them right from the start. The more that electronic shopping is taken up by the mass market and not just a limited target group, the sooner established brands will transfer effectively to the web. Manufacturers, retailers or service providers with strong brands will then find their e-tailing initiatives become a little easier.

Another set of arguments for using existing physical-world brands to front e-tail initiatives, is that existing brands and campaigns can be used at very low addition cost. For example a billboard 'real-world' advertising campaign can simply append the company's or product's web-site at no real additional cost. If the e-tail initiative uses this brand as its 'front' then web brand building (in one channel) costs nothing. This logic is reinforced by an argument that runs along these lines: all those who are 'early adopters' are already online; building the next set of customers needs physical-world advertising to emphasise web brands. Since these 'later adopters' spend less time online: their brand awareness needs to be built largely 'offline'.

So far the reality has been that new brands are what are fronting e-tailing. Newcomers in e-tailing, as well as established large companies, have tried to create new brands for the virtual world. In Germany, giant retailer Karstadt committed itself very early under the name '*MyWorld*'. In the UK we see online banks, which have been particularly successful, that have entered not as subsidiaries of traditional institutions, but as '*Egg*' (Prudential) or '*Smile*' (The Co-operative Bank). Stores group Arcadia operates online as *Zoom*.

There are essentially four arguments for *setting up a new brand*:

- ◆ As a young, modern medium the Internet favours *young, modern brands*. A traditional brand name like 'Prudential' didn't sound progressive enough to attract online customers and didn't appear to offer something new to the public, particularly not to a new set of target customers. So in the UK, blue-blooded pension-provider Prudential launched its innovative (and highly successful) online bank under the whackily chosen brand '*Egg*'. Early Internet stores need technology-friendly, modern brands.
- ◆ New Internet brands avoid possible damage to the *integrity of established brands*. The greater the importance of Internet activity for the company, the greater the potential conflicts with the 'core' business, as different market requirements lead to different strategies. A leading manufacturer with e-tail ambitions might be forced to offer his range at lower prices in his Internet store than through traditional retail-

ers, doing this to build rapid volume and presence with online customers. The exclusivity of the established brand in traditional channels would be undermined. In another case an e-tailer might be forced to carry new ranges in his Internet store that he does not carry in his high-street store. If Amazon had been a high-street book shop, it probably would not have been able to invest in the online pharmacy/ drugstore market without significant internal friction. Separating the 'heartland' brand from the 'e-tail brand' is also a way for manufacturers to reassure retailers that e-tail is only part of its mix of channels to the customer.

◆ Internet brands must be *capable of operating internationally*. E-tailers must set their sights on a global market. This requires the readiness and ability to form alliances abroad. A highly national brand name can be an obstacle, as the brand has to be usable internationally. Global fashion e-tailer *Boo.com* chose its name because it means the same, i.e. nothing, in almost every language.

◆ E-tailing as a new business brings new *risks*. If consumers in the core business come to regard the Internet initiatives as a 'failure' it may carry over to the established brand. Imagine the problems if an online bank, branded the same as its real-world parent, has to shut its business operations after the press publicises the fact that hackers have made several intrusions into it and made fraudulent transfers. The damage to the image of the core business would be considerable. A separate online brand can be a buffer against this risk.

Our bias so far has been towards recommending the use of a new brand when entering e-tailing. This was particularly the case for new e-tail sectors and where it made sense to build an independent business to exploit an online opportunity. Since the end of 1998 established market leaders have, however, started to find success on the web with their own brands. Brands like *Disney, Levi's, Wal-Mart, Macy's, Gap, Eddie Bauer, J. Crew* are now leading the way in their categories online. Studies are beginning to show that initial-purchase and repeat-buying rates for established brands in online shopping are higher than for new Internet brands. Established brands clearly enjoy a trust and confidence advantage. The more electronic shopping becomes accepted, the more existing companies *will use their established brand names on the web*. However, we still believe you should do this only if one of the following arguments is true for your company:

◆ Your established brand name can counter a *newcomer's competitive lead*. Internet stores are now established in nearly all categories of goods. The market position of the likes of Amazon.com shows that established companies are well advised not to let a newcomer's competitive lead become too great. Successful Internet shops are increasingly using traditional mass media for brand building so that in market segments where an established brand already has a position, it seems foolishly expensive to invest further in a new brand to take on the e-tailer, as we said a few paragraphs earlier.

◆ An established brand name raises *synergy* opportunities. The Internet is an outstanding information medium with whose help customers make their purchasing decisions. A high percentage of customers with traditional purchasing patterns are now finding out about goods over the Internet. The Internet store can leverage marketing activities in the traditional business. Traditional and new media can mutually support each other, if for example, an Internet store is linked to a manufacturer's television advert or a retailer's newspaper insert.

A good example of our thinking here is '*bol*', at one stage the largest investment by a German company in e-tailing. Bertelsmann took up a world-wide struggle against Amazon.com with its own online bookshop. The choice of brand was an important strategic decision for Bertelsmann. It was clear that:

◆ the new online bookshop had to work in the USA to be successful;

◆ the range must not be limited to books;
◆ the company needed strong partners in important countries; and
◆ the 'Bertelsmann' brand was only known in Germany.

The 'bol' brand is a good choice. The name has an echo of *AOL* the leading Internet service-provider (and a minority shareholder in Bertelsmann) so brings with it a flavour of market currency and success. The ending 'ol' generally signifies 'online' and so it has a clear connection with the Internet. The 'b' can be taken to mean both 'Books' or 'Bücher' , or even 'Bertelsmann' when building up the brand, without this connection being a long term obstacle. Finally, 'bol' in international terms is broadly neutral and creates no issues for joint ventures.

'Bol' is not used in the US. The joint venture between Bertelsmann and Barnes & Noble for Internet book selling uses the name 'barnesandnoble.com'. This was justified by the huge competitive lead that Amazon.com had. The best chance of catching up was with a strong brand. It will be interesting to see which ranges not sold by Barnes & Noble branches will be offered by 'barnesandnoble.com' and what conflicts will arise from that. So far Barnes & Noble have been poor at co-ordinating online and offline efforts.

Protect your brand!

The use of an established brand on an Internet store can also contribute to *brand name protection*. At the moment the number of domain names is limited. For example, at the domain *Computer.com* for weeks there was only one sentence: 'This name is for sale' (obviously to the highest bidder). The only effective protection for a brand is to ensure ownership of the corresponding domain name world-wide, especially the US ending '.com'. E-tailers everywhere should have acquired this in connection with their brand name, even if they are not yet internationally active. Whereas it was once enough to protect brand names for a specific group of goods in a limited number of countries, this smacks of negligence in the Internet age. Imagine a foreign supplier marketing goods to your customers under your brand name. This is a real problem for non-US companies with the anticipated globalisation of e-tailing and the increasing breadth of range offered by Internet stores. Anyone could set up a shop selling personal care products under the name of Bodyshop.com if the 'real' Bodyshop has restricted itself to Bodyshop.co.uk. For the same reasons e-tailers need to protect related names or variations of their brand name. Amazone.com from Scotland offers books, CDs and gifts and Dall from Sweden deals in Computers, Altlavista.com offers a link to a competing search site.

The law provides some protection in that no-one else can pass themselves off as you under your domain name. In the US and Europe there have been legal cases using this principle to protect established brand names. If this was not the case, in the early days of the web any individual could have taken an address like www.bmw.com and begun to sell cars off the site. In some quarters these legal cases have been strongly criticised as unduly favouring big business – the debate is likely to continue.

If two companies have the same brand name in different industries, then, irrespective of its size, the company who was there first has the corresponding Internet address. If the Internet address 'Next' is used by *Next Computing* (now owned by Apple) then the UK fashion retailer must be satisfied with *Next.co.uk*. As this example shows, ultimately a major US brand name could appear as an address in every country with a different ending and uncontrolled by the US firm. Even if it does not bother you that your e-tail brand is taken in, say, Finland by another company, it won't be long before this company might be supplying US customers. Conclusion: protect your brand world-wide.

Practise real-time marketing

When you have decided to become an e-tailer and have chosen a brand, you need to establish what tools you are going to use systematically to build your brand on the web. We talk about each of these as we go through the rest of the chapter. Much can be transferred from established consumer-goods marketing techniques, but there are many important differences to note. Most importantly, when marketing on the web you have to implement in real time.

Real-time marketing needs a new level of customer interaction and at the same time an efficient way of appealing to its target group (see Fig. 5.1). Traditional *mass marketing* is one-way traffic in terms of brand communication, directed in the same way to one, more or less homogeneous, target group. Marketing techniques like radio or television advertising employ a scatter-gun approach and are therefore lost on many people. At the same time it is not possible to measure very directly the success of advertisements. *Direct marketing* is a more efficient and more focused approach to the target group and reduces the scatter-gun effect. But scatter-gun losses in consumer business are still huge and you can only be sure of having reached the target group once you have generated large numbers of individual customers or transactions. But this is all still one-way communication. *Personal selling* is interactive and is the best way to sell complex products and services.

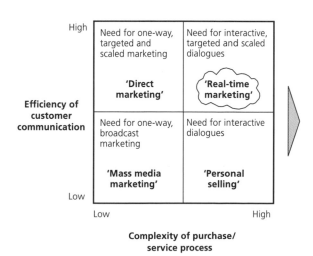

Fig. 5.1   Real-time marketing.

Real-time marketing combines the advantages of all the marketing approaches we have briefly touched on. The Internet is an interactive medium that can very effectively supply the customer with advice and information. The customer can access this faster, more objectively and more comprehensively than he can through personal contact with a salesman. A company can now supply information on the net at a fraction of the cost of a sales contact in person. Extending marketing activities to new geographical markets also now costs hardly anything. The one-way traffic issue disappears too, as information gained from interaction with the customer can be used specifically for segment and direct marketing. A savvy web store can examine, in real time, its number of customers, how many are first-time buyers, how they respond to specific banners, the number of complaints that arise from the different banners (if any) and from which other sites new customers arrive. This type of information can be rapidly converted into specific marketing activities. The tools are available to measure the specific effects of advertising on each customer contact. The Internet enables you to market in real time, building unprecedented flexibility into 'campaigns'. It allows companies to establish individual dialogues with specific customers. The critical message here is that there is a huge new range of marketing possibilities to exploit around this capability. The basic theme of direct-marketing innovation is something that should be in every e-tailers mind.

Use every level of Internet promotion

The Internet has already created its own specific tools for promotion. Some of these tools, and the whole discipline of Internet marketing, are still in their infancy, but they do give some early outline of what are successful approaches. Internet promotion takes place on four levels:

- level 1: on your web-site
- level 2: on other commercial web-sites
- level 3: on Internet communities

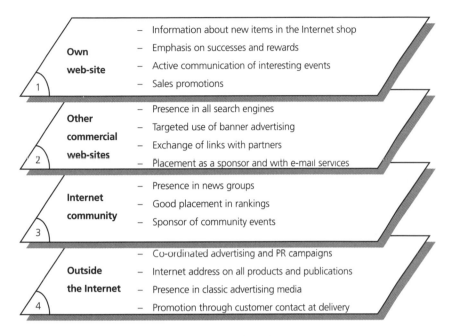

Fig. 5.2 Internet promotion on four levels.

◆ level 4: outside the Internet.

Level 1: Promotion on your web-site

Just like a manufacturer's product packaging, a mail-order firm's catalogue or a retailer's sales' floor, your web-site offers numerous possibilities for marketing to customers and customer contact. Promotion here equates to point-of-sale advertising.

Let your visitors know what's new in your e-store
Successful e-tailers constantly create new ranges and offers; this means maintaining a dynamic web-site. As the site becomes more and more comprehensive, visitors need to have changes pointed out to them. In particular, 'theme'-related innovations need to be clearly announced on the site's home page. The home page is close to the heart of the e-tailer's brand essence so it is here that excitement and dynamism need to be

communicated. Many web-sites provide a 'What's New' button, to help the visitor find out about changes since his last visit, which may not necessarily be 'headline' enough to be heavily marketed on the home page.

Boast about successes and awards

Internet stores like any other web-site, are assessed and given awards by various media and user organisations. If you receive such an award, market it just as you would a good assessment by a product-testing establishment. Quote positive press notices. Make use of customer testimonials in anonymous or attributed form. If you can show high numbers of visitors or sales, document your success quantitatively, perhaps by keeping a counter running on the site. Consumer electronics supplier *800.com*, for example, displays assessments of its products from third-party sources.

Mount events and involve your visitors

A good e-store always has something happening. As in the real world, you don't want to shop in a store where there is nothing going on and it is totally quiet. Point out in advance what you believe is interesting for your visitors and what will encourage them to return. Interestingly the most successful web 'events' need advertising in traditional media, beyond the Internet. A great example here was *Victoria's Secret* web fashion show in January 1999, which attracted more than 1.5 million visitors in a matter of minutes. The critical factor here? The event was announced in a television advert during the Super Bowl final.

Ask your visitors to give your e-store preferential treatment. If a visitor likes your store, he will visit a number of pages on the site. Don't be afraid to ask him to 'favour' you: remind him to 'bookmark' your web-site or list it amongst the 'favourites' in his browser. An invitation to register – as we shall show in Chapter 7 – is even better as it identifies those interested personally, but it must always be linked with an incentive for the visitor and come at the right time in a visitor's exploration of the site. An invitation, or requirements, to register too early can be a turnoff.

Screenshot: Victoria's Secret.

Promote, promote, promote

Promotions have to be interactive on the Internet, inviting the visitor to do something himself. Some of the favourites that have evolved are:

- specific offers 'just for Internet customers';
- discounts or free gifts for first time buyers;
- raffles;
- auctions;
- competition/games;
- appeal campaigns;
- subscription to mailing list, which regularly informs subscribers of new offers;
- time-expiring software to use prior to purchase; and
- vouchers which can be printed online and redeemed in-store.

The last of these, vouchers redeemable in a physical store as a reward for activity in the e-store, is worth a short aside. Technology now exists to allow these types of incentives to be offered securely, with no fear of fraudulent misuse. The underlying principle is a sound one too: web users, who may be natural experimenters and more 'promiscuous' rather than 'brand loyal' shoppers, should have a link with the physical store re-emphasised to them. They may be most at risk of switching to other web or physical stores for their purchasing. In a variation on this theme, *Voucherexpress* offers retailers sales that they would not otherwise have made. It focuses on enabling people living abroad to give UK residents gift vouchers for UK stores.

The practical mass application, and real impact in this area of all these measures is still uncertain, however.

Level 2: Promotion on other commercial web-sites

Just as a manufacturer has to exploit all the marketing channels available to him rather than just advertise on his packaging, so a mail-order firm has to go beyond the catalogue and a high-street retailer beyond its branches. In the same way, an Internet shop has to find outlets for its messages beyond its own site. One possibility here is promotion on other commercial web-sites.

Make sure you are present on search-engines, portals and web guides

Nine out of ten visitors still reach Internet stores via a search-engine or equivalent. It doesn't matter whether it's an independent portal like Yahoo or the start pages of an Internet service-provider like AOL or Freeserve. Make sure that your store appears when any relevant search terms and key words are used. There are whole books and extensive newsletters advising e-tailers on how specific search engines are structured for searching, with the aim of helping an e-tailer get their site to the 'top of the pile' when a specific search request is input.

We only comment in passing here on some simple steps to getting this done. Most of the search suppliers rely on one of a few software programmes (e.g. *Inktomi*). When you register, put down all the key words with which a customer could come across your Internet store. Use the maximum number of key-word entries allowed and scatter second-priority keywords over different search engines. On the one hand many surfers search for a term with several suppliers and, on the other, there are metasearch engines which filter the terms through several pro-grammes. Check that your Internet store appears in all the important web guides and remember that web-sites of many public magazines and newspapers offer ratings and rankings of the shopping offers on the Internet.

Readers who are not e-tail practitioners ought to be aware that some search engines will 'sell' key search terms to specific e-tailers. This means that the e-tailer's site will always be re-turned as the number one 'hit' in the list when a search term he has bought is entered. If the e-tailer buys rights to the first ten hits, a visitor might conclude that only that e-tailer's site offers the chance to purchase that category of goods on the net. Sophisticated visitors will click to see the 'next ten' sites when they realise that the 'top ten' all refer to a single e-tailer, but the less sophisticated may be duped. The Internet may in general create more power for consumers, but *caveat emptor* is still a relevant slogan.

Target your banner advertising

In the virtual world, banners and page headings are equivalent to prime-time advertising on TV. Pricing of space on the web reflects the real-world principles of quality and reach of the space. You can choose 'blue riband' volume sites or – for less money – look for an innovative niche. Here traffic may be lower but duration of visits is higher and visitors pay more attention to what is on the screen. E-tailers need to learn how to evalu-ate their advertising effectiveness more closely. The biggest ad-vertisers on the Internet such as Amazon.com, still pay on a 'performance' basis only, giving a percentage of sales gener-ated by the banners they place on other sites. Smaller e-tailers have to pay on 'click-through' (i.e. whenever anyone clicks on your banner, you pay). Only the least sophisticated pay on the basis of cost per thousand exposures (CPM), where each visitor and page-view counts.

It is generally the case that visitor-frequency numbers can be manipulated and should be used cautiously as an assessment standard. As an Internet surfer's exposure to the same banner rises, the probability that they will click on it reduces. Given this, it is vital to have more than one banner and one set of themes, and to animate them, so that the effectiveness of your banner advertising stays high. Banner adverts with a direct relationship to a web-site are effective at *Petcat*. This Internet community for cat lovers in the UK is organised by the market leader in pet food, Pedigree Petfoods. It offers an ideal platform for marketing their own products in a very light-handed way, as well as observing what cat owners like for their pets.

The art (and science) of placing banner adverts is becoming ever more polished. Banners can now be relatively simply made 'context specific' to what the visitor is looking at; or who they are; or how many times they have seen a specific banner. All these aim to raise the attention a banner receives on the

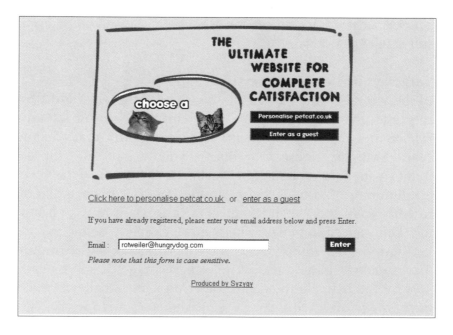

Screenshot: Petcat.

web-site. Keep the effectiveness of your banner advertising at the front of your mind. Click-through rates of more than three per cent are considered excellent. Effective banner advertising can give you significantly more control over your chances of an advertising 'success' than in the physical world.

One specific tool that innovation in online advertising has produced is the 'interstitial', which will also become a key feature in interactive television. For the geeks who dreamed it up, the interstitial is the 'killer app' of banner advertising. For those readers who are lost at this point, an 'interstitial' is one of those windows that suddenly opens up in front of what you were originally looking at, partially or wholly covering the window you had open. You have to click on the top right corner to shut it down.

These greet you when you sign on to AOL and have a habit of appearing on the Microsoft MSN home page. They are a 'killer app' because they can be made context-specific (order a shirt online and the e-tailer could fire interstitials at you suggesting you buy a tie, handkerchief, collar stiffeners and cufflinks) and you have to take notice of them to make them go away.

From a customer perspective they can be a pain in the eyeball! E-tailers, use them with care!

Exchange links with partners

In the spring of 1999 Amazon.com and Dell, announced that they were going to co-operate more closely in referring traffic to each other's sites and cross-marketing. Go into similar partnerships with other Internet stores. The most common form of co-operation here is the exchange of links between two Internet sites. One e-tailer's web-site shows the other store's range at a suitable place. One click takes the visitor to the relevant part of the other shop. Amazon.com has more than a hundred thousand links to its own web-site and as a result is almost omnipresent on the web. As well as this, the company offers a 'partner programme' through which each home-page owner can install a link to Amazon and get commission from the sales of customers who reach them in this way.

One of the prerequisites for exchanging links is that you must have a high volume of valuable visitors, otherwise you pay. Amazon has developed these 'bartered' advertising forms, because it derives huge advantage from having its banners close to 'subject areas' on which people might buy books. So if you're using Yahoo to look for a common term such as 'wine' or 'Florida', Yahoo gives both a range of web-sites on the subject as the result of its search, and provides a link to Amazon which, if clicked gives you tips for books on the subject. Exchanging links with international partners makes sense. Banners on some American web-sites now appear in German if you log on from Germany, the technology is there to make it happen. The good news on advertising via links is that you get the customers to jump into your store. You then have the chance of persuading them to buy. The bad news is that new technology is now emerging which can make sure that the customer pays only a timed visit to the 'advertising' store and is then returned automatically to the original web-site. More threateningly there is now technology to allow a customer to 'wash out' banner advertising entirely.

Use sponsorship opportunities

As well as banner advertising, e-tailers can sponsor whole sections of Internet communities, or commercial and non-commercial theme or event pages on other web-sites. In these instances, company name and logo and 'editorial' contributions are placed on a site visited frequently by the target audience. Hyperlinks take interested parties to the firm's web-site. Just like banner advertising, the value of sponsoring depends on matching the offer to the appropriate audience.

Provide an e-mail service in your store

Many independent service-providers and other media owners offer free e-mail services. Registered visitors with these services receive periodic newsletters from their e-mail provider. Many of these services offer e-tailers the chance to place 'infomercials' or straight advertisements for a small fee. Again the issue is one of qualified targeting to the group the e-tailer wants to reach. These are most likely to be used effectively by niche e-tailers. Such approaches are not effective in the mass-market. It is crucial in e-mail campaigns that the e-tailer invites the reader to visit his web-site. The e-mail should include a direct link to the store's home page.

Level 3: Promotion in Internet communities

Brand-building is also done by 'word of mouse' on the Net. Whether through chat rooms, forums or bulletin boards – communication and swapping experiences between consumers takes place at extremely high speed. Customer knowledge of many Internet stores can only be explained by this independent 'network broadcasting' that goes on. It can be actively promoted.

Making yourself known on the Internet
Early in 1998 *'ecompare.com'* opened, with no hint as to what it offered. Its owners left it to visitors to find out what was behind the entry page. They offered only one thing: each visitor could register and receive ten free shares in the company. Within a few weeks, ecompare had more than three million registered users. From this 'regular clientele', the company built up a virtual shopping network within a few months.

Such creative initiatives can ensure the beginnings of a rapid surge in visitor frequency. But how do such innovations spread on the Internet? On the one hand, each Internet user can tell hundreds of his friends in a few seconds by e-mail. On the other, there are special places where users can exchange information. First are the virtual communities in which like-minded people meet as if in their local bar or pub. In *Geocities*, one of the ten most visited web-sites, more than a million members share their views and preferences on all conceivable subjects. Exchange of information is through news groups, chat rooms, mailing lists and 'blackboards'. In this way innovations spread like wild fire. These new media laboratories have their own directories. The best known are *'liszt'* for mailing lists and *'Dejanews'* for newsgroups.

The same applies to subject-oriented communities for narrower target groups such as doctors, bikers, pensioners or homosexuals. There are often communities specifically related to a brand, like the Harley Davidson riders' club or those for fans of football clubs, famous or not. So, as well as the official home pages of leading Premier League soccer clubs, there are hundreds of unofficial home pages run by private individuals in their free time.

Companies that manage to build or buy a presence in their relevant communities can count on a positive impact of such presence if they stick to the rules of the game, giving information and not directly advertising. Community presence creates enormous potential to learn from customer feedback. Ignoring effective communication with communities can have very negative consequences. In the mid '90s a group of scientists showed that one of Intel's new generation of microprocessors could miscalculate when dealing with very large numbers and told the company about the mistake. The company ignored their

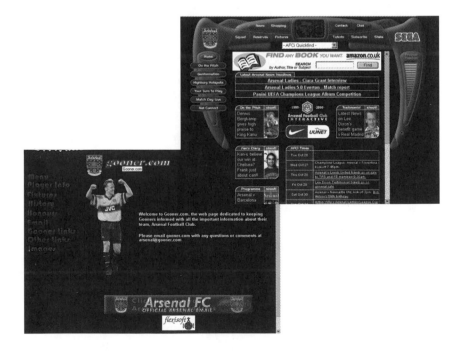

Screenshots: Official and enthusiast Arsenal web sites.

advice. The phenomenon was rapidly discussed by the scientists over the Internet and the error proven by many more experts. In a concerted action they sent hundreds of e-mails to Intel, who replied back with a standard e-mail. The story was then leaked to the press, and reported in news broadcasts all over the world, creating real damage to Intel's image. Had Intel rapidly and openly discussed the issue with the relevant community, the outcome would probably have been very different.

Exploit 'What's Hot' lists
Various 'What's Hot' lists make the rounds of the Internet shopping world. An evaluation as a 'Hot Site' or 'Cool Link' for example can attract thousands of new visitors. The problem is that the editors of these lists, like film or restaurant critics, judge by relatively personal and obscure criteria. Influencing their judgement needs particular creativity. Several agencies have already begun to specialise in this field and 'viral marketing' is now used to describe the user referral driven campaigns on which they concentrate.

Level 4: Promotion outside the Internet

Most companies in the consumer-goods industry – be they manufacturers or retailers – spend millions every year on advertising. Most companies can relatively easily find a few cents for the Internet store from every dollar spent in the physical world.

Co-ordinate e-tail and normal advertising
We have already talked about the benefits of co-ordination here. Make sure that the Internet store appears in all your company's advertising. Show your Internet store across your full range of media. Make your advertising agency work to link creatively your traditional and virtual advertising campaigns. A great example here is IBM and its e-Business campaign. The same applies to PR activities. Nothing is more helpful for your home page than when it is discussed on television.

Refer to the Internet store at every opportunity

Use every press release and conference to promote your Internet store. Put the web-page address on all your company's products, letterheads, company brochures, answerphone messages, annual financial statements, price lists and e-mails. Link your next collection of free gifts and samples to your Internet store.

Develop a specific presence in traditional advertising

E-tailers are increasingly using traditional advertising media. Those with small budgets should at least advertise in the web guides put out by newspapers and magazines to point out their own Internet home page. *Bol* are advertising on television in the UK to push the brand. Portal site *Excite* is committed to a significant UK awareness-building campaign on TV. In the US we have already seen many television adverts for Internet stores.

Exploit customer contacts at delivery

Most Internet stores generate a chance for physical contact with their customers only when they deliver their products. Most often the contact is made by logistics and delivery-service providers and not by the company itself. There are creative ways to overcome this sterility or absence of final customer interaction. An e-tailer's package can be made easily recognisable from the outside; it is much more exciting to know that your CD from CDNow has arrived than finding another brown package in the mail. In Europe Amazon has been know to include jelly babies and handwritten thank you notes with large orders of books.

E-tail searchlight on web-sites for Chapter 5

- Amazon   www.amazon.com
- eBay   www.ebay.com
- Barnes & Noble   www.barnesandnoble.com
- CDNow   www.cdnow.com
- Music Boulevard   www.musicblvd.com
- Egg   www.egg.co.uk
- Smile   www.smile.co.uk
- Arcadia   www.zoom.co.uk
- Boo   www.boo.com
- Nike   www.nike.com
- Disney   www.disney.com
- Levi´s   www.levis.com
- Wal-Mart   www.wal-mart.com
- Macy´s   www.macys.com
- The Gap   www.gap.com
- Eddie Bauer   www.eddiebauer.com
- Bol   www.bol.de
- AOL   www.aol.com
- Computer.com   www.computer.com
- Next Computer   www.next.com
- Next Retail   www.next.co.uk
- 800   www.800.com
- Victoria´s Secret   www.victoriassecret.com
- Voucher Express   www.voucherexpress.com
- Inktomi   www.inktomi.com
- Petcat   www.petcat.co.uk
- Ecompare   www.ecompare.com
- Geocities   www.geocities.com
- Excite   www.excite.co.uk
- Liszt   www.liszt.com
- Dejanews   www.deja.com

Chapter 6

Getting the Internet Store Right

An Internet store is one that can be entered from anywhere in the world. The web-site is the sales floor. Getting the set-up of the store right for an e-tailer is a core competence, similar to new-product development and production for a consumer-goods manufacturer, catalogue publication for a mail-order firm and retail format and layout for a high-street retailer. We are surprised by the number of would-be e-tailers we have met who believe that 'setting up the store' is something that can be outsourced completely. They are right at the technical level, in terms of system to operate a store, but are missing a point that the look and feel of the online store provides one of the major components of the e-tailer's brand essence.

Anybody who buys a branded good, such as coffee, in a store can pay a variety of prices between shops. Retail stores demonstrate differences in layout, in advertising range and in-store service. As far as Internet stores are concerned, web design makes the difference: how comfortable is the user, how good are the graphics on the site, how quickly can I find the desired product, how easy is it to pay?'

Klaus Eierhoff
(Board member, Bertelsmann, Germany)

E-tail searchlight illuminates Chapter 6

- *Context makes the difference*
  'Content', 'community', 'commerce' and 'convenience' combine to create a shopping context for the customer. Web-site creation should be built around these from the start.
- *Decide on the right type of web-site*
  Today's millions of web-sites can be classified into just five types – from the 'presence only' to 'virtual-shopping world'. Start with the right e-tailing site in mind.
- *Enthuse your customers*
  Provide attractive design, entertainment or excitement: offer your customers something special.
- *Make shopping easy*
  Provide suitable shopping help and make the user's buying process easy. Help your customers navigate the site and customise it to their needs.
- *Keep critically testing your web-site*
  Fast-loading, legible text, good site-descriptors and a simple path to a transaction constitute the fundamentals of a well designed site.

Context makes the difference!

Web-sites can be classified depending on whether they focus

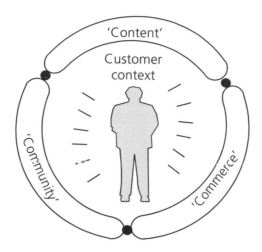

Fig. 6.1 Interplay between 'content', 'community' and 'commerce'.

on 'content', 'community' or 'commerce' for the user. We believe that successful Internet stores stand out because they create a successful interplay of these three factors, and also layer in convenience. Context is what makes great web-sites stand apart from the rest, and provides the online shopper with benefits beyond those available in physical stores. An e-tailer's website has to reflect this from its outset.

Web-sites offering 'commerce' alone are sterile, boring and unlikely to be successful. If an existing shop is reproduced on the Internet the customer never has the equivalent buying experience of the real shop. For this reason many early Internet shops failed. Those elements of the buying experience which are lost on the Internet, the smiles of the shop assistant, the ambience of the store, being able to touch the merchandise, cannot be balanced simply with technical gimmicks or wizardry. If you want to stand out you must have interesting content for the customer (to a degree mirroring but improving upon the sales assistants) and a new type of buying experience, which can be achieved through customer interaction. Any e-tailer who thinks that he can rely solely on the superiority and competitive pricing of products will very quickly fall behind the competition. The Internet shopper wants to be delighted, excited and 'wowed'. If they don't find it in one place, they can quickly seek it out elsewhere.

Web-sites offering only 'content' or 'community' find it very difficult to earn revenues, let alone profit. These find it extremely difficult to cover their costs as a widespread belief among users currently is that information and communities on the Internet should be free (see Chapter 11). The operators of these web-sites would have to have a very large number of users to be able to demand money for their services, on the basis that customers might be prepared to pay for access to a very wide network of like-minded individuals. So 'commerce' is a critical skill for all those intending to have a long-term presence on the web, particularly those whose model may major on 'content' or 'community'.

So provision of the three Cs should be top of the agenda when setting up an Internet store so that it has interesting context for the customer from the outset. Let us take an example. You want to open an online health and well-being store. As 'content' you want to offer information that is interesting for an appropriate target group. This could be:

◆ homeopathy and household-remedy books;
◆ recipes for healthy cooking;
◆ workout tips in different disciplines (e.g. swimming, jogging, aerobics);
◆ 'health weather' (ozone and smog levels, daily pollen counts for areas);
◆ links to/addresses of fitness studios, health farms, alternative-medicine practitioners;
◆ notes on events and health products (index by town);
◆ reports on healthy travel (e.g. walking holidays, cycling holidays);
◆ online advice on back problems for office workers;
◆ sun-protection recommendations for various skin types; and
◆ information on allergies.

This content has to be correct, up-to-date and clear so that it is of benefit to the customer. Information of this type is, of course, usually free, but it encourages the customer to come back to your web-site regularly. The health store needs to build up a 'community' of users. Of relevance here might be:

- chats with well-known sportsmen or models;
- themed message boards: 'Ask Dr. Winter about backache';
- discussion forum on weight problems;
- second-hand market for exercise equipment;
- massage or t'ai chi courses;
- moderated user forums on health products;
- online cooking courses with recipes from different customers; and
- database of customers' product recommendations.

The more strongly the customers feel that they belong to a community, the more loyal they will be towards a web-site. They will be, as it were, buying from their own club. Obviously different customers will behave very differently. Some will want to take part immediately. Others will be reluctant to take part, but they are no less loyal. A successful web store must provide these 'community' elements and consider how to match the special requirements of its users. The community itself can be a good source of self-generated content for the store. In this instance the network benefits we alluded to at the start of the book come into play: the larger the number of users, the more content is generated and, in the example of customer ratings, the more useful the content because of the larger base number of customers rating or recommending a product.

Last but not least comes 'commerce'. A critical set of decisions here is around the product range that the e-tailer wants to sell, particularly how much of the 'traditional' range is sold. Just as important, however, are considerations of visitor volumes and other sources of revenue, outside core-product categories. For example an e-tailer can sell someone else's minor ranges, set up auctions or let other shops participate on the site (the store in store concept). In terms of new revenue sources, manufacturers can be charged to publish information about their products on the site. If visitor-traffic volumes are large enough third-party advertising income may be a realistic source of additional revenue. Stimulating traffic may need co-operation with strong partner sites, in turn perhaps opening the way to new businesses.

At a very early stage the e-tailer needs a clear idea about how 'content', 'community' and 'commerce' are going to interact on the web-site. Looking at how competitors deal with the same factors is a good starting point. The ultimate decision around the interaction of these factors will have a great influence on the layout of the Internet store and its ultimate set-up and running costs. All three factors require different technology, resources and capabilities to be brought to bear to exploit them well.

A good example of an integrative site is *Baby Center* where 'content', 'community' and 'commerce' sit well together. The site is an Internet store and forum for pregnant women and young mothers. A fledgling example of where the three Cs are coming together is *PogoPet*. It provides great context for its target users, building a basis for long-term success.

PogoPet – a case study

PogoPet is a player in the particularly hotly contested market for 'pet portals'.

Stacey Estrella is a successful woman: a student at Harvard and Stanford, a meteoric career at Oracle and the founder of her own consultancy firm for fast-growing businesses. One day in the summer of 1998 she ran out of food for her beloved labrador retriever, 'Emma'. That day sparked an idea which changed her life. Stacey got together with Bruce Folge, an internationally known vet and author of more than thirty books about animals, and founded a pet portal. PogoPet offers a home on the Internet for pets and their owners.

PogoPet combines 'content', 'community' and 'commerce' in a way that is applicable to all portals:

◆ *PogoPet Care Centre* (static information: 'content 1')
Here owners can learn about everything that is important for their four-legged and other pets. All content on pet keeping is licensed exclusively and prepared specifically for the Internet. Asking a question about 'scratching' for example refers the user to a section on fleas and their prevention.

◆ *PogoPet Service Centre* (external service-provider: 'content 2')
A source of information on services for your little darling: from vets to dog groomers. This information is regularly updated.

◆ *PogoPet Neighbourhood* (exchange of experiences: 'community')
This is the platform where pet owners communicate with each other. It is the virtual equivalent of the guinea-pig club or dog club, but also for 'chance meetings in the street'. Pet owners like to chat – observe their behaviour on the street – there are few subjects that encourage communication more than animals.

◆ *PogoPet Shops* ('commerce')
Well, obviously, a place to buy products for and about pets.

The web-site also offers the opportunity for personalisation, the importance of which we discuss in more detail in Chapter 7. In *My PogoPet* you can enter the complete personal profile of both the pet and the household in which it resides. This area is linked to all the other parts of the web-site and contains, for example, an e-mail reminder service for medicines, vaccinations, birthdays and more. This is what a PogoPet's profile looks like:

Emma's Pogo Page

breed	labrador
colour	white
sex	female
born	13 October 1992
home town	San Francisco
favourite toy	sheepskin hare doll
friends and relatives	Hasso and Benjamin
favourite food	Frolic
favourite activity	swimming
favourite spot	terrace

If I get lost, please check my dog identification disc to find my owner.

rabies	xx23ghl
microchip	j4ftrl6qwd97
identification number	SF-123xyz

It is fun for most dog owners to fill in a page like this. The top part can be published in the 'Neighbourhood' section and provides a basis for communication. The bottom part has space for more important information such as the dog's identification tag number, which owners always mislay and usually can't find in an emergency.

A completed page gives PogoPet a wealth of information for personalised suggestions. A birthday gift? Vitamins for old age or as a supplement for their favourite food? A new cushion for their favourite spot? Are their friends already PogoPets? Every pet owner will quickly recognise the power of this interplay of 'content', 'community' and 'commerce'. The business potential is enormous. People love doing things for their little darlings, but they often forget their birthdays or can't think of a suitable something.

So how do people find out about PogoPet? At least two ways:

◆ First: marketing by the vets. These are people that pet owners trust and that have a great deal to gain from building this trust. A majority of pet owners forget to take their pets to the vet regularly. PogoPet reminds them. As a consequence, vets market PogoPet.

◆ Second: 'Word of mouse', or 'Viral marketing': The simple request – 'Please e-mail your friends about PogoPet.'

Perhaps the most interesting part of PogoPet is yet to come. When asked what will be sold in PogoPet's store, Stacey answers: 'No idea. We shall decide this later when we have a feel for what people really want. Many of our competitors are trying to make themselves different by offering the cheapest dog food. But the Internet is different: you have to get visitors and then you can start selling something. The strength of a web-site lies in customer allegiance and service partners. Cheap food is replaceable.'

Success on the Internet is not just a question of good ideas. Stacey and her team sustained their first Internet scars in the spring 1999 when a stampede for animal-owners' sites broke out, and suddenly everyone was rushing into the field. There were power struggles and intrigues between different venture capitalists and their chosen companies. Internet heavyweight Amazon.com bought the first pet web-site, PetShop. Forbes Magazine reported in June 1999 on the 'Piranha battle for pets'. In a year or so we shall know who, in spite of all the obstacles, has won the fight for investors and consumers.

Decide on the right type of web-site

There are millions of web-sites. More than 500,000 of them are related to electronic shopping. But very few of them actually generate any sales. Take a look round at the various Internet stores so that you can decide on what the right e-tailing entry is for you, right from the start. Web-sites can be classified in the following five ways:

- *Simple presence on the Internet*
  These web-sites provide static information about a company, are essentially text orientated and use only simple graphics. They take up few pages which are seldom updated. Investment requirements and upkeep expenses are just as small as the benefits. There are few reasons, other than seeking specific information, for a visitor to return to this type of web-site. Most commercial Internet sites are still of this type.
- *Image web-site*
  These web-sites contain company, product and advertising information. Text and graphics are increasingly being integrated, the layout is appealing. A simple menu leads you through the pages which reach into double figures. Image web-sites allow direct interaction between the customer and the company on a simple level. The focus of the site's development is ease of navigation and quality of information-content. It is updated at least once a month. Investment and upkeep in the first year require at least a five-figure sum.

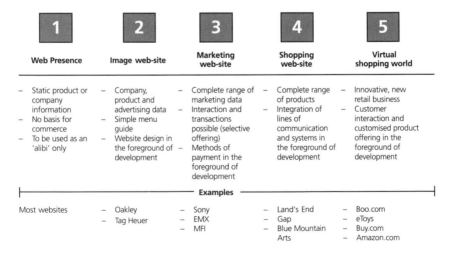

Fig. 6.2 Types of web-site.

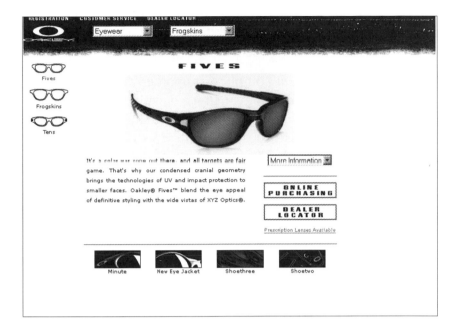

Screenshot: Oakley.

There are many such sites, but examples of unashamedly image-driven sites are those of *Oakley* and *Tag Heuer*. The critical issue for image sites is whether they can really lead to sales. An example of how image sites can draw users to transactions comes from *EMX*. The company manufactures products to combat the effects of high-frequency emissions from mobile phones. Its site provides a wealth of information on the issue, intended to capture the interest of users.

◆ *Marketing web-site*

These sites offer a company's complete range of marketing information. This is done by leading the user through a visual layout from which he can find his way around. The text is in the background. Both purchases and electronic transactions are possible but a complete product range is not offered. The focus of web-site development is the integration of payment systems to enable transactions. The number of pages usually runs to three figures and is updated at least once a week. Investment and upkeep in the first year requires at least a six-figure sum. A good example here is *Nike's* web-site which blends marketing with e-commerce capabilities; while *Sears* focuses in certain merchandise categories.

◆ *Shopping web-site*

These sites provide a complete shopping range with all the information and technology that go with it. They require comprehensive product databases and the integration of traditional business-processes with processes for web-selling. The focus of web-site development is linking online sales to all the necessary background functions and systems. The pages run to at least four figures. It is updated every day. Investment and upkeep require at least a seven-figure sum in the first year. Significant sales revenues can be attained rapidly. Good examples are found among the apparel retailers: *Gap, Land's End, JCrew.*

◆ *Virtual-shopping worlds*

These sites are new, strong Internet brands, which innovative retailers set up. They are context driven and offer a new shopping experience. They try hard to create real customer loyalty and offer the customer personalised ranges. Virtual-shopping worlds are leaders in target-group and one-to-one marketing and/or operate new types of market places. They systematically gather information on their customers' shopping history, and actively use this information, for example creating the first ranges tailored to a specific customer. These web-sites carry out intensive online promotions and set up links to a large number of other suppliers and business partners. They are quick to use technological advances and represent an ideal combination of marketing and technology. The focus of web-site development is customer interaction and personalisation of the products. Upkeep of the web-site is done in real time. Setting up a virtual-shopping world requires an eight-figure sum. Good examples are *Amazon* and *eToys.*

It is important to target the right type of web-site right from the start. Many companies adopt a stance that regards going onto the web as a learning process, allowing gradual evolution: 'just so long as we get something going we'll figure out what to

Screenshot: eToys.

do next later'. There are some good reasons for not adopting this 'suck it and see' approach:

- Unless you have the 'full Monty' of complete interaction and transaction with customers you will hardly learn anything useful. The learning comes from setting up to manage customer relations effectively and reorganising the appropriate business processes.
- Many potential customers will not come back to an Internet store if they have been disappointed the first time around – first impressions count (and second impressions cost lots of marketing dollars).
- The pace of Internet competition does not give e-tailers the time to develop and slowly 'test' several types of web-site.

Success lies in setting up a shopping site which has an interesting range to offer and a balanced relationship between 'content', 'community' and 'commerce'. Obviously at the outset not every possible function, product in the range and piece of related information will all be available, but development should be on a platform which will allow this and this should be the ultimate ambition.

Enthuse your customers

A successful shopping site should fire potential customers with enthusiasm in at least one respect. There has to be a hook, something that is out of the ordinary for the majority of customers. For potential customers the hook helps build preference for the specific site and word of mouth (or mouse) may encourage other Internet users to visit. The critical question here is what on the site offers the visitor something special. Enthusiasm can be inspired by, amongst other things, beautiful design, entertainment or exciting services.

Electronic shopping is mainly a visual experience. Beautiful design can lead to preferences and promote sales. *Garden Escape* understands that the 'garden' theme has to be an experience right from the home page, although clearly 'content' and 'commerce' are at the forefront. *Sephora* has one of the most graphically appealing web sites of all large companies. But 'commerce' is much too limited in it. *Violet* has chosen a good compromise. This shop offers design orientated gifts in six categories: '6 departments, no crowds.' Product details are well documented and the goods artistically presented on screen.

Online games ensure entertainment and can be used to attract parents into e-shopping with their children. Some commentators believe that the initial success of Microsoft Windows with users has been due in no small way to the fact that it includes games like solitaire and minesweeper. Games can be organised thematically and can appeal to a specific target-group, suited to the web-site. Multiplayer games can also promote elements of 'community'. *Sony* has online games as one of the core areas of its home page. There are even opportunities to organise games in which customers can win money. *Gamesville* has shown that with a skilful choice of games even the smallest wins can lead to a large number of visits.

Screenshot: Violet.

The best solution is if product presentation itself can be entertaining. In *Eddie Bauer's* Dressing Room you can dress a mannequin with clothes and try out more and more combinations as a game in itself. The Internet store of *Sharper Image*, the New York dealer in technical gift ideas, offers the visitor a 3D presentation of its products. The potential buyer can view articles 'as if they were in his hand', check them by looking them all over and even try movable parts and the individual functions of the unit by clicking on the mouse. The web-site of *Clairol*, US market leader for hair colouring, has a 'virtual mirror' in which the visitor can view various styles and hair colours. All that is needed is a digital photo stored on the user's PC on which various styles can be tried out. This spread like wildfire in US offices, offering users utility and, at the same time, the chance to have fun with friends and colleagues.

A further way to fire visitors to a web-site with enthusiasm is with exciting services. Customers who want to book a hotel room with *Lastminute.com* can have a virtual tour before booking. They view the hotel from the outside, all round, go into the

Screenshot: Clairol.

hotel foyer, check out the swimming pool and finally look at the room that they can book. Tickets for visits to major events will soon be obtained in the same way. *Ticketmaster* offers potential spectators at NFL American Football matches the chance to check out the view from their seats in a virtual stadium and use this as a price guide for tickets.

Services are exciting when customers do not expect them. Austrian builder/developer *Mischek* is working on a large residential construction project 'Donaupark'. The interested visitor (potential purchaser) to the web-site can take a virtual helicopter flight over his future home during the building phase and also check out the view from his future balcony and the position of the most important facilities in the area. In one of the empty flats he can move dividing walls himself and get an impression of the layout and the way the fittings can be arranged.

Special features of this kind are more than gimmicks, they enthuse potential customers as well as adding utility to the site or store. We are not saying that you can create a workable business model on the basis of unexpected services alone, but they help to set a site apart from its competitors and are one of the pre-conditions for building the frequency of customer visits and longer-term customer loyalty.

Make shopping easy for your customers

It may sound obvious, but e-tailers need to do everything they can to make it easy for customers to find the Internet store; to go in and find everything within it; to choose products and above all to buy them. Ensuring that the customer feels at ease during their shopping trip is just as important in the electronic world as it is in the physical world. E-tailers need to find what works to make their customers feel at ease.

As a first step in this direction, many commercial sites offer the visitor a *guided tour* as an aid, making it easier to navigate the site. Good examples of guided tours can be found on the sites of the information-provider *Express*, *Eddie Bauer's* customer-service area and the test portfolio of stock broker *Consors*.

Answers to so-called *FAQs* (frequently asked questions) are another useful way of putting customers at their ease. Answers to FAQs are intended essentially to avoid the cost of repetitive customer-service queries, be these ultimately handled over the phone or by e-mail. As a result FAQs are very popular (from the site owner's perspective) on commercial web-sites. They can cover a wide range of topics, from the overtly technical e.g. 'What does it mean if I cannot click and drag a product into my shopping basket' to the covertly encouraging e.g. 'How safe are my credit-card details if I give them over the net'. Critical subjects which influence purchase decisions and behaviour, like payment conditions or data protection, can be dealt with by FAQs in an objective and neutral form. Many FAQs are clearly anticipatory in nature, the e-tailer has pre-empted what his customers' concerns and questions may be. Formulating resolution of users' issues as a question-and-answer game can make even difficult subjects simple. The user does not have the impression that he is the only one with a lot of questions and may even feel that he is being catered for personally. Good FAQs like those on the *US Post* web-site offer links to additional information about the relevant questions. Some companies, like *Merant*, publish internal memos answering important questions on the FAQ page if they can help a customer. The first rule for FAQs, however, is 'Don't just list the questions, give the answers too.' We have found a number of web-sites which list the most frequently asked questions but don't give any answers.

Making it easy for customers to find and select products sounds like an obvious thing to do but there are some subtleties to think through. If a customer has problems deciding on an article which he can see on screen, offer him more information about the article. A web-site can potentially include more knowledge than a salesman could ever offer. The trick is to make sure that it is easily to hand rather than having to wait for the customer to ask for it. Just as in a store where many people too embarrassed or short of time to ask for help finishing a specific article, so those browsing a shopping site need easily accessible buttons to click which can provide further information. The best, most responsive, sites should be able to sense that an article has been displayed for longer than average, and fire a banner at the user, perhaps saying 'Not sure? For more information about our XYZ range click here.'

Finding innovative approaches to bring the product closer to the customer is keeping a good number of web experts in work. The *Gap* gives visitors to its web-site a *zoom function* with which they can see details on an article of clothing like buttons or the specific patterns on a fabric more clearly. At the same time further information on the quality of the workmanship in the garment is also supplied.

It is worth a word or two here on the topic of search capabilities on an e-tail site. Many retailers who have turned e-tailers have opted for search tools on their sites which allow you to search their (mainframe held) product catalogues. This involves a number of tricky systems 'patches' between the mainframe 'legacy back-end' and the 'web front-end'. These patches have to be put in place to translate the questions that a customer is likely to ask on the web front-end into language that the legacy back-end systems can understand. On the web a customer will ask questions much as they would in a store: for example 'have you got a Junior geo Safari' might be a question addressed to an online toy store; in practice translated by the customer into a simple filling in of a 'search our store' function with the words Junior geo Safari. This then has to be translated into a product (or stock-keeping unit – SKU) code that the legacy inventory or buying systems can interpret. This is when the fun (or pain) really starts.

There are at least six ways in which 'Junior geo Safari' could sensibly be entered as a search term in a search utility. The best e-tailers will have anticipated all of these, or have a programme which interprets what is written and throws back a number of possible answers. The less good e-tailers, probably retailers who have decided they must have a web store, will have taken the least complex route of allowing perhaps two variants to be recognised, but any other than these two variants will receive the response that the product is out of stock or not stocked. Result – a lost sale. All is not plain sailing for those using a programme which allows 'fuzzy' or 'close matching'. Customers can just as easily be put off by being offered five alternative products that appear to bear little relation to their request as simply being told 'we don't have it'. Search engine quality can differ quite strongly on different retail sites. Incorrectly enter a search for Sonny (rather than Sunny) Ade music on CD Now and it forgives your mistake. Do the same on Amazon and it offers you memorabilia of Muhammad Ali's fight with Sonny Liston!

Getting what appears to be a 'simple' function like searching what is stocked (and in stock) right can be hard, particularly if one has tens of thousands of possible SKUs on offer. There are no simple answers on how to get this right. Extensive pre-testing, observation of how real customers use the facility and up-front investment in thinking through the architecture of the site, to reduce the need for product-specific searching, are all part of the solution. We talk more about site architecture and navigation in a few paragraphs' time. Needless to say, pure e-tailers, without existing legacy information systems are at a distinct advantage.

Giving customers a *virtual shopping cart*, into which they can put articles while they are visiting a web-site has become a well established tool to build enthusiasm for online shopping – it mirrors the real-world experience and once the cart is reasonably full the customer is loathe to abandon it in mid-shop. *Peapod*, among the US's best known Internet based grocery suppliers, automatically gives its customers a shopping list of the articles which are usually bought each week or each month and which can be rapidly put into cart. Prompting repeat orders and making them easy to make are important.

Simplifying the *act of purchasing* is also a must. Actually ordering something is the moment when most would-be customers break off. Customers must, right from the first desire to purchase, have confidence that the company will fulfil what are essentially unseen performance promises. They need to have faith in the security of the transaction. Up to now this has been one of the greatest obstacles to generating transactions online. If a customer prefers to give credit card details over the phone to an automated recipient, or wants to contact the company personally, he should be able to do this easily. Access to a freephone call centre is an expensive must: *Dell* indicates this service on its home page: 'Buy Online or Call: 1-800-WWW-DELL'. The critical issue here is to try to avoid calls escalating and keep interaction to e-mail. Phone costs undermine the web cost advantage.

Easy shopping and user-friendliness

Amazon.com was one of the first e-tailers to convert massive numbers of their browsers into customers and still has a high conversion rate among first-time users. Amazon is quick to point out to its users the security of the transactions that they may make and gives further information if requested. It manages the first-time buyers process extremely well. The data it needs to collect to allow a first-time purchase, name, address, credit card details, etc., are just as comprehensive as in other Internet stores, but its steps are well structured so that the customer feels logically led to the purchase, rather than feeling 'I want to buy a book, why do have to fill in all this stuff now?'. Amazon also makes second-time purchasing easy by giving users a unique name and password. They also refer many times to their generous returns' policy. In this way it has achieved a high conversion rate for first-time users, which has been reflected in their rapid growth

As well as these 'tools', Internet customers expect to be able to navigate through the site easily. Many studies have shown that attention and patience are in extraordinarily short supply for the Internet user, and personal experience will tell you that they are right! Each time a visitor to a web has to think where he is and where he wants to go makes him more inclined to leave with the next click. For a customer, learning the way around a web-site has to be much easier than learning to use other software. It has to be similar in ease of use to picking up on a game show on the television. The challenge is to create a web-site that takes the visitor quickly to his goal without stress.

Users should be able to go through the site intuitively. A visitor to a web-site should be able to find his way around without any specific help. We distinguish two levels here: navigation, that is the arrangement of the pages in relation to each other ('streets') and labelling the navigation elements ('street signs'). Both elements have the task of setting out the routes to the individual areas on the web-site so that the visitor can reach the desired information easily and quickly.

There are two basic types of *navigation*: 'hierarchical' or 'networked'. Hierarchical navigation builds up a web-site's areas like a pyramid and leads the visitor from the general to the specific. This may mean, depending on the range of the web-site, several intermediate stops before reaching the desired goal. A typical web-site with hierarchical navigation is *Yahoo* ('**y**et **a**nother **h**ierarchically **o**rganised **o**racle'). Yahoo's information catalogue is divided deductively into sections through which visitors can pull themselves, hand-over-hand as it were, to the desired object. Similar navigation elements and short loading times ensure that this process does not last too long. *Altavista*, originally a search tool, now has a 'mixed' model.

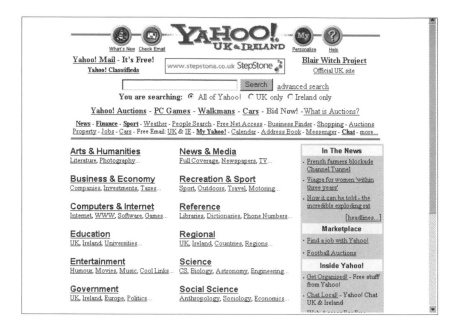

Screenshot: Yahoo.

Networked navigation sets up a web-site's areas as a network, in which everything is linked to everything else. Site maps, pop-up menus, indexes and search functions help visitors find their way around. While there are a few 'main roads' through hierarchical web-sites, many paths and short cuts run through globally navigated web-sites which allow for a more spontaneous buying experience. An example of global navigation is the web-site of *FAO Schwarz*, the famous New York toy store.

A good navigation system contains a healthy mixture of hierarchical and networked navigation. If the web-site is too hierarchical, it will be boring and predictable. If on the other hand it is too networked, visitors lose track more easily of where they are. The right mixture may also depend on the target group. Let us make some bold assertions here. Older people have usually learnt from books and prefer deductive and text-orientated approaches to navigation. Younger people more often think in a networked, picture-orientated way. If it is possible you should leave the user to decide on their preferred choice of navigation.

Screenshot: FAO Schwartz.

Labelling is an area of navigation that is often overlooked. By labelling we mean text labels and symbols (icons), which a web-site uses for navigation. It is best to keep to labels that are generally known on the Internet. Typical of this type of label are 'Home', 'Search', 'News', 'About us', 'Contacts' or 'Site map'. Because these terms and their functions have been established as standard, you should not reinvent the wheel. The same applies to established symbols like buttons, navigation bars or search fields. If no explanation is needed for these, the visitor finds his way round intuitively. Creating new words and new icons leads to confusion. Unleashing creative forces on re-labelling what have become standard signposts on web-sites can be dangerous – like changing street signs on unexpectant motorists: at best they just get lost, at worst they generate a bad case of road rage and avoid coming back at all costs.

Check the design of your web-site

The design of the web-site is essential to the success of an Internet store. Top management will, of course, leave web-site design to internal and external experts, but there are a few design rules which should be helpful to managers who are responsible for placing design orders. Readers who are more interested in the strategic aspects of electronic shopping should jump to the end of this chapter, although we have laid out our thoughts in a simple check list to allow swift reading.

Internet coding and programming language was not developed for designers of advertisements, even if pictures and photos can easily be mounted in a page. Despite much apparent comment to the contrary, current Internet technology places many hurdles in the way of successfully creating a web-site. The critical rule for those specifying the design of a site is not to allow a designer to have it all his own way. The following rules should help you judge whether your web-site design will help or hinder shopping success.

Rule 1: Short loading-time

Waiting-time is fatal for any shopping experience whether it is in a virtual or a real shop. The web-site design must avoid lengthy loading processes. You can drastically reduce the memory requirements of your web-site without cutting out content or layout if your designers heed the following tips:

- ◆ Use the same design elements on several pages! The user's PC recognises these during the visit and can download them faster.
- ◆ Use graphics instead of photos! Good photos eat up memory even if you can revise colour scales and resolution.
- ◆ Use vector graphics instead of bitmaps! Bitmap graphics are resolved in individual pixels like photos. There are various formats for this (gif, jpeg) with specific advantages and disadvantages. Vector graphics, resolve a circle for example,

not in individual dots, but describe it with a simple geometrical formula which uses up the minimum amount of memory.

- Use few large instead of many small pictures! Don't fill the pages with too much. You not only gain disc space, but also make the screen clearer for the customer. It usually makes it more attractive too.

- Don't put too much information on the first page. Use a 'splash screen', which draws visitors to your web-site and at the same time leads regular users to the desired transactions!

- The ideal Internet 'appearance' is only as fast as the slowest modem. Make sure that pictures build up in steps. The visitor can guess what is coming while he is waiting or will recognise shapes.

- Before you release your web-site, go through it systematically for areas hungry for disk space! Reduce the number of colours used on pages and revise the colour scale and resolution of photos and graphic elements! This does not usually make any discernible difference to the look of the site. As a rule of thumb, the memory requirements of a page should be less than 30K.

- Shop the store while simulating the access speed of a customer with an analogue connection and a slow modem at busy times!

- Make sure you have enough server capacity! Think about the maximum requirements and the best case demand you could expect for the next six months! Bottlenecks accessing the server have an immediate effect on your customer hit rates, they prevent potential sales and alienate potential first-time buyers, who may not come back in a hurry.

Rule 2: Make text layouts legible

Do you enjoy reading instructions for use? If so, you'd like some of today's web-sites. Most customers do not want to, and will not read long, obscure texts (including legal agreements)! Your designer should heed the following tips:

◆ Choose the font you use carefully! (There are special fonts just for the Internet obtainable from Microsoft's web-site). The font should be pleasant to read and work well on all systems and with all browsers. Investing in a high-quality font is always worth it.

◆ Be careful with coloured writing. Less is often more here, especially if you use coloured graphic elements at the same time. Standard text should be black.

◆ Avoid empty lines and drawn horizontal lines to create text blocks. Use indentation and colour blocking (especially for tables) instead. Lines not only take up more disk space, but have to be processed visually by the reader. Even in the real world, graphic designers have been battling for years against such overloading of text.

◆ Avoid long lines of text. Diagrams today are predominantly in landscape format because with a large font the lines of available text are too short. But try reading the text of a book in A4 landscape format. You quickly find it a strain. The same goes for web-sites. Graphic-orientated pages should be wide. Text-orientated pages, like detailed product-information or press releases, are best kept narrow.

◆ Avoid margins that are too narrow. Clear margins simplify reading. Take care that even on small screens the right-hand margin does not disappear.

◆ Avoid annoying background pictures. The only real background for text is a single colour. Black text on a light background is the most easily read.

◆ If it is feasible, offer your visitors the possibility of choosing between text and graphics. Many customers are interested in fast access to information. Frequent users especially want to forgo pages which include lots of graphic elements but not much information.

◆ Check whether the text can be shortened. As Goethe once put it: 'I have written you a long letter because I didn't have time to write a short one.'

Rule 3: Attractive layout

Take your visitors through a virtual world in which they would like to spend a little time. This assumes the use of graphics and brings you into a potential conflict with the aims with rule 1. One critical thing is to make sure that the web-site looks attractive:

◆ Avoid technical errors like dots in pictures and lines, visible pixels and shadows in photos and graphics. These mistakes are noticed by customers and annoy them.
◆ Emphasise an up-to-date feel. The Internet is a modern medium, that is visited by technically aware people. If in doubt, make your web-site feel more modern rather than less. But keep within the boundaries of your corporate design.
◆ Don't shy away from changes. It is quite usual to re-create a web-site after a few months of e-tailing, when you have experience from customers to guide your changes. Consider offering your customers a new experience from time to time without confusing them; there should be some continuity from one change to the next.
◆ Invest in design quality. Go to just as much trouble with your web-site as with a new advertising campaign.

Rule 4: Remember your commercial goals

By remembering your commercial aims for your site, you can ensure that it is not just design awards that your web store collects. The key here is to think creatively about drawing visitors to the site and making them want to return.

◆ 'Only three clicks away' – Customer behaviour on the Internet is easily measured. Research indicates that within three clicks visitors must either be captivated by the site or have reached their specific goal, otherwise they will leave the store. So helping them get to the point of purchase rapidly is a must.

◆ Fill your first page with key terms that the general search engines can latch on to! This is the most obvious way to draw interested traffic to the store. The key terms used on your home page can be invisible and only found by search engines. One key point here is to make sure that your terms make sense to the broadest range of users. For example a soft-furnishings retailer in the UK might use the term 'curtains' but forget to use the US equivalent, 'drapes'.

◆ Confirm that the layout of your web-site works with all current browser versions and operating systems. A perfect demo version in your office may not work well everywhere. Simulate the different types of access through which the customers find their way to you. Test Netscape and Microsoft browsers, work with Windows and Mac. Check direct access through the World Wide Web as well as through AOL or equivalent portals. Customers must be able to buy easily from everywhere.

E-tail searchlight on web-sites for Chapter 6

- Baby Center   www.babycenter.com
- Oakley   www.oakley.com
- Tag Heuer   www.tagheuer.com
- EMX   www.emf-bioprotection.com
- Nike   www.nike.com
- Sears   www.sears.com
- Landsend   www.landsend.com
- JCrew   www.JCrew.com
- Amazon   www.amazon.com
- Microsoft Networks   www.msn.com
- Garden Escape   www.garden.com
- Sephora   www.sephora.com
- Violet   www.violet.com
- Sony   www.sony.com
- Gamesville   www.gamesville.com
- Eddie Bauer   www.eddiebauer.com
- Sharper Image   www.sharperimage.com
- Clairol   www.clairol.com
- Lastminute.com   www.lastminute.com
- Ticketmaster   www.ticketmaster.com
- Mischek   www.mischek.at
- Express   www.express.com
- Eddie Bauer   www.eddiebauer.com
- Consors   www.consors.com
- US-Post   www.usps.com
- Merant   www.merant.com
- Peapod   www.peapod.com
- Dell   www.dell.com
- Yahoo   www.yahoo.com
- Altavista   www.altavista.com
- FAO Schwarz   www.fao.com

Chapter 7

Building Individual

Customer Relations

In e-shopping, the most important and most rewarding investment is in building individual customer relations. One-to-one
sales to individual customers is a trump card that every e-shopping player needs to hold. In Chapter 5 we discussed how you
attract visitors to your web-site. In Chapter 6 we showed how
you should set up your web-site so that your customers never
leave it. This chapter discusses how to win customers' interest,
permanently.

E-tail searchlight illuminates Chapter 7

◆ *True customer loyalty to a site is becoming more and more important but more and more difficult to win*
The more e-tailing develops, the more critical strategies to develop customer loyalty become. Internet users' acceptance of simple 'push strategies' is rapidly waning. Offer your customers specific benefits for giving you information, helping you build allegiances to your site.

◆ *Build individual customer relations in stages!*
1 get to know and understand your customers;
2 address customers individually;
3 let customers create the buying experience; and
4 promote customer communities.

◆ *Recognise the value of your customers!*
Learn how to judge the lifetime value of a customer, the profitability of different customer groups and the value of customer networks.

True customer loyalty to a site is becoming more and more important but more and more difficult to win

Even in today's sophisticated retail environment, most companies do not know their customers well enough, do not value customer data sufficiently, often fail to reach their full potential audience, and can only win new customers at considerable expense. There are certainly exceptions: manufacturers of nappies and baby foods have developed distribution skills which allow them to reach nearly all young mothers. Airlines such as British Airways have well-developed customer loyalty programmes. In general, however, the possibilities of direct-to-customer communications which drive loyalty have been well developed by only a very small number of companies. The main focus of considerable investment in customer-data projects has been on winning new customers away from the competition.

The Internet world offers the opportunity to do *direct* business with individual customers and to win them for the long term with *individual* offers. Every individual customer's electronic transactions can be identified, buying patterns watched and evaluated. By the same token individual customer satisfaction becomes measurable. This is a key part of every e-tailer's basic know-how and represents a huge competitive edge over traditional retailers.

Customer loyalty is becoming more and more important

Success as an e-tailer comes in three steps: winning individual customers, getting to know them well, and making them come back. The more e-tailing develops, the more critical customer-loyalty and return-rate measurements become. In the early days of the Internet it was a question of making your own products known and acquiring new customers. Only when the ma-

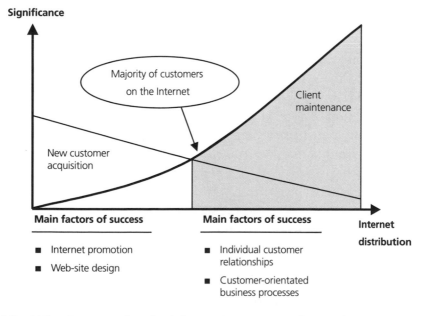

Fig. 7.1 Customer loyalty is becoming more and more important.

jority of customers in a target group use the Internet as their shopping centre will regular customer loyalty become more important than winning new customers for all suppliers. Setting up the brand and creating shops are then less important than building up individual customer relationships and also creating customer-orientated business processes.

Internet shops need to use the customer information available to them from their earliest stages of operation to establish trusting relationships with individual customers, to gain a competitive edge. We discuss the necessary tools to do this during this chapter. Building customer loyalty really means creating switching costs, which prevent customers using another supplier's Internet shop. Switching costs are currently very low on the Internet because each Internet web-site is only a click away. Deliberately creating switching costs is therefore the bedrock for permanent differentiation in e-tailing. Customer information, customer loyalty and switching costs are the three pillars of successful customer relationship management (CRM).

But winning customer loyalty is becoming more and more difficult

The Internet shopper's tolerance of 'blunt instruments' of customer loyalty is rapidly falling. Simple 'push strategies' like unsolicited e-mails are becoming less and less acceptable to Internet users. There are now a number of service providers who manage customer data in the interests of the customers and act as middleman for transactions. In California companies must now pay a $50,000 fine per e-mail if they send e-mails to customers who have expressly said that they do not want them. There is a growing demand for software which protects Internet users from banner advertising and e-mail news (see Chapter 9). Finally it is significant that there are more and more would-be e-tailers trying to establish their Internet shops. Marketing methods which worked for the first successful Internet store no longer attract so many, increasingly sophisticated, custom-

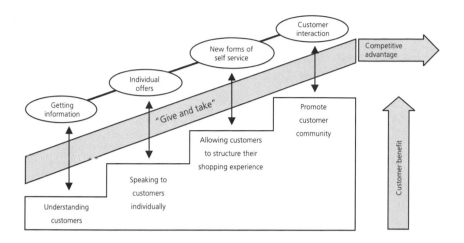

Fig. 7.2 Customer benefits from customer relationship management.

ers. The early e-tailers have a significant advantage over those who have only come into e-tailing later.

What does that mean for you? Prepare yourself for the fact that the refrain 'It's good for you, it's good for me' must become the e-tailers' mantra. Internet customers expect specific rewards for giving out information about themselves, and are increasingly less tolerant of having their details distributed to different suppliers. Without concrete benefits, customers will fight information collection or, worse, avoid your shop. 'Give and take' begins at the collection stage and the customer must feel the same thing in all customer-loyalty programmes. This has to be reinforced with a high degree of data protection. Treating a customer's information as privileged is the only way to build long-term customer relationships.

Build individual customer relationships in four stages

Direct customer relationships are the e-tailer's trump card – if they are built up properly. Most would be e-tailers on the Internet have few visitors, very few first-time buyers (less than three per cent of visitors) and hardly any repeat buyers (less

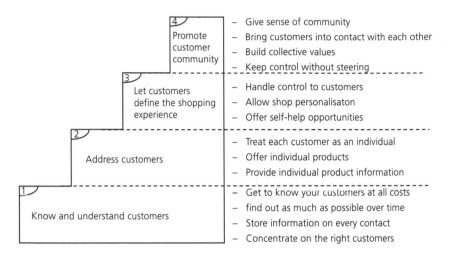

Fig. 7.3 Building customer loyalty in four stages.

than one per cent of visitors). This is not a very encouraging background for getting into direct customer relations. Customers don't come on their own, they want to be wooed and won. E-tailers must always do something to 'wow' them into staying. Building customer loyalty successfully involves the following:

1   get to know and understand your customers;
2   address them individually;
3   let customers create the buying experience; and
4   promote customer communities.

Step 1: get to know and understand your customers

You must get to know your customers!

You must persuade your visitors to leave their key details with you right from their very first visit. Avoid a long-winded registration process when they first visit the site as there is no greater turn-off in a customer's eyes. Ask your visitors for feedback instead. It is often more effective to offer visitors both the possibility of writing comments in a guest book and actively asking for their opinion on various topics as they do so. It is during these self-initiated processes that customers can be required to leave their details.

Incentives for registration make sense. Participation in a competition, an invitation to an event in the area, innovative free gifts, a voucher for the first purchase or an invitation for a test purchase in which the first article is free, are all methods in current use. The most common type of registration takes place at the time of purchase itself. As we have already mentioned, it is at this moment that most visitors leave Internet shops. Given this dynamic it is better to know the customer already, or offer a particular incentive for handing his details over. Clarity to customers concerning which registration fields are mandatory and which optional is also an important point.

In some instances 'members only' sections, which provide additional information, can be used to collect customer details as an entrance fee. Such 'members only' sections can have a certain VIP air about them but should have several levels of membership so that members still have a prospect of raising their status. If the entrance fee is only a few standard items of information, you will not be able to maintain the appearance of exclusivity for long.

Try to find out as much as possible about your customers over time!

A returning customer represents your first success. Tracking the 'progress' of customers within your Internet shop yields a great deal of learning about their behaviour. You can soon recognise patterns of behaviour that form the basis for further development of your web-site utility and/or products tailored to the individual.

Site-usage profiles are part of this picture. More important is the creation of user profiles. According to eTrust more than 40 per cent of all users leave a web-site when personal details are asked for. Of those remaining, almost 25 per cent leave false details. A particularly popular e-mail address, when asked, is gates@microsoft.com. However, almost 90 per cent of all visitors claim to be ready to give information if they receive an adequate reward for it. Motivating your customers to give you more information is an e-tailer's skill.

Hallmark, US market leader in greeting cards, offers both electronic greeting cards and a free reminder service. Their customers are given plenty of notice of an impending event. From Hallmark's perspective they are more likely to buy an electronic greeting card. The key here is that, to get a reminder, customers must give out a large amount of personal data such as partner's name, the number and ages of any children or the size of a circle of friends that would otherwise probably not be revealed.

On *Barbie*'s web-site the young and the old can put together their personal Barbie doll. By tracking customers' favourite Barbie 'make ups', Barbie conducts almost-free market research on what's in demand. Barbie records the favourite doll models and the most requested accessories – both those that are purchased and those that are not purchased because their profile creators are too young to give a credit card number. The information gathered in this way is used to revise the product range for traditional sales channels. Even if they do not sell very much over the Internet, the web-site is a very valuable resource for understanding the customer.

Store all the information on every customer contact!

Set up a comprehensive data record for each customer with all their available information. Ensure that the data from each customer contact is recorded – each purchase, each delivery, each visit, each complaint. The old days of data storage being too expensive and software being too cumbersome to interpret the data are gone. *Microsoft* has perfected the gradual collection of customer information, building extensive profiles from multiple visits. Customer details, well assembled and understood, are one of the sharpest weapons that leading Internet traders have against newcomers.

Make the information stored available to the customer. Customers should be able to access their shopping history at any time. Don't be afraid to let them correct their own data. Many are prepared to give further information if they can see their own profile. Or take the case of an acquaintance who recently gained a doctorate and has two bank accounts: one with a large bank and one with an online bank. Months after being allowed the use of the title he had not got round to asking a bank employee in his branch to add 'Doctor' to his customer details, but with his online bank he did it himself, and has found himself preferring to use his online bank credit card which has his title on it. Another reason to give customers access to their data profile is simply cost: why retain expensive employees to alter addresses or credit card details?

Use all the information available to understand the customer!

Suppliers who already have individual customer information have a strong starting position as potential e-tailers. Obvious players here are mail-order firms or retailers who have built up archives of customer cards. These information resources shouldn't be forgotten as a first line of inquiry into the potential customers for your Internet shop. With some judicious manipulation and re-cutting of data held originally for catalogue distribution, they can often yield useful strategy insight into potential core customers. Remember, however, that the Internet provides reach beyond your existing customers; don't become over-focused on those you know. Those you have yet to meet count too!

An important second step is to link individual customer data from the physical world with the information about your Internet customers. Customers expect you to have all relevant information about them if they've given it to you once. There is nothing more frustrating than interacting with an organisation where 'the left hand doesn't know what the right hand is doing'. Ask your customers for details once and once only and make them available to your staff regardless of point of contact, be it Internet, telephone, fax or letter. Again, repeating information, often in the course of the same phone call, drives customers to despair.

Learn from your growing hoard of information!

E-tailers have to be fast-learning organisations. Your hoard of customer information is going to grow quickly but can constantly open up new possibilities for you. The systematic collection of every piece of customer information related to interaction with the company and customer transactions, creates the opportunity both to offer products tailored to be of benefit to the individual customer, and to evolve whole ranges further.

Dell is a good example here. Dell's sales success has given it so much customer information that the company now has offers for different target groups within their own Internet shop. Dell discovered that customers from large companies, univer-

Screenshot: Gigabuys from Dell.

sities, the public sector and small companies not only demanded different products, but also purchased in very different ways. So in Europe Dell built five 'shops' to match their customer segments, and reached from the main site. Dell also understood early on that with direct contact their business customers allowed them to collect a large amount of information about end users. In March 1999 Dell's *Gigabuys* opened, supplying software and computer accessories to consumers. This business extension was made possible only by mining the customer information that Dell had available from its hardware business. Online auctions are a further addition to Dell's web presence. These are an excellent way to sell refurbished, ex-lease PCs which , given that they were built to order, would otherwise be hard to sell.

Concentrate on the right customers at the outset

Not all visitors become attractive customers and not all early customers have a high lifetime value. Try early to judge which of your customers are high-value ones to you. Concentrate your efforts on building up direct relations with those in this group. Give these valuable customers preferential treatment. In the early stages you can fall back on your experiences with different customer segments in your original business. Soon, however, you need to make a further assessment of which customers are most valuable with the help of customer information gathered over the Internet.

Take the example of airlines and car-hire firms that have comprehensive customer-card programmes. US market-leaders *American Airlines* and *Hertz* initially aimed their Internet offer at members of their customer clubs. Both companies offered their loyal customers special services and special offers over the web. They increased the loyalty of their existing members and acquired large numbers of new members. If your Internet store is a success for your most important customers, you can open it up – or at least the standard services – to a wider range of customers. American Airlines offers one of the web's best air-travel agencies with online booking and travel planning. The company calculates its prices based on Internet bookings. Travel-agent customers pay a higher price.

Not all purchasers actually make the purchase decision. Make sure that your Internet store is attractive to the real customer. Take the example of successful express parcel services. *United Parcel Service* and *Federal Express* have aimed their websites not at the requirements of the purchasing departments of their business customers, but at those people who actually use the service and most need to know the status of a delivery. Users can follow important consignments at any time until a package is finally received.

The same also applies in consumer businesses. It's a statement of the obvious, but baby goods and toys are not sold to small children themselves. In many clothes shops more men's clothes are bought by women than by men. Make sure that your Internet store is aimed at the right decision-maker.

Step 2: address customers individually

Treat each customer as an individual!

Address each customer by name when he comes back to your web-site. This is the least you can do to build up a personal relationship. Some companies employ staff to generate standard answers to e-mail enquiries, while signing them with their name to build up a feeling of a personal contact. Alternatively they provide answers or recommendations through a specific person who has gained the customer's trust and begun to develop a relationship with him.

One of our clients, an early Internet pioneer, hired a student called Jenny to answer e-mail requests. Jenny could not answer all of the specialist questions that arose but she took a great deal of care over every individual query until 'her' customers were satisfied. Rapid growth in the company meant that the amount of e-mail increased rapidly, but Jenny's exams got closer and closer. She left to take them. The company took on two 'professionals'. After only three days the e-mails began to mount up asking: 'Where's Jenny?' Now the company employs four 'Jennys', who answer e-mail queries according to their own revised Jenny hand book, which she helped write after her exams were successfully passed!

It is surprising that the Internet, which is by nature a rather impersonal medium, can clearly offer a personal experience to many people. Always remember that you are dealing with individuals who want to be treated as such. Today's technologies can do this efficiently and at reasonable cost. There are systems available that enable automatic answering and personalisation at the same time. Personalisation takes many forms some of which are obviously clumsy, others more subtle. Answering queries and addressing the customer by name is a start. Mentioning that other customers in the same town have had the same query could take it further. Monitoring what 'works' for the customer is critical. If the customer feels the response is 'personal' it works; if not you can't blame the software.

Remember that e-mail is the most widely used (and abused) Internet function. Companies must ensure that e-mail queries are answered within 24 hours – it's what customers expect. Despite this, more than a quarter of large European retailers do not use e-mail as a method of contact with customers. A third have an e-mail address but do not answer simple queries. This is catastrophic for relationships with online customers, and costly; answering the same question through a call centre costs ten times as much.

For traditional companies implementing a robust e-shopping initiative, one of the critical elements is to manage the customer relationship across multiple channels, for one-to-one marketing, sales and customer service. Innovative technology providers have been addressing this issue. The one we like best is RightPoint (see box).

Offer the customer individually tailored products!

It is now common practice for personal computers to be configured

RightPoint – building 'real-time eMarketing'

RightPoint addresses a fundamental issue of so-called 'clicks-and-mortar' businesses, i.e. companies that have a strong real world as well as on-line presence. How do you manage a customer relationship across multiple channels and touch points, in terms of

◆ giving the user the choice of the channel and touch point at any time
◆ using the most effective and efficient channel to contact the (prospective) customer and assure mutually reinforcing interaction across channels
◆ managing your customer database across channels in real time
◆ using your data effectively to tailor offerings to your customers?

RightPoint has a solution that not only incorporates all touch points: the web, e-mail, fax, call centres, POS and – yes – snail mail; it also inter-operates with all common back-office systems to provide efficient profiling and 'matchmarketing'. It combines excellent data collection and storage, profile management, analysis and reporting, rules management and dynamic algorithms to tailor offerings. Recently it introduced RightPoint.net, an innovative real-time eMarketing portal, which constitutes a unique Internet subscription service delivering real-time marketing decisions to the web-sites of e-shopping players.

No wonder RightPoint has already acquired early customers who are sophisticated web players, like Babycenter or iVillage, as well as companies with very strong traditional businesses such as American Express, Halifax Bank and GTE. One of RightPoint's most successful services is for outbound marketing campaigns, on the web as well as via call centres or other media.

'One of our challenges in explaining the RightPoint solution to customers is that we are rather unique in our value proposition', says CEO Gayle Crowell. 'People often want to put us in a "box" they know and it can be a long sale until they grasp the full potential of our offering. As soon as they understand it, however, they want the RightPoint solution to be implemented yesterday.'

for individual customers. In online computer stores, such as Dell, customers configure their computers without sales assistants. The same goes for cars. Hardly a car today – with the exception of special models – is fitted identically to another. Pre-conditions for individual products are corresponding built-to-order systems, which create the customer's individual article in a reasonable time – 48 hours for computers, a few weeks for cars.

Internet stores offer unique possibilities for selling articles tailored to the individual. You can supply information for complex products faster and better than the best sales assistant could. When a customer configures his own product, there are hardly any service costs, and you can give the customer demonstrable benefits in terms of price or value. Individually tailored products present the most interesting opportunities for customer loyalty. *Levi's* offers made-to-measure jeans on the Internet. Imagine giving your measurements once and being able to order, in a very short space of time, made-to-measure suits and shirts at off-the-peg prices. For some people there's a great incentive to do all their shopping in this way in the future – as long as the supplier maintains product-quality and delivery-performance standards. There are already companies offering made-to-measure shirts on the net; for a Jermyn Street example visit *Charles Tyrwhitt*.

A pre-condition for individual products is a working built-to-order production system. But you do not have to produce everything yourself. Find a third party who can do this for you at the right quality and cost. Make sure that customer orders are transferred directly over the Internet to your business partner so that there is no delay in the delivery process. But avoid the manufacturer having direct access to your customers.

Enable your customers to find out about the benefits of your products individually!

If you cannot or do not want to offer individual products, ensure that customers can find out about the benefits of your products for themselves. *Land's End*, one of the leading US branded mail-order clothing companies, was one of the first to adopt this principle. On their web-site you can create a 'personal model' that represents your own appearance and personal measurements with the help of an online doll. Your personal model is ready for you round the clock to try on Land's End products, to check the fit and to match the colours with your hair, eye and skin colour. If you want, the model gives you tips on different styles and combines suitable outfits. Several disadvantages of electronic shopping for clothes have been overcome using these personal models.

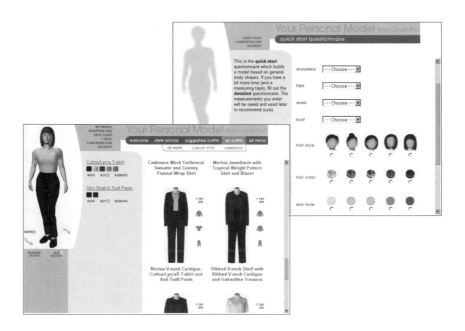

Screenshot: Land's End Personal Model.

Clothing has become 'more accessible' and decisions enriched with more information, for example, whether jeans also look good from the back! Such services can raise customers' emotional allegiance and perceptions of value provided, potentially encouraging satisfied customers to come back and repeat order without chasing after special offers.

J.C. Penney offers a personal model for their female outsize customers. The model in *Just4meplus* has extensive personalisation capabilities and can be turned through 360 degrees so that the fit of the clothing can be checked from all sides.

Another interesting example is *Garden Escape*, the leading supplier of garden items on the Internet. *Garden.com* proves that even articles that are supposedly not suitable for electronic shopping can be sold over the Internet when you get it right. Garden Escape sells both garden tools and equipment as well as plants and seeds. It offers a complete range and is by far the leading supplier of these goods on the Internet.

Garden Escape offers both a comprehensive catalogue range and a complete world of experience in the garden with its own

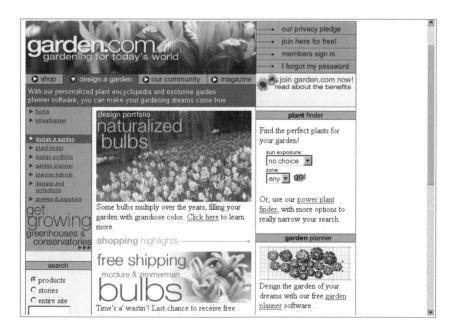

Screenshot: Garden.com.

gardening magazine and updated daily content. Customers get highly individual benefits from links to a detailed database that enables Garden.com to give each individual customer specific recommendations for their garden – depending upon the size and composition of the garden as well as its geographical position. The database recommends the right plants and equipment for individual customer needs and also gives recommendations for maintaining each individual customer's garden. A complete product range, which simply cannot be held in inventory by a high-street store, and links to a huge fount of knowledge (in this case an intelligent database) are the key to the superior offer of this e-tailer.

Garden Escape achieves great customer loyalty by linking its stored knowledge to its customer details. Each customer can set out his own garden on the web-site and recreate it. The customer can go back to his virtual garden at any time and receive recommendations and product information. In this way there is a close attachment to Garden Escape. Anybody who has set up his garden – still quite a laborious process – will use it again and again and not change to another supplier.

Garden Escape's best shopping idea, however, was to make sure that people could order products once they had created their virtual garden just by clicking on the mouse and making the link from 'laying out' the garden to 'buying it' almost seamless. The average order of customers who have set out their garden is about ten times higher than other customers. The repeat-purchase rate of these customers is five times higher. Garden Escape appears to have found the key to the problem of how customers can be made extremely loyal to the company. The company is now among the strongest Internet brands and has 'revolutionised the gardening industry'.

Bond your customers to you so that they won't want to change suppliers!

Land's End and Garden Escape show how customer loyalty can work on the Internet. At the same time, good customer-loyalty tools create obstacles to customer switching. A pre-condition is a superior or at least a competitive 'standard' service; failure to meet a customer's basic requirements leaves no room for trying to impress with additional benefits.

The best approach is to offer the customer superior personal benefits, which he will find only with you or can receive only by investing a great deal of time with a competitor (e.g. setting out his garden again). Alternatively give him the incentive of being able to increase his status, so that it is worth his while staying put; for example, a bonus programme which works in the same way as the airlines' air-miles collections. In this way you build in switching costs which are the basis for distinguishing your relationship with the customer versus those of the competition in the long term. An interesting variation on this theme, although not one that guarantees longer-term loyalty, is one used by *TheMutual.net*. This is an aspiring Internet community which at launch promised to provide each of its early users with a share in its future public offering.

When you are certain that you will not lose or deter your most valuable customers, you can try to bind them to you contractually. One good example here is the *Wall Street Journal*, which has managed to win more than 300,000 subscriptions to its interactive edition. More than two-thirds of these subscribers are completely new subscribers, while subscriptions to the newspaper have also risen. Fears over cannibalisation appear unfounded. The interactive editions offer a large amount of information which is obviously also in the paper but is tailored to the individual and has more than a single day's stories easily accessible. The *Wall Street Journal* has succeeded in winning paying subscribers for what is an information service, and binding them to it permanently; more than 80% of electronic readers renewed their subscriptions in the first year.

Step 3: let customers create the buying experience

Give customers control over the whole business relationship!

Early on, the Internet was something free and almost anarchic. Early Internet users were independent, technically aware people who generally avoided the net's commercial opportunities. A hint of these origins is still evident today in customer behaviour. Marketing experts soon saw the potential of electronic shopping for aggressive direct marketing: the customer leaves his e-mail address once and can then be bombarded with offers. The customer buys one or two things and then receives e-mails that offer him products that supposedly match his personal profile. Experience shows that these apparently obvious methods do not necessarily work well on the Internet.

Most customers would like to have control over their relationship with businesses. They will accept individual offers but largely only when they have asked for them explicitly. Offers have to give the customer the feeling that you are doing him a service if they are to generate any real desire for them. Let the customer decide how he will interact with you. If he would rather place an order over the telephone after he has inquired on the Internet: no problem. If he would like to pay by credit card rather than direct debit: no problem. If he needs another type of invoice: no problem. If he would like to rummage around your Internet shop in text mode and can do without lots of graphics: no problem. All of these have consequences for the economics of your store, but you have to respond to what customers want.

You must therefore ensure that you record your customers' wishes. An extreme example was reported to the board of the New York's Bergdorf Goodman department store. A customer complained that an article he had ordered had been sent to his home, although the company should have known that at that time of year he was always at his holiday home in Florida.

Offer the customer the opportunity to set up his own shop!

One of the oldest marketing ideas in the Internet is individual web-sites. *Yahoo*, the Internet's most-visited domain, provides personalisation of its offer through 'My Yahoo' as a matter of course for millions of visitors. An individual customer is unlikely to use the whole range of your Internet store, just as you are to visit, at one go, all the shops in your favourite shopping centre or all the aisles of your supermarket. It is technically relatively simply to offer each customer an individualised range; reduce the complexity of visiting the store and avoid what may be irrelevant information. *LaCravate*, an Internet supplier of ties, offers a simple method of browsing yet finding the one tie from the whole range that suits your taste. A zoom function brings the articles closer to make the decision easier.

Bluefly offers customers the possibility of creating an individualised store from its whole catalogue. Users enter which types of goods and brands they prefer and what sizes they need; creating a personalised range at the same time, while the company receives valuable information on customer preferences.

Bear in mind that excessive personalisation can prevent fast access speeds. So ensure that the speed of your web-site stays high. Some e-tailers avoid offering individual ranges and prefer a targeted shop-in-shop approach. Critically important is to let

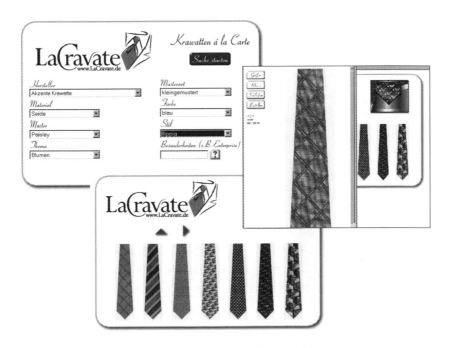

Screenshot: LaCravate.

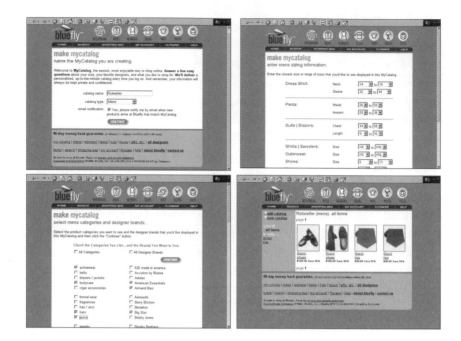

Screenshot: Bluefly.

the customer decide which section of the range he is interested in. He should be aware that you are creating his own individual shop for him – but that he can change this creation at any time.

Let the customer design personalised products!

Give your customers freedom to choose which offers they wish to take up. American Airlines allows its frequent flyers to construct the special offers they would like to have. Each customer confirms which destinations, airport, dates or price class interest them and, if an offer is available, it comes to them. Customers feel that they are treated as individuals and perceive real benefit from this approach. At the same time American Airlines gets a great deal of information on the preferences of its most valuable customers.

FragranceCounter offers a 'gift adviser', to help find a perfume as a present without smelling it. The customer enters what relationship he has with the intended recipient and their preferences and what the gift is for. This generates a short list of recommended scents. Again, FragranceCounter gets a great deal of customer information but in return for a valued service.

Many shoppers value good product recommendations, but buy on the basis of different types of recommendations. *Amazon.com* is a well known example in this area. Here is the first of two examples.

Choose a book from Amazon's web-site. You get not only general information on the book, but also the book's sales-ranking at Amazon, and reviews by the author, the publisher and readers. Reader rankings work on a simple 1–5-star rating system, plus commentary. The more visitors, readers and buyers Amazon has, the greater the benefit of this information. Amazon will also give you further book recommendations on this same subject area. Most tempting, however, is the listing of the three most frequently purchased books that buyers of the same book you are considering also bought. Few of those browsing can resist looking at these recommendations. Since introducing this method of indirect recommendation, Amazon's average order has risen considerably. The customer feels that this type of recommendation is of value: it is more 'neutral' than a 'direct from Amazon' message and does not regard it as pestering. If you want to go further with Amazon's recommendations, you can provide your own evaluation of a number of books you have already read, creating a profile of your taste, from which Amazon generates new book-recommendations. One can see elements of this approach being useful in many other categories, for example in the sale of clothing accessories and even holidays.

Somewhat more controversial has been Amazon's recommendation list based on summaries of what groups of employees of specific organisations have been reading.

In the second example, Amazon.com's music shop, try visiting the 'Recommendation Centre'. Amazon has painstakingly researched what kind of recommendation customers respond to and offers seven types of music recommendation. The customer can choose from:

Screenshot: Amazon Recommendation Center.

- ◆ recommendations by Amazon on the basis of earlier purchases by the customer;
- ◆ recommendations on specific artists;
- ◆ recommendations on specific types of music (e.g. classical);
- ◆ recommendations of a well-known artist (changed weekly);
- ◆ subscription to an e-mail magazine with current news on the music scene;
- ◆ list of 'essentials' (i.e. recordings that everybody should have); and
- ◆ 'mood matcher': (recommendations for situations or mood-creation (e.g. getting-up, parties, driving the car, feeling low, sport) or even quite specific (e.g. Valentine's Day, or 'painting like Andy Warhol').

Give customers the opportunity to help themselves!

Online banks, like *First Direct*, or online brokers, like *Charles Schwab*, let their customers work for themselves. Customers carry out transfers and keep an eye on their portfolios. Many customers don't see this as the basis for getting more favourable terms, but as an additional benefit. Let the customer check his orders, deliveries and invoices himself. Give him the chance to contact you however he wishes, but make sure that the level of service is the same whichever means of communication is used.

Dell and *Cisco* have shifted their customer services almost completely to the Internet and have saved millions of dollars while increasing customer satisfaction. Cisco would have found it hard to grow its business so fast had it continued to provide traditional customer service interactions. As one of the largest travel agents in the world, *American Express* offers a new type of corporate service. A business customer can register its travel policies, and each member of staff can book online according to these policies. This has tied business customers to American Express, increased private sales with staff, and acquired new credit card customers.

Customer forums offer the visitor the opportunity to ask each other questions about specific category issues and potentially the supplier's products. In this way interested customers can exchange information on specific products and their applications. *Frys Electronics*, a Californian company, hosts an uncensored forum for its customers' comments. If you do not want to leave customers to their own devices, there are several technical possibilities open to you. One US software house supplies a system with which the customer relations officer of a company can control the mouse on his customer's computer and can help and advise online. German consumer electronics retailer *Brinkmann* offers online advice via Internet video with which a customer can talk to a personal adviser.

Step 4: promote customer communities

Give your customers the feeling that they belong!

People like to feel that they belong to a community. At its creation, the World Wide Web itself existed as a virtual community, often of scientists or technicians who exchanged common experiences and interests. Leading international publishing group *Reed Elsevier* for many years produced a large number of highly regarded scientific journals with small circulations, read by a few interested experts who often knew each other. These journals existed primarily for the publication and exchange of scientific views within a community of scientists. Much of this information exchange now occurs online and underlines the value that scientists place on being part of a community.

Make use of the special features of virtual communities and integrate them into your Internet store. *Diesel*, the fashion retailer, has built its own successful community, based on a club concept. It offers members sneak previews of collections and new products to stay ahead in the fashion stakes.

Set up interactions between customers with the same interests. Some of your Internet customers will be willing to take part and encourage others to do the same. Amazon's customer reviews increase the credibility of their range and are extremely popular. Let your customers exchange mutual experiences in your chat rooms. You will be startled at how much valuable information you can gain about customer behaviour by observing their conversations. Involve customers in problem-solving and product-development and bring them together with your internal experts and business partners. Finally let your customers help each other. *Dell* and *Cisco* fulfil one part of their customer-service tasks by passing on tips from one customer to another.

With these customer-to-customer interactions it is important to ensure that the perceived benefits increase rapidly with the number of active participants. Ensuring that your community grows quickly becomes critical. Promote interaction with attractive content, actively encourage the participation of your customers and let 'guest speakers' and 'VIPs' play their part. Find out early what types of customers can be encouraged to take part and target them to be involved.

Promote the creation of mutual interest!

Remember that your customers have their specific reasons for choosing and using your products. They are not interested in maximising your profits, but have their own interests at heart. Building a clear set of common values which create involvement of customers within the online community and with your company should be your goal. If you do not succeed in creating such a value-set and in setting up a lively community, you run the risk of being replaced, because you are no more than an order mechanism, and because you fall into direct competition with intelligent agents, simply searching for the lowest prices available (such as *MySimon.com*). Creating communities of mutual interest around your own e-tail site is a necessary pre-emptive strike against communities which aim to turn the tables in retail and shift power from suppliers to buyers. Examples of such sites, attempting to aggregate individual consumers' demand in order to extract better prices, include *Mercata* and *AccompanyInc*.

One example of a vibrant virtual community is *golfweb.com*. This web-site was once the hottest spot for golfers on the Internet. Golf fans found a virtual 19th hole where they could meet and exchange information. Now golfweb.com is the leading retailer for golfing equipment on the Internet. Users have the opportunity to submit product criticisms and comments as well as take part in live discussions about golfing equipment. Golfweb.com offers an immediate opportunity to order products discussed, and has built a huge online catalogue of golfing goods. The value to users has constantly been increased as more and more visitors log in. As user numbers have grown, suppliers of related services such as organisers of golfing holidays have joined the network.

Retain control without controlling!

Obviously the community created around a store should not exclude the e-tailer altogether. You must be in a position to ensure that it is taken seriously and to prevent destructive criticism, or worse, being generated. Such problems have been reported on a very small number of commercial sites. Otherwise let the community have free rein without precisely planning everything and organising everything. If the community opens up sales opportunities for new product-groups or services, seize them; even if they are not part of your traditional core business.

Hagel and Armstrong describe in *Net Gain* (HBS Press, 1997) how they believe managers of virtual communities should behave. They recommend the role of a gardener who sows, looks after, and tends. 'Sowing' means bringing a community and other sub-communities into the world and awaiting their development. 'Looking after' means providing suitable resources for promising sub-communities and new attractive offers. 'Tending' means switching off empty chat forums and disruptive behaviour.

For an e-tailer, a virtual community is equivalent to building a university of Internet marketing. It produces understanding of individual customer relationship management which can become a permanent competitive edge for the company.

Recognise the value of your customers

Many companies today not only do not know their individual customers in any meaningful sense, they do not appreciate the value of each customer. Companies have a tendency to be driven by short-term sales pressure into how they interact with customers at an aggregate level, losing sight of the value of individual lifelong customer loyalty. The food sector is a good example. A regular customer's value is high, given that an average household for a decade buying its basic needs every week in the same store will account for a six-figure sum in sales over this period. The lifelong value of a food customer combined with the frequency of purchase makes the industry a natural centre for building up long-term direct customer relationships. Imagine the competitive edge that a retailer would have if he could identify customers for whose custom he did not have to compete.

As a general rule, an existing customer is more valuable than a new one so at some point you have to scale back new customer acquisition. A loyal customer can become more valuable each year, if he is spending a higher proportion of his income with you. Good purchase recommendations both reduce customer relationship costs proportionately and can shift customers to being less price sensitive. In the face of static consumer goods markets, the largest growth opportunities are to be found in exhausting existing customer potential. Existing customers are many companies' greatest growth opportunity.

Despite this, most retailers lose 15–20 per cent of their customers each year. Spending to retain customers is always cheaper than spending to gain them, so every current customer is much more valuable than a new one. As an example, the costs of winning a new mobile-phone customer have been shown to be 8–10 times higher than the costs of keeping an existing one. This logic applies even more to e-tailers because an alternative supplier is often just a click away.

The *profitability of different customer groups* is highly variable. We've worked with one food retailer to show, from customer profitability analysis, that it has just as many customer segments returning an operating loss as those making profit. Good information around profitable customer segments' behaviour can drive specific measures to increase their purchase frequency or average spend. In this instance the retailer geared staffing at checkout tills to reduce queues at times when the most valuable customers shopped, dramatically increasing satisfaction ratings in a core group of shoppers and their frequency of visits. Nothing was done to retain unprofitable customers. The overall result was a slight decrease in customer numbers and in sales but a significant profit uplift.

E-tailers have to examine the value of their customers from every possible angle. They must be aware of the lifetime value of a customer and try their hardest to invest in valuable customers from day one. Doing this means evaluating the potential value of a customer early on and selecting the correct customer groups to target. Focus on creating a large network of the 'right' customers rapidly. The size of the customer network ultimately determines your value as an e-tailer.

E-tail searchlight on web sites for Chapter 7

- Hallmark — www.hallmark.com
- Barbie — www.barbie.com
- Microsoft Networks — www.msn.com
- Dell — www.dell.com
- Gigabuys — www.gigabuys.com
- American Airlines — www.aa.com
- Hertz — www.hertz.com
- United Parcel Service — www.ups.com
- Federal Express — www.fedex.com
- Levi's — www.levis.com
- Charles Tyrwhitt — www.ctshirts.co.uk
- Land's End — www.landsend.com
- Just4meplus — www.just4meplus.com
- Garden Escape — www.garden.com
- The Mutual — www.themutual.net
- Wall Street Journal — www.wsj.com
- Yahoo — www.yahoo.com
- LaCravate — www.lacravate.de
- Bluefly — www.bluefly.com
- FragranceCounter — www.fragrancecounter.com
- Amazon — www.amazon.com
- First Direct — www.firstdirect.co.uk
- Charles Schwab — www.schwab.com
- Cisco — www.cisco.com
- American Express — www.amex.com
- Brinkmann — www.brinkmann.de
- Diesel — www.diesel.com
- MySimon — www.mysimon.com
- Golfweb.com — www.golfweb.com
- AccompanyInc — www.accompany.com
- Mercata — www.mercata.com
- Merant — www.merant.com

Chapter 8

Create Customer-centric Business Processes

Customers can't just be won, they have to be satisfied. An electronic shopper faces a new shopping experience, new suppliers, new products and new services. As many Internet users are beginning to test the waters of e-shopping, it is critical that e-shopping suppliers meet the explicit or implicit promises they make in terms of delivery and efficiency. E-shopping players need business processes that are set up and driven from the customer's point of view. Successful innovators go beyond this with built-to-order products and business processes which have a focus on customer needs at their heart.

E-tail searchlight illuminates Chapter 8

◆ *Built-to-order products will revolutionise industry activity chains*
Efficient manufacture of products tailored specifically to the customer will be the next step change in many industries. Real success as an e-tailer will come from providing a range of products tailored to the customer right from the beginning.

◆ *Create new business processes*
E-tailing requires completely new business processes which focus on the customer, involve all supply chain participants and are secure.

◆ *Outsource and use partnership*
Almost all an Internet store's essential functions can be provided by a third party. Beyond the customer and the supplier; web-hosting, web applications, fulfilment logistics and transaction-processing can be outsourced.

Built-to-order products will revolutionise industry activity chains

The Internet will promote efficient manufacturing of products tailored to the customer just as much as it will encourage direct marketing to 'the segment of one'. Built-to-order ranges will allow the manufacture of individual customer orders using a unit construction-system that guarantees fast delivery and low complexity-costs. Such ranges are already quite usual in the PC and auto industries. Most cars and PCs are made to specific customer specifications. The consequences of mass personalisation go beyond the manufacturer and affect the whole activity chain of the relevant industries. The radical restructuring of the auto industry and their supplier-base is perhaps the best-known example. Over the last decade the world's largest car makers have been radically reducing their number of suppliers, shortening their lines of communication to them and making their production lines more flexible. The activity chain of the PC industry has also altered dramatically but in a much shorter space of time. *Dell* is arguably the leading built-to-order supplier, whose far-sighted perspectives on how to e-tail on the Internet have left many competitors trying to catch up. It is now so efficient that it operates with negative working capital.

We are convinced that many more industries will be changed by e-tailing and e-shopping in a similar way. In the US there is already much discussion of 'consumer to business' e-commerce in connection with build-to-order products. An ability to offer customer-specified products is rare, and can be a great competitive differentiator. At the same time, built-to-order ranges reduce direct comparison and therefore price competition. These are two strong drivers to ensure that many industries will follow the example of the PC industry. Companies who manage to influence and change the value chain of the whole of their industry will have the greatest opportunity to create new sources of profit and growth.

Most companies claim that they put the customer first. In e-tailing this primarily means providing customer-orientated core processes for your Internet store. We set out the essential features of these processes later in this chapter. These are relatively quickly becoming an 'entry' standard. If you are looking for real success in e-tailing, you need to provide a range of products tailored to the customer from the outset. However, do not expect to be able to demand higher prices for personalisation. The benefits will flow from altering capabilities in the relevant industry and participating in the rewards to follow.

Let's demonstrate our ideas with two examples, the clothing and the furniture industries. The *clothing industry* has traditionally produced garments on a 'fashion cycle' which is up to 12 months ahead of what consumers are buying in the stores. Integrated clothing companies like Benetton or Hennes & Mauritz have revolutionised the industry by offering fashion at a reasonable price which reaches the market on a production cycle much shorter than 12 months. The next developmental leap for the clothing industry in the Internet age is to create ranges of customer-specified products, tailor made but at off-the-peg prices. Those who know the economics of the industry know that preparation of material and cutting tend not to allow very flexible production techniques. At the same time, retailers and manufacturers have a built-in bias towards creating stock for a 'core' range in order to reduce their stock risk in more 'outlandish' styles, colours, etc. This means they manage their risk of failure, but can also reduce their chance of success. If something is truly 'hot', the cycle of retail feedback, manufacture of further stock and placement of stock in store, can take so long that the item rapidly becomes out of stock or can only be replenished for next season. Built-to-order fashion allows greater prediction of what may be 'mainstream' fashionable (to help production forecasting) and a low-risk way of addressing 'unusual' demand (in terms of style, colour or sizes). Fashion e-tailers will increasingly supply reasonably priced 'tailor-made collections' – from tailor-made shirts to suits right up to silk ties with individual patterns. *Land's End* already allows its shirt-buyers significant choice of specific features of the shirt (style of collar, length of sleeve, button styles). The whole clothing industry is facing a potential revolution.

A similar situation exists in the *furniture industry*. Customers typically wait weeks for furniture manufacturers to supply their orders. Sofas can take six to eight weeks or more, while recent inquiries for a new mattress in a UK store suggested a waiting period of an astonishing sixteen weeks! Ordering and delivery are time-consuming and cost-intensive processes with high rates of error and are criticised by many customers. Shops selling self-assembly furniture, such as *Ikea* and *MFI*, have revolutionised the industry by offering customers flat-pack furniture and the opportunity to eliminate the whole ordering and delivery process and reducing purchase costs significantly too. The next step for part of the furniture industry in the Internet age should be a range of reasonably priced specifically commissioned items with a short delivery time. Internet customers could order the furniture direct from manufacturer with order details fed into the manufacturer's flexible production system in real time. Consumer ordering and flexible, reasonably priced production imply a unit construction system. Many of today's manufacturing and retailing structures cannot cope with mass personalisation like this, so Internet furniture shops trading with traditional manufacturers will probably have only limited success. However, somebody who manages to influence the value chain has the chance to revolutionise the whole furniture industry.

It is our opinion that most industries are suitable for built-to-order ranges. The requirement for personalisation assumes a minimum degree of customer involvement with the product. There are categories, like cars or clothes, which have a high degree of involvement. In these industries, built-to-order ranges will have a huge impact in the long term. With other categories, like toothbrushes, crockery, and bicycles, most customers' involvement is small although the interaction may be high. But this does not apply to all customers. Consumers today show a complex combination of high and low involvement. Take the once humble 'sports shoe' or 'training shoe' as an example. To some sections of the population these are utility shoes which are, generally, not 'office' or 'smart' shoes. One pair covers a mass of occasions and sports. To other sections of the population, they are fashion items, but for serious amateur athletes and keep-fitters they are almost tools of the trade. Any of these groups may perceive benefits in being able to 'tailor-make' their own shoes, a service offered by German company *Creo*. In bicycles 'tailor-made' services are an important aspect for enthusiasts, a demand met by US companies, such as *Made 2 Order Bikes*, *Waterford* and *Hujsak*. There is potential for made-to-order product in more categories than one might at first imagine. In your industry you should examine objectively how much potential there is for mass-personalisation. A pre-condition for it is that cheap, flexible business processes exist within the supply chain, or that customers can communicate efficiently direct with manufacturers.

Create new business processes

An Internet store needs no business premises, no till and no sales staff in the conventional sense. It operates with a new type of 'staff': servers, hosts, and service providers. Other customers help in selling! Running an e-shop needs new business processes.

Design processes for customers – not for you

The online customer is uncertain: Anybody who goes into a department store to shop knows exactly what he has to do and in what order: he looks for the goods, goes to the till and pays. Do you know how to shop on the Internet? There is still no 'standard' for virtual shopping. Create the shopping process by looking at it through the customer's eyes. It has to suit the customer down to the ground, because the competition is always just a mouse-click away. 'Customer oriented' has long been a business catchphrase. The Internet makes it possible in many new ways. Resist the temptation to want to make the process easy for yourself; it makes it less easy or satisfying for the customer.

Use the customer's knowledge

Many country-specific backpackers' guides are available in book form. But the very latest hot tips are also available on the Internet from readers who have just returned from their trip. Even on the day of departure, a holidaymaker can find out current information on hotels, pubs, discos, opening times and beaches. This information is then included in the next edition. Readers become authors, and publishers save on expensive local research. *Lonely Planet* does this in travel and *Zagat* restaurant guides also use the same principles. Look on your customer as an expert user of a product sold by you. He knows it better than you do. Accessing customer knowledge and experience promotes customer involvement and can provide the basis of a competitive advantage.

Let customers, suppliers and service providers help you

At Amazon readers write short reviews of books they have bought. A professional salesman in a traditional bookshop could not provide better advice. Who undertakes data management in the electronic world? The customer too. He looks after his own details himself, of his own freewill and free of charge. But it's not just the customer who lends a hand in the Internet store. You don't need to know what your products look like or technical details when creating your catalogue today. The manufacturer can look after technical information in your catalogue while logistics providers look after delivery to the customer, so that the costs of logistics turn out to be very low. And even when it comes to payment, you let others do the work for you: Visa; a specialist payment clearing player; or your telephone company will take care of payments.

What the e-tailer focuses on is the draw to the store – the e-tail brand. Internet-only fashion retailer *Boo.com* (yet to fully launch at the time of writing) is a proponent of such a brand-centric, process-outsourced business model.

Collaborate with suppliers and service providers

Obviously the business of e-tailing is not limited to your managing the division of 'the real work' between the others involved in the process. Suppliers and service providers rely on the e-tailer to facilitate efficient information exchange, and for good reason. Electronic shopping offers significant opportunities for collaborative e-tailers to obtain a competitive edge from close co-operation with their suppliers and service providers, without having to give away the trump card of owning the customer relationship at the same time.

Security for all involved

No shopkeeper leaves the till open. This applies in the virtual

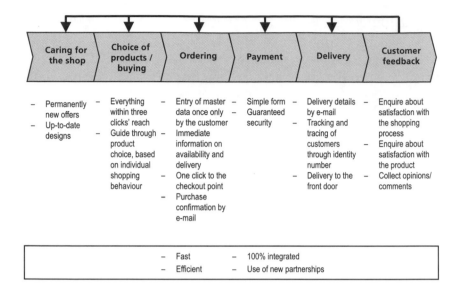

Fig. 8.1 The business process in electronic shopping.

world too. Just as organised bands of pickpockets roam the streets in some large cities, hackers surf the net looking for booty. Passwords and coded algorithms are replacing padlocks and signatures; customers and suppliers will exchange data with you only if they trust the security of your systems. Doubt over payment security and fear of data misuse are still the main perception-driven obstacles to electronic shopping. Trust in a store's security standards and guaranteed data protection are pre-requisites for business success on the Internet. We say these are perception driven because systems available today can guarantee more secure transactions (see Chapter 9) than the 'real' world. A recent study on the US mail-order trade found that payment fraud and the number of payment-related complaints in Internet trading were 50 percent lower than in the mail-order catalogue sectors. Customers' focus is again paramount: create your business process for your customer's comfort and not for yours.

What effect do these peculiarities have on business processes in electronic shopping? From the customer's point of view, the e-tail experience must be fast, efficient and highly integrated. Let's consider the mail-order sector a little further to bring out how Internet-based retail processes are different.

Looking after the Internet shop

A mail-order catalogue appears quarterly. Internet customers expect constantly up-to-date ranges, so that business have to do 'Business @ the speed of thought' (Bill Gates). Looking after range in e-tailing is more important than creating catalogues in a mail order business. The online catalogue has to be kept up-to-date in real time, reflecting stock positions for multiple variants of size, colour, and style. The Internet store operator is plagued with technical questions. These start even before a customer gets into the store: Netscape or Internet Explorer: which browser in which version should the store support? HTML, CGI, JAVA or XML: which language should the pages be programmed in? These would be considered merely technical questions at first glance, but they are decisions on which the performance of the store will depend. It may be an obvious point, but it is worth emphasising. The technical performance of the store is as much 'part' of the e-store as the pictures and layout are of a paper mail-order catalogue. This business process which creates the mail-order catalogue is not experienced by the customer. In the online world it is much more transparent and closer to the customer. Looking after the e-shop has more potentially critical process elements than its closest real-world parallel, the mail-order catalogue.

Select products and make sure they are bought

From a business-process point of view, the interface to the customer is critical. On the Internet there can be days between product choice, payment and delivery. On the other hand, the customer possibly does not notice that he is making demands for performance that will incur costs. Therefore, in the Internet shop he must take a definite step, make a special 'click', that results in a purchase. This click makes the visitor to your web-site a cus-tomer. With the help of 'cookies' (storing the Internet shop's identifier on the customer's computer), you can determine whether he is a visitor or a new customer. With a new customer, first his relevant data is sought. It is not an employee, but the customer himself who enters all his details into the system by means of an Internet 'dialogue'. We have seen that in the anony-mous Internet all available customer details are relevant. As far as possible, they are validated as soon as they are put in. The e-mail address and the customer's credit rating are checked. As soon as the customer is registered, his account is opened.

Triggering orders

The following steps take place on the Internet store transaction server – usually in fractions of a second. First, depending on what type of payment is used, the customer's payment capabil-ity is checked with the payment centre via electronic data ex-change. To help avoid fraud, the customer is sent an order confirmation by e-mail. Then a process similar to that of a mail-order firm takes place. The manufacturer (or warehouse) checks delivery capability and confirms it electronically. To reduce despatch costs the current order is combined with previous or-ders by the manufacturer. Once the manufacturer confirms that the goods have been despatched, the customer's payment is processed. A prerequisite for all of this is the electronic con-nection of supplier and logistics service provider to the Internet stores systems. In this way irregularities in order handling or delivery can be picked up by the relevant systems. The supplier automatically informs the e-tailer of supply bottlenecks or model changes, and this information can be passed to the customer.

Handling payments

The payment process on the Internet is actually the transfer of an authorisation of payment to the customer's payment centre. It doesn't matter whether it is a credit card, digital cash or direct debit: the Internet shop server sends the data to the bank, credit-card company or the customer's Internet service-provider and thus triggers the payment process. The failure risk depends essentially on which payment conditions were negotiated by the store with the payment centre. For payments within the payment-centre's responsibility limit (e.g. credit card limit) the payment is guaranteed to the Internet shop operator. For accounts that are over this amount, and with invoiced deliveries, the traditional invoicing and payment system is used.

Delivering the goods

The goods are transferred from the manufacturer or wholesaler to the logistics service provider. He gives them an identification number and informs the Internet shop by electronic data transfer of their dispatch. An e-mail informs the customer of the intended arrival of the delivery and, using the identification number, he can check at any time on the current progress of his delivery. If he wishes, delivery can take place at any address and at a time agreed with the customer.

Receiving feedback

We've emphasised the anonymity of the Internet as much as we have discussed individual customer relations. There are good reasons, therefore, to set up feedback systems at the end of the business process. The Internet gives e-tailers the ability to question their customers automatically, individually and almost for free.

Outsource and use partnerships

E-tailers should, in extreme cases, be able to reach very significant sales with only a handful of staff – if they organise their

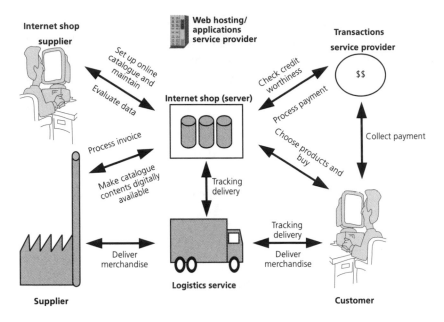

Fig. 8.2   The participants in the e-tailing process.

business processes properly. One characteristic of the Internet-retailing age is that almost all retail functions can be outsourced to a third party. New entrants to the e-tail arena have been quick to spot the advantage of this approach. Outsourcing saves capital, allows a business to be scaled very quickly and to adapt to changes in market conditions flexibly. As well as suppliers and customers, a *network of partners* is critical to the e-tail business process. The most important service providers for e-tailers are those offering:

◆ web hosting
◆ online applications
◆ transaction
◆ logistics.

Web hosting

Operating an Internet store creates a large number of challenges in infrastructure. Above all, systems have to work for 24 hours a day, 7 days a week, and be scaleable almost at will. A breakdown in the EDP system immediately leads to losses of sales, customers and money. In some instances system failures have created significant shifts in stock prices and company valuation, as e-Bay has experienced. Given this, many companies have decided to entrust the operation of their web-site to a professional web hosting company who provide space on dedi-

Case study – Frontier Global Centre

Frontier Global Centre is one of the pioneers of *high-end web hosting*. It currently processes some 8.8 billion page-views a month and 1.8 billion 'hits' a day. Its most important customer is Yahoo, for whom Global Centre operates the majority of web-sites. Others such as Compaq, Lycos, Playboy, The Washington Post, Electronic Arts, Salon Magazine, The Motley Fool, USA Today and many other well-known Internet companies use their services. Frontier Global Centre supports 70 per cent of all online financial services and 60 per cent of all Internet search processes.

The business system is simple: Global Centre is building huge data centres in the USA and increasingly in the rest of the world where companies can rent 'racks', i.e. two square metres of large computer and routing racks including maintenance and band-width on the Internet. A rack costs approx. $1000 per month and the band-width per megabyte is about the same. If you exceed the band-width ordered, you will pay a higher price, but the service level is guaranteed.

Global Centre plans to grow at more than 200% a year, half of this being generated by an increase in existing customers. Together with Exodus and Digex, Global Centre has so far dominated the upper end of the web-hosting market.

cated servers in a large data centre, large amounts of band-width to the Internet and a 24-hour service.

Web hosting comes in all shapes, the simplest form being the so-called 'shared server', by which a company rents space on a server. This can be enough for a pure information site, but is not really any good for professional e-tailing.

All Internet service providers and telecommunications companies have become involved with at least low-end web hosting. As well as basic services, these companies generally also offer a call-centre service for customers.

The critical point with web hosting for e-tailers is always the connection back to data or functions on the company's 'legacy' systems. This integration is complex and one which, for web hosting, companies can master, as many of them have concentrated on being 'pure' Internet players, because they themselves have no legacy systems. As established companies enter e-tail, integration of new front-ends to old legacy back-end systems is rapidly becoming one of today's hottest issues.

Applications services

An e-tailer has a large number of information-driven functions to perform electronically. These place massive demands on application software and its interplay with internal databases and external companies. Packaged solutions have already been developed for some standard functions and processes.

Despite solutions for some specific functions, most applications related to e-tailing are today still self-developed or laboriously patched together using software from various suppliers. This is attracting the software giants into the field. Microsoft in particular is currently developing a whole e-tailing package which, as usual, has defects in individual applications but works as a whole quite seamlessly.

For e-tailers the big problem is that many systems are too inflexible and, once created, an IT structure which cannot be scaled easily, soon becomes a strait jacket. A solution in the offing comes from *application service providers* – companies that

Case study – Intershop

Intershop is one of the few European software companies to have become established in electronic shopping.

Intershop offers complete 'front-end' software solutions for selling goods to an end user over the Internet. Their software has now been installed in over 20,000 companies, making Intershop one of the leading global companies in its sectors.

The company itself is one of a new generation in Germany, financed by venture capital and one of the first to float on 'Neuer Markt'. Founded in Jena, East Germany, it soon relocated its head office to San Francisco. Interestingly, although company founder Stephan Schmalbach lives in California, most of the development and an essential part of its marketing still take place in Jena and Hamburg.

promise that you can obtain 'applications software on demand'. The idea is that, as with band-width, you only take the applications you need, and then adapt these to your requirements at any time. Unfortunately this is clearly more difficult with software than it is with data transmission capacity.

Early suppliers of this type were start-ups like *Corio* and *USInternetworking*. Now both IBM and various telecommunications suppliers have followed suit and are offering applications software on demand to your requirements. None of these players has yet focused only on the e-tailing market, although the product concept should be of much interest in this quickly changing field.

The provision of functions relating to *directory services* and *e-mail management* should be of interest. While call-centres have widely improved in the last few years, most companies are not prepared to have the primary customer interactions by e-mail. Several web-hosting companies have made a first attempt at plugging these gaps in the market, by offering applications to do just that.

While the underlying processes for e-tailing continue to need integration of the old and the new, systems integrators are busy. Even here Internet specialists have established themselves with start-ups *USWeb*, *Viant* and *Scient*, making life difficult for the market leaders of the old world like Andersen Consulting. It is difficult to predict how the existing market for applications service providers will develop, but it is clear that there will be a massive demand for them, and that e-tailers should get used to using them.

Transaction service providers

The Internet shop has no cash till. A customer pays for goods with the electronic currency of his choice. Service providers take care of collection and guarantee the Internet shop operator payment. At the moment payment methods are limited to:

- ◆ *Credit and debit cards*
  These are the most common forms of payment on the Internet. In the US, credit card companies are on marketing offensives because of the boom in electronic shopping, many offering comprehensive transaction services to e-tailers. Transactions handled according to the secure electronic transaction process (SET) enjoy the same status in law and fee levels as credit card payments made at the till, with signed receipts and card controls. Transaction simplicity is one of the main points in favour of Internet business using credit cards. One issue for e-tailers is that credit card penetration is at its highest overall in the USA. Elsewhere, particularly in Europe, credit card ownership and usage are relatively low
- ◆ *Internet service providers' invoice*
  AOL, T-Online and other Internet service providers offer payment for purchasing on the Internet via online invoicing. At month-end the ISP invoices the customer online for

all purchases made. For the customer this is the simplest way to pay on the net. Apart from user identification to the service provider, no further user recognition is necessary. For the e-tailer, implementing this type of transaction can be complicated because each ISP may support a different payment protocol.

◆ *Bank deposits, COD*
Although not in use in the US and the UK for Internet shopping, these mechanisms are a distinct possibility elsewhere in Europe (for example Germany and Italy) where they are already in use for mail order. These payment methods have higher transaction processing costs than others, and therefore may be suitable only for larger ticket items.

◆ *Electronic cash*
Several firms are offering digital-currency solutions (Intershop, First Virtual, etc.). With these, the customer essentially buys digital money units with traditional cash (or credit), and these are stored on a virtual purse on the customer's PC. If the customer buys over the Internet, money units are taken from his purse. This method has the advantage that even small transactions can be handled simply and cheaply. There are as many different types of supplier as there are concepts for digital transactions. At the moment this whole area is looking for a standard, so electronic cash still does not play a major role in consumer retailing.

Payments through transaction service providers are well established on the Internet. Outsourcing the whole transaction to a supplier like Telecash is a further logical step. As soon as a payment is to be made, the customer is connected to a Telecash computer. The transactions are executed here and the result transferred back by secure connection to the Internet store server. The customer knows nothing about this. He imagines that he is still on the Internet shop site. The transaction fees are handled according to the e-tailer's preferred payment methods. The opposite case is also possible. The dream for transaction service providers is to provide an 'electronic purse'. Millions of customers would give the service provider (e.g. their bank or their Internet service provider) all their data relating to payment just once. The customers' transactions with all Internet shops would then go through this purse, administered by a single clearer. The disadvantage for the e-tailer is that he no longer receives customer details himself. In the worst case, the customer remains completely anonymous.

Logistics providers

Logistics companies play a similar role to that executed for traditional mail order, transporting the goods from suppliers and warehouses to the customer, in some cases taking over collection of payment. To an e-tailer a logistics partner is useful only when he has set up systems to allow automatic order handling and despatch processes. In the future each individual customer will be able to chase his deliveries at any time. UPS, Fedex and other large service providers will link e-tailers' sites to their logistics systems. Once a package number has been allocated, the e-tailer will get a detailed online record to allow tracking of the consignment and its current location. This 'tracking & tracing' information needs to be accessible via the Internet store site. Electronic shopping does not necessarily mean home delivery in every case. Deliveries to local pickup centres or to offices play their part. Growth in e-shopping means that e-tailers and logistics providers need to think creatively about these kinds of delivery to avoid the creation of huge logistics problems.

eBay, finding that its packages accounted for around 15% of the US Postal Services' parcel volume, has recently acquired a physical world participant in the hosted mailbox business.

The role of the supplier

Suppliers will have special demands made on them by e-tailers, particularly as far as linking to the Internet store systems are concerned. Suppliers can potentially be integrated to all the stages of an e-tailer's business processes. This extends, for ex-

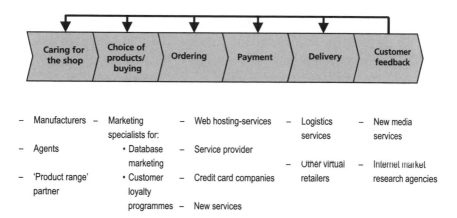

Fig. 8.3 Service providers for each phase of the business process.

ample, to a close co-operation in which the supplier and e-tailer develop future ranges together and the supplier provides a built-to-order range directly to the customer base. Supplier integration will lead to considerable competitive advantages as far as delivery speeds and build-to-order are concerned. Those e-tailers who work their supplier relationships effectively will generate significant points of differentiation from their competitors.

As we've said, nearly all Internet store core processes can be executed by a third party. Figure 8.3 makes it clear that outsiders can play an important role in each area of the business activity. The range of potential providers covers established companies like AT&T, British Telecom or Visa, and a host of new service-providers. Amongst these are numerous creative-design web agencies; e-tailing software houses, such as Intershop; online market researchers like *MediaMetrix, W3B*, or Nielsen Net Ratings; feedback agencies like *Facilitas*; e-mail services like *MessageMedia* or administrative service providers like *Employease* – to name but a few.

We believe that setting up a strong network of external partners is critical for every e-tailer, but it takes real effort. The individual parts of the network that are created have to be co-ordinated and points of interaction tightly managed so that the overall e-tail process runs smoothly for the customer. Add to this the need to have a resource base for the business that is rapidly scaleable to follow the rapid growth of the Internet store, and you have a challenge which needs a lot of human resources to solve it and hardly any capital. Our experience is that suitable management and staff are in short supply, so you will have to fall back on the services of external consultants in the early stages of development, to be able quickly to set up the underlying e-tail model, including a network of suitable partners.

E-tail searchlight on web sites for Chapter 8

- Dell   www.dell.com
- Lands End   www.landsend.com
- MFI   www.mfi.co.uk
- Ikea   www.ikea.com
- Amazon   www.amazon.com
- Lonely Planet   www.lonelyplanet.com
- Zagat Survey   www.zagat.com
- United Parcel Service   www.ups.com
- Deutsche Post
  eCommerce Services   www.e-cs.de
- Creo   www.creo.de
- Made 2 Order Bikes   www.mtob.com
- Waterford Bikes   www.waterfordbikes.com
- Hujsak Bicycles   www.hujsak.com
- Entertainment Express   www.entexpress.co.uk
- Frontier Global Center   www.globalcenter.com
- Exodus   www.exodus.com
- Digex   www.digex.com
- Intershop   www.intershop.com
- Corio   www.corio.com
- USInternetworking   www.usInternetworking.com
- USWeb   www.usweb.com
- Viant   www.viant.com
- Scient   www.scient.com
- MediaMetrix   www.mediametrix.com
- W3B   www.w3b.com
- Facilitas   www.facilitas.com
- MessageMedia   www.messagemedia.com
- Employease   www.employease.com

Part III

Towards the Digital Economy

In the first two parts of this book we have dealt mainly with the strategies and success factors for e-tailing of physical goods. A look at the future, however, opens up a new vista: that of a fundamental change in our information and service companies driven by the Internet. We will all be living at the epicentre of a digital earthquake, driven by the emerging digital economy.

This digital economy has enormous forces for change at its centre, created by digital products and new services linked to a new infrastructure and a capital market for intangible assets. All business models in e-tailing and e-shopping will be fundamentally influenced by it.

The infrastructure of the future, which will create the conditions for the digital economy, is discussed in Chapter 9. The

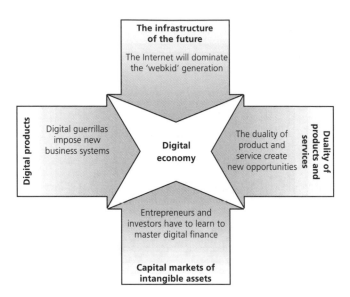

Fig. III.1 The epicentre of the digital earthquake.

term 'infrastructure' includes the availability of suitable access devices, software and supporting services. Although the infrastructure of the digital economy is only in its embryonic stage, it will develop at breath-taking speed; here we can only hope to introduce its essential elements.

In Chapter 10, *It's Free – the Age of the Digital Product*, we discuss the often paradoxical effects of the Internet on the value of digital products. More and more products are becoming digital – music, books, news, photos and games. Consumers are becoming digital guerrillas, challenging established industry leaders. Our recommendations here serve as a compass – the maps for this new land still have to be drawn up.

In Chapter 11 we discuss the effects of the Internet on services leading to a *Brave New World of Services*. E-shopping principles will conquer the service area creating an even more profound revolution than in the physical goods business. Entrepreneurs and established companies creating new business service models need to take careful account of the duality of goods and services.

Finally in Chapter 12, *The capital market – a survival kit*, we deal with questions of finance and a company's value in the digital economy. The world of e-shopping with its rapid growth possibilities and the dominance of intangible assets requires equity investment, and will set the financial markets many new challenges.

We hope you enjoy yourself diving into the digital economy.

Chapter 9

The Infrastructure of

the Future

Tomorrow's infrastructure will be dominated by the Internet and its associated technologies to a degree still underestimated by many. The Internet is the backbone of the digital economy. In this chapter we look at the dramatic changes that the Internet will undergo in the next few years. This will in turn affect all our industries. We concentrate on those aspects that are relevant for electronic shopping and e-tailing.

E-tail searchlight illuminates Chapter 9

◆ *Total dominance of the Internet*
The Internet is 'new media': it will supersede books, newspapers, telephones and televisions, but be more than the simple sum of these components. Our children, the web generation, will be permanently online.

◆ *Anytime, anywhere access*
The Internet will dominate new user devices. Interactive televisions, mobile 'smart phones' and even household appliances will be connected to the world wide web. Electronic shopping will hit a second phase in its development. Web-sites in the future will have to be designed for delivery in multiple formats.

◆ *The Internet 2*
Broad band access to the web will be achieved with a variety of technologies. It will allow graphics-based content to be rapidly distributed and will create new possibilities for shopping and 'infotainment'. 'XML', a new universal language, will provide new structure to Internet content and enable it to take a further quantum leap forward.

◆ *Data security is sufficient*
The technological conditions for secure payments on the Internet are to a great extent in place. Customer acceptance is rising. Service providers are ready. Excessive security can create 'big brother' fears.

◆ *The customer strikes back with Virtual Intelligence*
Intelligent agents will make life in cyberspace easier. The application of these 'bots' to purchasing, privacy protection and creation of a user-defined context will be the customers' weapons against the Internet shops' marketing initiatives.

Total dominance of the Internet

Many people are watching spellbound as the Internet grows exponentially, as we described in our first chapter. What they often do not realise is that the Internet is not only a fascinating new interaction medium, but that it will completely dominate our society.

Previous generations knew books, newspapers, telephones and televisions. The first three were essential aids to life, two text-based, the third speech-based. Anyone who was denied access to them was disadvantaged in our society. The picture-based medium, television, helped to bring the world closer to home. But it condemned the viewer to passivity and has been more a hindrance than a help in aiding individuals to develop new skills and capabilities.

The Internet will unite all the traditional media and push them further. Most significantly, this is the first time that pictures will be used interactively for information, communication and development of skills. Even today, everyone who uses the (still underdeveloped) web is able to catch a glimpse of the potential of the medium in this direction.

Our children will grow into a web generation. They won't log onto the Internet occasionally, but will be online all the time. Fortunately they will be significantly more active than the TV-dominated baby boom generation. Those who are denied access to the Internet completely or partially will be enormously disadvantaged. They will be lost in our digital society.

Obviously access will not be as it is today: slow, unstructured, available only through the computer. We will have intelligent tools for tapping undreamt-of possibilities. We can glimpse the beginning of these developments in many places. Shopping over the Internet of the future will be the obvious thing to do, regardless of whether the goods are ultimately delivered or fetched in person. Both the time-short and time-rich will love using the web in this way.

Regardless of whether you agree with our views, you should read on. It is important for every e-tailing and electronic shopping strategy to understand in detail what dramatic changes the Internet will undergo in the next few years.

Anytime, anywhere access

'The first 200 million Internet users used a PC – the next 800 million will use another device.' This is Eric Benhamou, the head of 3Com, producer of amongst other things the beloved 'PalmPilot', an organiser the size of your hand, talking in the spring of 1999. Although we do not agree with his view when delivered so provocatively, and believe firmly in the future of the PC, there will certainly be numerous new devices for Internet access. Many will be particularly suitable for certain forms of electronic shopping.

Today 'interface' devices for the electronic world fall into three categories: telephone, PC and television. The telephone and the television were network-orientated devices from the beginning. They had a specific use: speech-based one-to-one communication on the one hand and picture-and-sound-based broadcasts on the other. The PC was initially a stand-alone calculating machine which was gradually networked and became a communication unit. It has been quite a long evolution. Douglas Englebart, the often unacknowledged forefather of the modern PC, not only invented the mouse, but as long ago as 1964 in his Stanford Research Institute, was propagating networking in its primitive forms. His early efforts were precursors of what we now call 'hyperlinks' on the Internet. Interestingly even Apple founder, Steve Jobs, who copied much from Englebart and marketed it, did not take this aspect of communication between PCs very seriously at first.

With digitisation (still only partially achieved with the telephone and the television), the three categories, telephone, PC, TV will merge. This does not mean that multifunctional devices will dominate the market place, although these are clearly possible. After all, a medium like the radio has not disappeared although the radio function has long been integrated into TV sets. For most of today's radio listeners TV sets are inappropriate. Digitisation of all devices does mean, however, that new applications and functional extensions will be possible. Overall we see three far-reaching changes for Internet access and electronic shopping:

- ◆ the comeback of the television;
- ◆ an increase in mobile devices; and
- ◆ the growth of 'easy use' equipment (intelligent fridges and much more).

Surrounding these elements of tomorrow's consumer infrastructure are a number of burning questions, e.g. who will provide the operating system which allows them to function? And who will provide the Internet access to them? Fortunately as an e-tailer you can wait and see.

The comeback of television

A debate has been going on for a long time about whether the PC or the television will win as a preferred method of access to the Internet.

A few years ago, a Japanese delegation visiting Silicon Valley asked Regis McKenna: 'Which will win – the TV set or the PC?'. 'The microwave oven' was his stunning reply. We love it, because it not only underlines the fruitlessness of the discussion, but emphasises that – thanks to Moore's law – we will see many more unconventional Internet access devices. We discuss these in more detail below.

Still, television deserves some special attention. With digitisation, it is on a technological collision course with the PC and many people believe that this means that one device will have to go. A long and pointless discussion has begun about whether the greater functionality of the PC or the wider distribution, better graphics and greater ease of operation of the TV set will win through. Combination units (PCs with which you can receive television broadcasts or TVs on which you write e-mails) are already on the market. So far they have not met with much success.

The reason is simple: the 'egg-laying wool-producing milk-providing pig' is impractical. In the foreseeable future there will be a device with a keyboard which primarily specialises in communicating and processing information and which will be compact to a degree or even portable – let's call this a PC. There will be another device that is big, though no longer clumsy looking, that specialises in high-resolution graphics and films – let's simply call this a television. This television can have an infrared keyboard connected to it but usually it will be controlled with its simpler remote-control unit. You will be able to interchange the two units to a certain degree, but the so-called 'look and feel' is clearly optimised to one type of application.

The critical fact is: *television is becoming suitable for the Internet.* This trend cannot be stopped. Most new and some proven Internet content is strongly picture-based and therefore particularly suited to television. Accessing it will not require a keyboard just as videotext or programme guides do not. The ultimate breakthrough for TV as an Internet device will come with broadband connections. Interactive TV will embrace Internet content as an add-on to TV programmes. We showed you a foretaste of this in Chapter 5 with Victoria's Secret's Internet fashion show which attracted more than 1.5 million TV viewers in January 1999.

For a long time it has been thought that video on demand (i.e. downloading films for payment) will be interactive TV's 'killer application', i.e. the decisive buying incentive for interactive television. Now it is clear that many people think that they would like video on demand but hardly anyone would pay for such a service at today's prices. Thus the so-called 'full service networks' (FSN) based on this (such as Time-Warner's notorious attempt in Orlando) have all failed so far. The good news was that Time-Warner's FSN worked; the bad news was that it cost the company about $12,000 per connected household.

It seems clear that an offer of a television including elements of so-called 'lazy interactivity' represents a sensible step forward. This provides:

◆ additional information windows: for example interrupting long-winded live broadcasts such as Oscar award ceremonies, coronations, slow sports like golf or baseball, concerts with news;

- ◆ 'buy' buttons in advertising and events;
- ◆ direct voting capabilities; and
- ◆ interaction in live auctions.

These offers can be linked to a 'picture-in-picture' segmentation or windows within the television screen. For example, users in the UK of Sky's digital TV offer will be familiar with the ability to change camera angles and call up player statistics while watching sporting events.

A big problem for TV-based Internet access today is still the lack of standardisation of the necessary set-top boxes. As consumers don't want to risk having to buy several of these boxes, many are playing a waiting game. Now PCs have become so cheap in the US that it will soon be possible, for under 400 dollars, to put a simple PC on the television set and to solve the rest of the problem with software. A nightmare, by the way, for all those who want to use set-top boxes to break Microsoft's stranglehold.

The US is the sparring ground for the big players in the Internet TV world and they are now heading for battle. The market-leader is currently *Microsoft* with *Web TV* and its 800,000 subscribers. Microsoft has taken a five per cent share in *AT&T*, who, after acquisition of TCI has become the largest cable TV supplier. As part of the deal, AT&T plans to install Microsoft software in 7.5 million set-top boxes. In another corner, *AOL-TV* has been announced. As US cable access was denied them, in June 1999 AOL took a 1.6 billion dollar share in Hughes Electronics, the operator of satellite-based *DirecTV* systems with eight million subscribers. *Hughes Electronics* is also the manufacturer of AOL's set-top boxes. Bertelsmann, co-owner of AOL Europe, wants to introduce AOL-TV into 'the old continent'. Here they face real challenges as the mixed infrastructure in European countries will need multiple solutions.

The future for television as a medium is firm but the future for many television broadcasters is uncertain. Cable TV players in some countries have got used to a pay-TV model. The advent of broad-band technology allowing TV to be watched on the

Internet threatens all this – as it becomes possible to charge subscription fees on the Internet.

Broadcast.com, taken over by Yahoo in spring 1999, has shown what is possible on the web using streaming technology. Broadcast.com, amongst others, has acquired Internet rights for sports broadcasts and is waiting for these to become accessible via TV sets, at which point it will be in direct competition with traditional broadcasters.

For e-tailers and e-shopping suppliers this means that, within the foreseeable future, they will be able to reach the whole television-watching community. They will, of course, have competition from television broadcasters like home-shopping channel *QVC*, which is moving the opposite way into the Internet. Note that as they prepare to migrate to TV, Internet sites must be adapted to be TV-acceptable with larger fonts, more pictures and navigability without a keyboard!

The growth of mobile companions

The meteoric rise in *mobile phones*, portable computers (notebooks and palm-tops) and personal equipment like 'organisers' emphasises the enormous significance of mobility in today's society. Mobiles, with Internet access will soon flood the market.

A prototype in this respect – perhaps ahead of its time – was the so-called *Communicator* from *Nokia*. It is a mobile telephone and small computer combined. Like most combination units it has suffered because it was not ideal either as a telephone (too big and clumsy) or as a computer (screen and keyboard too small). In addition, it was too expensive and thus not accessible to the mass market. With increasing miniaturisation, less weight, longer stand-by times and the growing importance of the Internet, these *smart phones* will gain mass market appeal. In what form and in which user-segments is still not clear. There will be significant struggles for market share and standards.

Some peculiarities will remain: the mobile spectrum will always be scarce and units will mostly have a small screen. Companies are feverishly developing technology to adapt the content of Internet sites to meet the requirements of such units, among them *Nokia* and *Ericsson* in Europe.

In mobile access in general, Europe is in a good starting position with the leading international GSM-Standard. A standard for transfer to the Internet – *WAP* (wireless application protocol) – has now been set and should be in the first mobile telephones by the end of 1999. It will enable those in Europe to call up simple web information and e-mails on their mobile phones.

Anybody who wants insight into products for these segments should look at developments in Finland, which is playing a leading role with its Internet euphoria and a mobile phone penetration of more than 60 per cent of the population. For a few years now it has been possible for Finns to buy a can of coke from a machine or pay for a car wash, all using a mobile phone.

Even *Organisers*, mobile units first used more for their calendar functions and address management than shopping, are forcing their way into electronic shopping. Retail chain *Safeway* in England has started a pilot project with organiser producer *Psion* to link an electronically managed shopping list with an organiser and make ordering possible from anywhere. Mobile units could also be used as a news service. Nokia and CNN have got together to develop this business.

Electronic shopping suppliers will find that, once enabled with these new tools, people will make spontaneous purchases which will soon become significant in certain categories (flowers, gifts). It is important for e-tailers to understand these developments and to continue to watch them so that they can adapt their strategy and specific ranges to the requirements of such purchasers (small band-width, fast purchase).

Growth of easy-to-use devices, intelligent fridges and much more

Apart from TV sets and mobile phones there is still a mass of new ideas for equipment which will enable Internet access and electronic shopping. The motto is *access anytime, anywhere*. Ideas in this area are pretty much boundless. An essential ingredient is user friendliness to break down 'technofear' and resistance to use. An example here is the so-called web phone.

Alcatel introduced its Screen Phone in 1998. It looks like a telephone with a small screen; at the press of a button, a keyboard slides out. This device should have made Internet access simple and cheap. A few user-unfriendly characteristics, however, caused it to flop. An improved version called 'webtouch' will now be launched on the market with a specific aim: to migrate the 15 million users of Minitel in France to the web.

Simple units usually have a significantly lower price level than the PCs of today. With the future distribution of devices likely to be disproportionate among certain customer groups (such as pensioners), the would-be e-tailer must make sure that his range is accessible with these simple devices. There are the same requirements for band-width and user friendliness as with other electronic tools.

IP telephony, however, we believe to be of secondary importance to electronic shopping. The most important aspect is that IP telephone access to the Internet becomes a matter of routine and the number of users will increase further.

Another very active experimental field involves web capable *embedded devices*. These are units with built-in chips, connected to the Internet and able to exchange communications and to control signals. Especially popular is kitchen equipment; fridges or microwaves. Many of these can be linked with intelligent electronic shopping: *Electrolux* together with ICL and Frigidaire have developed an innovative fridge that can trigger orders by itself, if supplies run low. What a hit for a certain segment of the population if the fridge would re-order more beer as soon as it ran low! For food manufacturers and retailers it is certainly interesting to follow these developments. New technology-enabled shopping concepts are appearing everywhere, but their practical significance lies, at best, well into the future.

We hope that the descriptions above have illuminated some of the most important trends in devices and their significance

@Home: a pioneer of fast Internet access

@Home, actually now 'Excite @Home', since its acquisition of the search engine Excite, is a pioneer in fast Internet access through television cables. @Home is controlled by US telephone giant *AT&T* and operated in conjunction with local cable TV companies. Although access is through a TV cable, the connected device is still a PC – the television will only be connected through a set-top box.

@Home's idea is constant, broad-band Internet access for a fixed price of $40 a month. The connection is constantly running, i.e. you do not have to take a lot of time and trouble logging onto the Internet. There are no time-dependent fees – the standard for Internet access in the future.

In this model high access speed is not restricted by a clogged up Internet node or a slow 'backbone' line. Content that is often called up is copied and stored locally, and a high-capacity 'backbone network' supports rapid content access. Although by the end of 1998 only 330,000 US households were connected, @Home has ensured exclusive access rights to 44 million US households by contracts with cable companies. AOL has already asked the regulatory authorities to examine this potentially (they fear) monopolistic position, but so far in vain.

@Home is up and running in England and in the Netherlands. The latter country has the highest European cable TV penetration with 95% of households connected.

@Home's customers are enthusiastic. Anybody who has experienced broad-band access will never willingly go back to narrow band-width. In the UK, *BT* has also observed the success of broad-band access and is soon to offer high-speed access using ADSL technology. This allows very high-speed connection but over existing telephone lines.

for electronic shopping. The trend to anywhere, anytime Internet access is clear. It is very worthwhile keeping one eye on the changing device technologies if you are an aspiring e-tailer or a supplier of e-shopping support services. Apart from television and mobile devices we would, however, exercise a certain caution with regard to the real importance of new 'gimmicks'. What is an unavoidable fact is that in future, web-sites must be available in at least three formats: for TVs, PCs and mobile phones.

The Internet 2

The broad-band data highway is coming

'Gilder's law' states the observation that the bandwidth available on the globe doubles every four months. At the same time transmission costs are falling: the cost to transmit 1 megabyte of data from the west coast to the east coast of the US has fallen from $100 to 1 cent in the last 20 years. Despite these advances in the backbone, most users experience Internet access today using a telephone line and a 'normal' modem with up to 56 'kbps' (kilobits per second data transmission speed). This is fast enough for almost all text-based content, but is too slow for complex graphics, let alone films. The speed problem, however, is not exclusively in access. Anyone who uses the Internet in business over a broad-band connection knows that individual nodes on the net specific servers also represent bottlenecks. An essential prerequisite for comprehensive Internet use is a high-speed infrastructure right into the home. The example of @Home gives a glimpse of the second-generation Internet.

As well as television cables, a large number of other technologies have been developed to enable broad-band access to the Internet. As setting up a completely new infrastructure would be too slow, they are all following the same principle. You take whatever line is available into the house and convert it to broad-band access. So far television cables, good old copper telephone wires and electricity cables have all been adapted

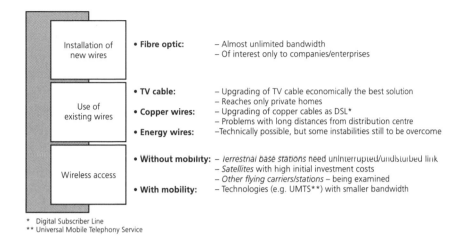

Installation of new wires	• **Fibre optic:**	– Almost unlimited bandwidth – Of interest only to companies/enterprises
Use of existing wires	• **TV cable:** • **Copper wires:** • **Energy wires:**	– Upgrading of TV cable economically the best solution – Reaches only private homes – Upgrading of copper cables as DSL* – Problems with long distances from distribution centre –Technically possible, but some instabilities still to be overcome
Wireless access	• **Without mobility:** • **With mobility:**	– *Terrestrial base stations* need uninterrupted/undisturbed link – *Satellites* with high initial investment costs – *Other flying carriers/stations* – being examined – Technologies (e.g. UMTS**) with smaller bandwidth

* Digital Subscriber Line
** Universal Mobile Telephony Service

Fig. 9.1   Broad band access technologies.

accordingly. Some radical thinkers have even considered water mains! Satellite broadcasting and other cable-free technologies complete the broad-band picture. Figure 9.1 gives a summary of broad-band access technologies.

One thing is certain: an 'always-on', broad-band data highway will come to the home and even to the car. A clue to the beginnings of this can be found at *Onstar* from *General Motors*. On the second-generation Internet, data will be essentially *pictures* and *graphics*. There will be more picture-based information than text-based communication, providing entertainment (music, games, films), shopping and education.

For those involved in e-shopping, broad-band access brings new possibilities for web-site creation and interaction with customers. 'Always-on', *constant Internet access will become the norm*. Within a decade, the vast majority of all households will be equipped with broad-band. In the meantime, e-tailers must be able to connect to both narrow-band and broad-band frequencies.

XML will become a new lingua franca

Interaction on the Internet is about to undergo a profound transformation. A new language – *XML* (extensible markup language) – is the magic wand to be waved. XML really has only one advantage but it will have dramatic effects: it will be possible to relate a *category* to a term that can be *recognised by a computer*.

That may not sound very exciting, but to grasp the significance of this simple fact you have to know how the world wide web of today works. Today's web is based on a language called *HTML* (hypertext markup language). HTML is purely text-based plus inserted links, its so-called 'hyperlinks'. These hyperlinks were a great innovation. They created 'surfing' on the Internet as we know it today: jumping from one place to another. The problem with HTML is that it is pure text. For a computer, today's web site reads like incomprehensible blabber:

> *Bla, bla, bla ... <link> bla, bla...<link> bla, bla ...*

The PC itself can't begin to do much more with this than print, store and connect to various lists. On the other hand, in XML the computer can be taught to recognise particular elements of the site:

> *Bla, bla* <goods category> *bla, bla* <Price> *bla, bla* <Size> <Colour> *bla, bla* <link> *bla, bla ...*

This *structured* information is very useful. It has such a profound effect that *business-to-business interactions* (communication and transactions between companies) will go *over to the web 100%*. Old EDI (electronic data interchange) systems provided such a structure and is why many business users have not so far, or only reluctantly, transferred to the Internet.

We cannot go into a long discourse on the multitude of advantages of structured information for electronic shopping and e-tailing. We just note that *efficient searching* for e-shopping information is hugely simplified. You can limit the exchange of information to essential criteria (e.g. price) without constantly having to send files backwards and forwards between buyer and seller. Current transmission waiting times will be considerably reduced. In addition, information can be stored efficiently (even in a media-neutral format).

XML can be universally understood. It has only one disadvantage: there is currently only a *syntax but no semantics*, so the structure is pre-determined, but meaning must still be defined by its user groups. In some ways XML is a 'meta language', allowing suitable languages to be formulated for specific requirements. Countless standardisation committees and large IT companies like SAP and Microsoft are trying to fill these gaps, which could in fact delay a universal introduction of XML.

Data security is sufficient

Discussions of e-tailing and e-shopping always used to begin with something on the theme of 'Security of the payment process'. There was good reason for this because fears about *security* were by far the greatest hurdle to users widely adopting electronic shopping. The technological pre-requisites for security have now been drawn together. We may even have the opposite: too much data security!

Credit cards are the most widely used payment method on the Internet. Many customers were wary at first: 'I would rather write my credit card number on an advertising hoarding than unprotected on the Internet' was a common sentiment. It is true that when online banking began, there were huge security problems. For example, the Chaos Computer Club made a name for itself very early on in Germany. In 1984 it ridiculed IBM and what was then the German Post Office (Telephone Division) when it broke into their jointly operated BTX service for electronic banking. It managed to get a Hamburg savings bank to ring its site constantly. There was a charge for this access and in one night the equivalent of over $50,000 was transferred to its account. The club gave it back after publicising its action. Other well-known cases have been less good-natured.

Absolute security of transaction is not attainable anywhere, even on the Internet. But users have increasingly accepted that payment on the net is appropriately secure. In the US the shift came in 1998 and now the majority of transactions are dealt with on credit cards. *Digital Cash*, a widely propagated alternative to other payment methods, has largely been a failure. Once highly valued, suppliers like *Cybercash*, *First Virtual* and *Digicash* have lost a large part of their market value and some are in financial difficulties.

Today's *asymmetric encoding* technologies, coupled with a *digital signature*, make payments on the Internet as secure as you should sensibly make them. Alternatively there are *electronic purses* with limited contents and an automatic maximum to limit fraud and errors. Greater security can be provided if one uses hardware solutions, for example a separate *card reader*. This provides a remedy against 'bugging' the keyboard (with software smuggled onto the computer) – a weakness that neither passwords nor encoding can prevent. Further improvements to these technologies are provided by personal identification procedures, such as confirming fingerprints or the iris of the eye. All these technologies are interesting, but they could easily suffer the same fate as digital cash. Ultimately users may accept what they know best (the credit card) and learn to live with a 'sensible' level of fraud risk.

Our view is that more and more payment security systems will provide only marginal benefits for the private user. The truth is that security problems are not around the transaction itself but in other areas:

◆ Does the customer use the technologies?
◆ Does he protect his access rights?
◆ Are these periodically checked/changed?
◆ Who has access to the computer (or other relevant equipment)?

These are severe security issues but outside the individual transaction.

Some payment processes, however, do need innovative solutions. Micropayments (for small cash payments) are still an unresolved problem. They are needed mostly for digitally transferable 'goods', where very low-value payments are still commercially sensible because there is no physical distribution. One possible solution to this problem has been created by Israeli firm Trivnet, which can provide a statement of micropayments via monthly invoice from the Internet service provider.

With data security in general there is a constant 'arms race' between attack and defence. *Firewalls* will have a great importance in the digital economy. A single virus, let loose over the Internet, could destroy the business of a major software house. For anybody who is interested in an exciting simulated battle on a high technical level, we recommend reading the October 1998 edition of *Scientific American*.

It is possible that we actually have a problem with *too much data security*. In the trial dealing with the monopoly complaint against Microsoft, a large number of the company e-mail files were analysed and embarrassing, very incriminating reports brought to light. The surprising thing was that these e-mails could be reconstructed although they had been erased long ago and the relevant hard disks had been overwritten many times. *E-mails are forever* is now an oft quoted saying! Could it be that we are worrying about data security when we are already on the way to a 'big-brother' state?

These issues apply to general Internet use, but for the e-tailer only two things are important:

- ◆ Most customers accept today's security standards if their first experiences are positive. Meanwhile today, standards will constantly improve.
- ◆ There are enough service providers for payment handling who offer insurance protection against fraud. These service providers will help to overcome many of the remaining real risks for the shopper and, with them, customers' psychological obstacles to shopping on the Internet.

The customer strikes back with virtual intelligence

Many users currently surf the net in a trial-and-error fashion. Attracted by strong brands or transported by search engines, they look for information step by step or complete transactions manually.

Their behaviour today will, in a few years, seem surprisingly naïve to us, because it is an expensive, risky and time-consuming way to reach a goal. Even today it is neither necessary nor appropriate to use the Internet in this way.

The Internet has prompted a re-birth of certain forms of artificial intelligence which we have christened *virtual intelligence*. The relevant intelligent agents are *bots*, a pet name used on the Internet for robots.

There are bots for almost everything. From *chat bots*, which can hold almost sensible conversations and thus fit seamlessly into the level of a typical chat-room, right up to *career bots*, which take care of job searches and salaries. If you want to go further into the world of *bot*, you will love BotSpot.com, which offers a complete summary of bots.

Bots will play a major role in e-tailing and e-shopping. They will sift through databases on company servers and recommend purchases. There are many that can be employed on the e-tailers side, which we discussed in Part 2, so we introduce here some that are fighting on the consumer's side:

- shopbots
- virtual doubles
- context builders.

Shopbots

There are few people who never ask themselves when shopping 'could I get the same thing somewhere else cheaper?' Well, on the Internet this *smart shopping* is 'only a mouse-click away'. See the case study on shopbot *MySimon* for how these work.

It is no accident that Amazon.com altered shopbot Junglee completely after taking it over. They removed books and music from the search fields. Supposedly the user would have no interest in a comparison of 'the minor price differences' with these goods!

Case study – MySimon

One of the most impressive price comparison services on the web is MySimon. The company was only founded in 1998 and is one of the few independent shopbots on the Internet. On the strength of its performance, MySimon has succeeded in making a name for itself alongside giants like *Jango* (Excite @Home), *Junglee* (Amazon), *C2B* (Inktomi) and Yahoo Shopping.

If you have never used a shopbot, you must try MySimon. With standard articles it only takes a few seconds to type in a description. The search takes hardly any longer. The experience will astound you. Even with such apparently competitive categories like books or CDs, the most expensive supplier in the USA – often a big brand name – is usually twice as expensive as the cheapest. Unfortunately MySimon has not yet reached Europe. Hopefully it will be by the time this book comes out.

MySimon's business system is simple. There are currently many thousands of e-tailers connected to its service. For each purchase MySimon receives between two and five per cent commission from the dealer. The service is free for the consumer. Many online shoppers prefer to click on MySimon for each purchase because the mouse click is worth it.

Why are e-tailers listed on such a service? It is very simple to identify the shopbot's knock at the store door and stop it there. The answer is that bots are just too well established, generating valuable visitors, to shut out. In addition, sites do not want to risk putting across a negative 'bots not welcome'.

Although undoubtedly they are the most useful, price comparisons are, of course, not the only function of shopbots. Goods searches, generating personal recommendations and the automation of auctions are further examples of their application.

If you want to get an impression of the state of advanced technology related to searching for information on the Internet, then try the web tool *Mata Hari*. As suits its illustrious name, Mata Hari is a meta-agent, controlling the services of many other search machines. It manages a wide range of complexly formulated queries ('Boolean algebra' in technical language).

It does not need much imagination to work out what the potential effects of virtual intelligence on the shopping process could be:

- Bots seek out the best price offer.
- Customer loyalty exists only when there is some reward for it (e.g. bonus points, discounts, preferential delivery times, complete ranges etc.).
- Advertising is completely ignored.
- Individual suppliers' defence mechanisms against bots are relatively worthless because there is almost always a substitute.
- Auctions take place between 'robots'.

No one can yet predict where the developments will take us in the long term. However, it is certain that the more shopbots there are, the more *differentiation* counts. Suppliers of standard goods like Amazon will be particularly hard hit. Internet shops will have to set themselves apart, as we have already discussed, with strong brands, linked to customer-specific products and built-to-order ranges. Even a certain lack of transparency in prices, which can be created by combining additional services, bonus points etc., will help against direct price comparisons. In every case electronic shopping companies must anticipate these developments and adapt their strategies accordingly.

Virtual doubles

Many web marketing advisers imply that web customers are highly transparent and can be easily prompted to buy if their online behaviour is accurately understood. Although the

Lucent Technologies' virtual double

Bell Labs, one of the most famous research labs in the world, has created a unique system for consumer protection which goes by the name of 'Lucent Personalised Web Assistant' (LPWA). The system works by generating a virtual *alter ego* for you using proprietary software. If LPWA users are asked for personal information on a web-site, they enter:

User name: \u
Pass word: \p
e-mail: \@

Lucent converts the symbols \u, \p and \@ into a new randomly generated identity for each e-mail address. For the consumer this is wonderful. They have all the benefits of a regular customer and in addition do not have to remember a password, (a standard problem for regular e-shoppers). They have given no clue to their true identity because they are being represented by a team of virtual doubles. E-mails will be sent on to the consumer unless they feel it is a nuisance and reject it – they can do this for each website individually.

Lucent's system is attractive as it allows e-tailers to do their marketing analyses in spite of anonymity, so that it serves both buyers and sellers.

Internet creates countless possibilities for one-to-one marketing, we have already emphasised that this will only be possible on the basis of a clear benefit for the customer. In this section we describe briefly how technologies will contribute to a customer's 'armoury' in electronic shopping.

The basis of all effective marketing is the collection of customer information. As well as omnipresent questionnaires and the analysis of purchasing history, e-tailers use *Cookies*. Not the tasty biscuit kind, but mostly Java-based agents that are transferred to the web surfer's computer and pass back details about their surfing.

Cookies are not the only way to obtain interesting customer details. In March 1999 the *New York Times* reported on the 'Globally Unique Identifier' (GUID) in *Microsoft's Windows 98*, which stored personal details in a global database and linked it with data generated by them. Once publicised, Microsoft suspended use of this immediately and spoke of an 'oversight', claiming that the function should really have been activated only at the customer's express wish.

There is currently intense discussion on the amount of regulation needed to protect privacy on the Internet. The problem with regulation is that e-tailers need information for many of the services they provide to consumers. *We have not lost our privacy, we've sold it piece by piece.* Although technically possible 'cookie blockers' (like Luckman Interactive's 'Anonymous Cookie' software) are only of limited use because you are throwing the baby out with the bath water. But even here there are innovative solutions to the problem of providing enough information while maintaining privacy. Lucent is an example here with LWPA.

To close the section on virtual doubles, we give you another example which deals with respect for personal details in exemplary fashion. If you have problems planning your free time effectively, the Internet knows how to remedy this. Get hold of a 'Funbot' like Open Sesame's *eGenie*.

Besides its impressive functions (on which we are not going to dwell here) it is concerned above all that you should never consider it is a nuisance or feel threatened by it. It does not bother you with questionnaires but learns from your surfing behaviour. To remain unthreatening it will allow you to take a look at what it has learnt anytime.

If the first thing you ask eGenie about is 'what's on at the cinema?' and then examine the *What I have learnt* section, you will see 'You are interested in the cinema and next time I will show you what's on at cinemas.'

With eGenie you also have an *opt out* option, enabling you to erase private information at any time. This gives the user the security of having full transparency and control over personal information, and creates confidence in providing such details.

Context builders

Today most people see web-sites just as they were set up by their operators. The visitor's context and the ways of forming this are pre-determined by the operator. This need not be the case. German technology giant *Siemens* shocked the advertising world with the introduction of its *Web-Washer*, a proxy browser which *automatically removes all advertising from web-sites*.

The principle is simple. The format of advertising banners on the Internet is standardised and web-washer blocks the downloading of these formats. Even if its Version 1.0 does not always work one hundred per cent, it is still surprisingly effective. An interesting side effect is that sites can be downloaded up to 45 per cent faster. The idea is not completely new. CERN's Web Filter and other software programmes all promised similar things. Web Washer is unique in being the first product suitable for the consumer market given its ease of use. Also attractive is that it is currently being offered free. If advertising can really be erased, it will have a dramatic effect on many web business systems.

Filters are still really in their infancy as tools to form one's personal context. *Zadu*, a Silicon Valley start-up, is pursuing a potentially far-reaching idea. They have a system based on a companion to the web browser which allows a visitor to a web-site to contact other visitors to the site. You can choose whether you would like to see all visitors or only selected groups and whether you want just to annotate the web-site with notes only visible to other user groups or communicate directly with other visitors at the same time. You can then interact with fellow surfers via annotations, combining all synchronous and asynchronous web-based communications. In addition Zadu's partners can choose keywords that will then appear highlighted to Zadu users on every single Web page on the Internet and linked to the partners' site. This 'overlay technology' shifts the power on the web. Suddenly you can attract browsers on someone else's web site without the consent of the author of the site. At the same time the user is always in control.

Finally in the area of 'context', the idea of a subscription-based Internet 'overlay' is in the air and many people are racking their brains over what could be suitable services to offer as part of this. You could imagine having a page translated, or activating price comparisons at the press of a button without first having to break off to go to another site. Ultimately, in future a visitor will be able to decide for himself which way he will 'consume' an Internet page.

This ends our brief description of the infrastructure of the digital economy. We have concentrated on those aspects which in our view are most important for e-shopping. Our only exhortation is to take timely note of the dramatic developments in the offing.

E-tail searchlight on web-sites for Chapter 9

- 3com   www.3com.com
- WebTV   www.webtv.com
- DirecTV   www.directv.com
- Hughes Electronics   www.hughes.com
- AOL   www.aol.com
- Broadcast.com   www.broadcast.com
- QVC   www.qvc.com
- Nokia   www.nokia.com
- Ericsson   www.ericsson.com
- Psion   www.psion.co.uk
- Alcatel   www.alcatel.fr
- Electrolux   www.electrolux.com
- @Home   www.athome.net
- Onstar   www.onstar.com
- Digicash   www.digicash.com
- FirstVirtual   www.firstvirtual.com
- Cybercash   www.cybercash.com
- Trivnet   www.trivnet.com
- BotSpot   www.botspot.com
- MySimon   www.mysimon.com
- Mata Hari   www.thewebtools.com
- Junglee   www.junglee.com
- Lucent PWA   www.lpwa.com
- eGenie   www.opensesame.com
- Siemens   www.siemens.de
- Zadu   www.zadu.com

Chapter 10

It's Free – the Age of

the Digital Product

Anyone accepting the developments we have described in the first two parts of this book as likely has to believe that they will fundamentally change our lives and our economies. The next question is: what happens when products themselves become digital? The perceived zero cost of (re)production and distribution of digital products will lead to a radical restructuring of the competitive landscape. These changes will not be triggered by innovative start-up companies, but by the behaviour of individual consumers world-wide. In this chapter we consider the consequences for e-tailers of this upheaval.

E-tail searchlight illuminates Chapter 10

◆ *Stand by for a digital insurrection*
Established industries built around digitisable content
(e.g. software, music, media) are facing a digital guerrilla
war. Manning the barricades to protect the old order is
a lost cause. Embracing a fundamental change to today's
business systems in these industries is the only way to
secure the next generation of consumers.

◆ *Be ready for a legal no-man's-land*
The value of digital products, appropriate taxation and
duty is hard to determine. Copyright protection and
unauthorised copying on the web are difficult to police.
Legal decisions on Internet issues in most countries are
based on laws developed in a totally different context.
Legislating sensibly for the digital economy is still an
open issue.

◆ *Exploit opportunities in digital products*
Attack is the best form of defence in digital markets.
Completely new business streams are available, particularly related to intelligent distribution concepts, personalisation, 'versioning' and next-generation services.

Stand by for a digital insurrection

Many goods are digital or can be digitised, amongst them all
types of information, software, and practically all media (tel-
evision/films, radio/music, newspapers/magazines, books and
games).

These goods are becoming increasingly significant in the
digital economy.

The combination of digital goods with the Internet as a distribution channel creates an explosive mixture. It is leading
more and more people, all over the world, to avoid today's established business systems. Consumers – not businesses – were

the first to recognise the potential of digital goods. Early 'rebels' used 'free' distribution on the Internet to copy software and distribute it to their friends on the web. In some countries these consumers are acting in a grey area of the law, or they are breaking seldom enforced – and in many respects inadequate – laws. The rebels are mostly well educated, largely penniless students. We call these groups of people 'digital guerrillas'. In conceptual terms we see a guerilla war being fought. The broader mass of consumers behave like the population in an insurrection. On one hand they can see the illegality of the guerillas' behaviour and the danger in destroying accepted frameworks. On the other hand they realise that the rebels have basically recognised where the future lies and are revolting against forces for conservatism. Not least, they sympathise with the courage needed to strike out against the powerful controllers of the current order. Increasingly consumers will begin to take part in the rebellion themselves. You find ambivalence toward the guerillas. Some see them as terrorists, others as freedom fighters.

For a deeper discussion of these themes we need to highlight a few specific *characteristics of digital products,* especially in connection with the Internet:

- *Originals and copies are equivalent*
  Differentiation becomes pointless.
- *Marginal costs are zero*
  This applies to the (re)production and distribution of goods; digital goods are often seen as 'free'.
- *Indestructibility*
  The quality of goods does not decrease with the passage of time.
- *Easy modification*
  On the one hand, adaptations are easy: on the other, it is not easy to guarantee authenticity.

Bearing these characteristics in mind let's look at the various phases (Fig. 10.1) of a digital guerrilla war.

Rebellion	Battle	Adoption of guerrilla ideas
– Revolutionary technologies disturb the peace – Rebels starts to use new technology – Internet growth broadens the rebel base – Increased bandwidth and new hardware increase the effect of rebellion	– Established businesses defend high-value content – Search parties, trials and police force fight the guerrillas – Intense efforts to standardise protected formats – Islands of 'free content' legalise the rebellion	– Significant elements of the rebellion are taken into the mainstream – Reforms in the retail structure pacify the majority of customers – Prices drop, consumption increases – New intermediaries and 'clearing houses' regulate legal traffic

Fig. 10.1   The phases of a digital guerrilla war.

Rebellion

Revolutionary technologies for creating, compressing or distributing digital content break up existing business structures. Established companies try to limit these, because their current business would not be able to stand up to them. The early rebels begin to use their new tools actively. The growth of the Internet rapidly broadens the rebel base. Increasing band-width and the development of suitable user devices increase the effectiveness of the revolt.

Battle

Established companies systematically begin to take defensive action. They purposely seal off high-value content. They take on search troops to seek out distributors of unlicensed digital products and take legal and commercial action against infrastructure providers or manufacturers of enabling user devices. Meanwhile the whole industry, still locked in their old ways of doing business, is trying to develop protected formats and implement them as standard. At the same time suppliers of 'new' content appear who aggressively exploit the opportunities for digital products. These 'islands of freedom' reinforce the rebellion in a way which forces fundamental change upon established businesses.

Adoption of guerrilla thinking

We have yet to see a digital guerilla war being settled. But any resolution will have to include the adoption of central elements of the rebellion. Reformed companies allow consumers to take full advantage of the potential of digital products. Prices fall drastically, but the economic effects of this are offset by higher consumption. New service providers and intermediaries are created.

Now let's look at how this guerrilla war is being waged in some industries.

Industry no. 1: the software industry

The software industry is the stronghold of the digital guerrilla. The movement has already reached the mass market. In 1998, 40 percent of the software available in the world was allegedly acquired without payment, a potential value of at least several billion dollars. In countries like Bolivia and Paraguay, more than 85 per cent of software is not licensed. The greatest damage is done to the software industry in countries with large populations like Brazil, India and China. But much more important is the fact that free, legal software ('freeware') is now available in many product areas, and the industry is gradually beginning to learn how to deal with it.

The *rebellion* began in 1985, when anonymous FTP servers (*file transfer protocol*, a data transfer standard) made unlicensed software available over the Internet. The spread of the rebellion was accelerated as access to greater band-width became available to users at work, (where most users made illegal copies). The Internet itself provided readily comprehensible, and efficient search engines to find sources of software.

The *battle* was delayed for some time. All attempts to encrypt software resulted in failure because its complexity reduced user-friendliness and hence sales figures so quickly that they were rapidly abandoned. Instead the industry decided to defend itself with regular, only partially compatible upgrades which rendered old versions unusable. At the same time, rebel-held islands

The emergence of freeware

Freeware is free software, which can be downloaded from the Internet and further developed. It is the legitimate child of the digital economy. In its beta-version form, freeware is now a firmly established component of most software developments.

In 1991, a 21-year-old electrical engineering student from the University of Helsinki put the following article on a hackers' newsgroup page: 'Hello out there ... I'm working on a (free) operating system (only a hobby, nothing big or professional). I would very much like to know which functions people would most like to have.'

The student was Linus Torvalds. No-one dreamed that by 1996 his operating system, *Linux*, would grow into robust system operating software with a wide range of functions, boosted by the enthusiastic inputs from a community of more than a million developers worldwide. The basic idea was that everyone could suggest a software code which was then assessed and accepted, improved or rejected by an international Internet community of 'peers'. Linux is essentially more elegantly written and better documented than most proprietary software programmes. As a reward for collaborating in its development everybody can download the software free. A *new, free operating system* has emerged. In 1999 Linux was accepted by all the big IT companies – from IBM and Hewlett Packard to SAP. Linux is now an alternative to Unix, but also competes with Microsoft NT.

emerged. The most famous campaign was 'Netscape Now' which distributed 'free' browsers into the world and forced Microsoft to follow suit. The rebels have now broken into the protected fortresses of complex operating systems with the emergence of freeware such as *Linux* (see box). Just as successful as Linux is the freeware product 'Apache' – a free web server with a world market share of almost 50 per cent. Organisations like *Opensource* and servers like *Shareware.com* distribute such freeware.

The *adoption of guerrilla thinking* is beginning to happen in the software industry. At the same time, the risks of supposedly 'trifling offences' in using unlicensed software are revealed by the Year 2000 problem.

As most readers should know, the Year 2000 problem has arisen because old programmes stored the year 19XX as two figures, rather than four, so after the millennium they cease to function accurately. Coping with Year 2000 problems requires the co-operation of manufacturers, which will be provided only if software licences have been paid for. In a country like China, with its large number of illegal copies, this represents a serious threat. It also underlines that a licence includes the services of the manufacturer and that this can be very valuable.

Buying software on the Internet is rapidly becoming standard practice. There will be great pressure to establish a generally applicable and 'sensible' business system for doing so. A certain amount of protection against copying will be introduced. Digital 'clearing houses' like Ingram Micro or Tech Data will simplify distribution. In addition, an Internet licensing register will be supported by the major players. Companies such as *RedHat*, building a business around Linux freeware, will develop rapidly as new players in the field. All this, however, is just the beginning of a fundamental restructuring of the software industry.

Industry no. 2: the music industry

In view of the sales success of CDNow or Amazon in CDs, you

could be forgiven for thinking that the music industry has already made good progress as far as e-shopping business systems are concerned. The exact opposite is the case. The digital guerrilla has only just sprung his first attack in this industry and you will be able to experience the exciting tussle live. 'The revolution will be televised'!

First of all a bit of background. The music industry is largely controlled by an oligopoly of five 'Major Labels': Sony, EMI, BMG (Bertelsmann Music Group), Universal/Seagram/Polygram and Time-Warner. Together they control about 85 per cent of the market and nearly all the big stars have contracts with one of these studios. The success of a label depends heavily on the big names. About 50 per cent of sales and 100 per cent of profits are earned by best-selling titles. Another industry feature is that the main earner of sales, pop music, is very short-lived: for an average hit title 90 per cent of the sales are made within a few months of initial release.

Digitisation and the Internet are causing a major problem. And it all started so beautifully: migrating to digital compact discs (CDs) earned music companies large profits because of the industry's pricing policy. A CD cost less to make than an LP, but was often sold for more than an LP. The difference went to the artist, to marketing, distribution and last but not least to the producers' profits.

In reality, however, the CD opened a Pandora's box. The same ease of reproduction that made CDs so cheap to produce made them easy to copy – and each copy is a perfect 'original'. Just as with software, in countries with large populations, mainly China and Brazil, the music industry has lost billions every year because of high-quality, flawless rogue copies. Nobody knows how to get these rogue CDs back into the box. One thing is certain though, the media industries have learnt from their mistakes. The CD will be the last digital format to be released without copyright protection. The film industry has only just promoted its first digital format on the market – DVD (Digital Video/Versatile Disk – which is reasonably well protected against copying.

The real rebellion in the music industry, however, began in 1998. As a by-product of a multimedia standard, a compression format called MP3 reached the market. This allowed CD-quality music to be sent over the narrow-band Internet. The German Fraunhofer Institute was the leader in the development of MP3 but released it for a licence fee. MP3 compresses music data to about a megabyte per minute. Downloading is so fast that if you have an ISDN or fast modem connection you can hear music 'live', from the likes of Spinner.com.

Within a year of its release 'MP3' was the second most-used search term on the Internet (after 'sex'), and is one of the rebels' critical weapons. Now you can – often still illegally – download more or less any existing music title from the Internet. Web sites with interesting content go onto the net for a few hours and then close down again before they can be found by the media companies' search troops. The number of legal web sites for MP3 downloading is increasing too. Just like freeware servers with software products, *mp3.com* offers free legal music. In spring 1999 mp3.com concluded a comprehensive licensing agreement with the American association of composers, authors and publishers (ASCAP), which has at least 85,000 members. Free distribution of music will certainly be an important component of a commercial strategy and has a valuable place in the future music industry. That new technology has a massive role to play in restructuring the music industry is underlined by the stock market performance of mp3.com. Floated on NASDAQ in July 1999 it is capitalized at around $2 billion, having been as high as $7 billion.

At the same time there are attractive, reasonably priced walkman-like players for MP3 music. In the US the most well-known MP3 player is probably the Rio from *Diamond Technologies*. In Europe German manufacturer *Pontis Electronic* offers a more advanced device.

The big names in the music industry were at first so stunned by the new developments that they were unsure what to do. It was not until the second half of 1998 that their empire struck back. At first, Diamond was sued. The complaint was based on a little-used law governing the introduction of digital radios and on the argument that the MP3 player was being sold only to listen to unlicensed content on many servers. The courts re-

Pontis Electronic's MPlayer3

Pontis Electronic's 'MPlayer3' introduced in 1998 was one of the first players for Internet music on the world market. It weighs about 170 grams, fits easily into your shirt pocket and, with two normal batteries, has a playing time of around 10 hours. The music is stored on small multimedia chips, originally developed by Siemens. The chip is similar to a mobile phone card and just as robust.

The playing length of the two small chips is more than 75 minutes. The player is completely resistant to vibration and is especially favoured by sportsmen. MP3 slots for the chip cards will soon appear in car radios. The days of the audio cassette and soon even the CD appear numbered. The chip's interface is standardised and can be used by future generations of chips. This means that the consumer will be able to put future chips into today's players. It is a dramatic advance on the CD, where players have effectively suspended the consumer in a long obsolete stage of technology.

jected an application for a temporary injunction. At the same time there were efforts to create a general standard for protection against copying and distribution, marked by the setting up of the Secure Digital Music Interface (SDMI) committee. Its aim was to create an international security standard before the 1999 Christmas rush. But the alliance appears to have crumbled. While *Sony* and *IBM* began to work on a system together, *Universal* forged ahead using *Intertrust* technology. Universal now have their Internet music partner, the Bertelsmann Music Group (BMG), as well as Matsushita and AT&T to back them up. It seems we are heading for a standards battle, just like the Beta/VHS one for video cassette players.

Would-be rebel *Real Networks* has gone into battle on IBM's side. Using proprietary software the company, with its website *Real.com*, enables even the slowest Internet connections to take music from the Internet – at least for listening to samples of acceptable quality music. The RealPlayer software has already been downloaded 70 million times and hundreds of thousands of downloads are being made everyday. The Real.com web site numbers almost as many visitors as Amazon and eBay. Real recently joined the MP3 wave with its RealJukeBox, whose user base has exploded to more than 12 million in a matter of months.

Whether any one of the planned systems will be used against the MP3 rebels is still not certain. Hardly a day goes by when a further chapter is not added to the history of this fight. 'Adopting guerrilla thinking' is being hotly discussed behind the scenes. The beginnings are discernible in some small markets, on theme-orientated web sites. However, the established companies are still mainly aiming to put in place defensive measures to protect against copying and seeking fines from transgressors. They have even considered taking the weakest part of the line of defence, the CD, with its flawless unprotected content, off the market quickly.

Innovation lies ahead. Music is an exciting field and you will be able to witness the digital guerrilla war live. The music industry is not alone here. A similar development is currently taking place with *images*. The flames of revolution will be fanned by the increasing availability of digital cameras. The biggest setback for consumers with *filmed images* is that they do not have access to broad-band. Elsewhere the emergence of the first digital content sites like *Film.com* or *Sightsound.com* signal that the rebellion is spreading to movies.

First attempts at digital film distribution have already taken place for business use. In October 1998 the film *The Last Broadcast* (87 minutes) was recorded digitally for less than $1000 and edited on two PCs. It was then sent by Cyberstar via satellite to five cinemas in MPEG2 compression format and shown on digital projectors. Later it was transferred by Roadrunner onto the broad-band Internet. You can think what you like about the content of this film, but technically it shows the way to the future. From 2000 the Sundance Institute, set up by Robert Redford, wants to allow digital films at his prestigious festival. In the UK, TV producer and movie distributor *Carlton Communi-*

cations have bought into digital movie distribution, acquiring 49% of *Real Image Technology* via their US subsidiary *Technicolor*. Change is in the air.

Industry no. 3: books and printed media

Print media businesses are under siege too. Transferring and storing content here is possible without compression. The lack of suitable electronic access devices for readers, and content that is available permanently on the Internet have led to what has been an atypical, although no less dramatic, development.

One of the most impressive and long-lasting examples of the power of digitisation in books is the rapid collapse of the *Encyclopaedia Britannica*.

Those who think that books will never be replaced can be shown that it is happening right now. The Internet has also become established as an efficient distribution mechanism for printed media. In *university libraries*, magazines and books are in retreat. Publishing giant *Reed-Elsevier* now markets more than half of its scientific publications exclusively on the Internet. All the important periodicals for the general public are now more or less available completely online. Most major newspapers in the USA can be read in their entirety on the Internet, right down to the smallest articles – but free of charge. The *Wall Street Journal* is one of the few newspapers online to have built up a successful paid subscription service. It now has more than 300,000 members of whom more than two-thirds are new subscribers.

Similar developments can be seen in all 'updating' media like travel guides and timetables. But let us not kid ourselves: computers are no use for reading. The 'look and feel' of paper is so superior that the majority of texts available over the Internet are printed out at their destination.

However, *electronic books* are making their way onto the market. The first manufacturer was *NuvoMedia*, with its *Rocket-e-Book*, a star at the Frankfurt book fair in 1998. The product is now commercially available, comes in paperback format, weighs

The fall of the *Encyclopaedia Britannica*

The *Encyclopaedia Britannica* was a perfect exemplar of a traditional print media business system that has had its day. Knowledge was collected and documented with painstaking spadework and aggregated into huge volumes. Then it was printed and sold by salesmen door-to-door in individually numbered editions for several thousand dollars.

At the beginning of the nineties electronic encyclopaedias arrived, headed by Microsoft's *Encarta*. This fitted nicely onto a CD-ROM and cost less than a hundred dollars. Right from the beginning it used multimedia, for example you could hear Edward VIII's abdication speech. Additional windows, pictures and maps illustrated connections and, by clicking on the mouse, you could leap to linked terms. In this way *Encarta* enabled an essentially intuitive interaction with information, and effectively contained more information in spite of its small number of search terms. Many people were not happy with the first *Encarta*, but it was enough to demonstrate the potential of the electronic format. It was not available online, but knowledge that was regularly updated was within the consumer's grasp.

It's no wonder then, that *Encyclopaedia Britannica* customers were put off buying their 'encyclopaedia for life'. Within a year of Encarta's release the business nosedived and the company was sold. An interesting footnote here is that the company has only now (October 1999) made its full content available free on the web. Change is in the air, but perhaps too late.

a pound and costs $500. A standard edition contains 20 novels and the battery lasts 20–25 hours. Other American manufacturers like *SoftBook Press*, *Glassbook*, *Librius* and *Everybook* have followed suit. These manufacturers are about to adopt a standard (Open eBook) to encourage customers not to delay purchase on the grounds that they are unsure as to what is compatible with what.

Everybook is copying the 'expensive' book. It folds and is bound in leather, comes in colour and costs a hefty $1500. At the other end of the scale, the *Librius* model can be had for only $200, and prices will come down even further. To promote adoption, there will be hardware subsidies, similar to those used in the mobile phone market. Members of electronic book clubs will very soon receive their hardware for nothing. Softbook is concluding contracts with schools in the US, which will make pupils' satchels lighter. The school district of Davis in California has applied for state subsidies of six million dollars to buy 3000 electronic books for its pupils. Perhaps the time is not very far off when each pupil and student will load the whole year's curriculum onto an electronic book, and merely update it as necessary. You can imagine how quickly reacting to the habits of the young would revolutionise the whole book market.

Although all of today's manufacturers are from the US, the pioneer of electronic books was actually a European: the *Acorn 'Newspad'* marketed a European Union financed electronic newspaper at the end of 1996 in conjunction with the Spanish 'El Periodico de Catalunya'. Unfortunately, because of a lack of infrastructure, downloading to the 'paper' had to take place overnight by television transmission. Altogether the system was ahead of its time and was not accepted by consumers.

You can see how intensive preparations are being made for electronic books in the *fight for rights*. Today's publishers have no automatic contractual rights over electronic formats – a situation they are remedying in their new contracts as quickly as possible. In doing this they drove the famous 'Author's Guild' in New York to man the barricades in May 1999: while the authors of paper books typically receive 15 per cent of the wholesale price as a royalty, they are being offered less than 5 per cent for e-books. Publishers have tried to point out that the costs of publishing and marketing electronic books are considerably higher – in stark contrast to the general expectation that they would make enormous savings. As a book's sales-life is often more than 20 years, the different remuneration regime proposed is a serious point of debate. E-book manufacturers like *Nuvomedia* are very worried about publishers' strategies, because delayed distribution of content will seriously damage the business of e-book manufacturers.

Figure 10.2 is summarised partially from a study by Forrester Research, and looks at the status of the most significant industries with digitisable products.

Industries are classified by how much digital content they offer today; what standards they have with regard to compression and protection from copying; how available access-devices are distributed; and how Internet-based licence systems have been established. As you can see, the software industry has made the most progress, whilst printed media and videos are just starting to develop.

The media industries have recognised the increasing convergence of digital media formats. They are now forming commercial groupings which have the whole multimedia domain in their sights in terms of licensing and content management.

One camp is gathering round *IBM*. Amongst them are *Sony* and *Real Networks*. The other camp is grouped around *Microsoft*,

Criteria \ Sector	Software	Images	Audio	Video	E-text
Offer of digital content	Beyond.com Download.com Shareware.com	Corbis	EMI / Liquid Audio MP3.com	Film.com Sightsound.com	barnesandnobles.com rocket-library.com
Standards for compression	ZIP	Bitmap GIF JPEG	MP3 MS Audio Real G2	MPEG	ZIP
Standards for copyright	Digital River GLOBETrotter Preview Systems	eSafe FlashPix	a2b IBM Liquid Audio	IBM Macrovision Microsoft	Open eBook
Distribution of equipment	Palm V PC PlayStation	PC Casio E 100 Sony Marica	PC Rio MPlayer 3	Web TV AOL TV	Rocket-E-Book Softbook Glassbook Everybody
Existence of licensing systems	Digital River Intertrust Reciprocal	eSafe FlashPix ThingWorld	IBM InterTrust Reciprocal	IBM Reciprocal	?

Fig. 10.2 Status of digital product industries (June 1999).

with *Reciprocal* and *Intertrust* as the most important members. With the development of media-independent storage and transfer formats, these groupings will become increasingly powerful.

Before we examine the success strategies for businesses with digital goods, we need to touch on some further issues.

Get used to a regulation-free zone

Nicholas Negroponte, director of the multimedia laboratory at the Massachussets Institute of Technology (MIT) in Boston, in his visionary book *Being Digital*, was one of the first to discuss the challenges that arise when goods are distributed as 'bits' and no longer as 'atoms'. The essential legal 'headings' under which to consider digital goods are:

- value of goods – duty, taxes and arbitrary jurisdiction
- copyright – protection against copying and controls.

Value of goods: duty, taxes and arbitrary jurisdiction

A well-known paradox has arisen around quoting the value of a laptop when crossing a border; is it worth $3000 for the hardware or $300,000 for the software containing all the owners' work from the past year? Luckily the border officials are currently asking for duty only on the hardware. The problem with the software is this: if on the server at home there is an identical copy of the software, what is the software on the laptop worth? If it is destroyed, nothing has been lost. To stick with our customs example: should the official change his mind and suddenly want to you to pay duty on the software, you can quite happily have it 'confiscated' and download a new copy from the Internet later. For the same reason the term 'theft' of digital goods is essentially meaningless. At best there is a violation of copyright. So how do you assess the *value of digital goods*?

If this question seems overly theoretical to you, calculate what duty and taxes are imposed on digitisable goods today. These 'local' taxes cannot be maintained in their current form. One can no longer specify accurately when and where a border has been crossed. In the music industry this already has real impact. Music rights are regulated nationally, so that an electronic sale abroad is illegal – a prime example of an antiquated law. But if music created by an American is on a server in Bermuda and a German downloads it whilst on holiday on the Red Sea, who gets paid what licence fee? And what rate of sales tax applies?

Just as complicated is criminal law. What happens if texts or pictures are forbidden in Arabia but are legal in Bermuda? In the USA such a situation can occur from state to state.

In Europe in the last few years there have been some sensational judgements in this area. In spring 1998, Felix Somm, managing director of the German subsidiary of American Internet service-provider *Compuserve*, was convicted of 13 cases of complicity in distributing pornographic texts on the Internet, fined the equivalent of $50,000 and given a two-year suspended prison sentence. The facts of the matter were, in short, that illegal pictures listed in a newsgroup on a server in the USA could be downloaded in Germany. The sentence and the judge's reasoning were heavily criticised. Ultimately, not only the defence, but also the public prosecutor's office(!) pleaded for acquittal. The law in Europe in this area says that access providers are not responsible for third-party content and only responsible for content they have provided themselves insofar as they know about it. A similar case came up at the beginning of 1999 in France, when the Internet service provider, *Altern.org* was fined damages of $60,000 for the unauthorised distribution of nude photos of the model Estelle Halliday. The complaint was directed at the 32-year-old owner of Altern.org, Mr. Lacambre, although he had offered to name the real compiler of the web site. The service provider was held to be in an equivalent position to that of the editor of a magazine. Mr. Lacambre had to liquidate his company to pay the damages.

Both judgements have been hotly disputed – but until there is a clear legal ruling, more cases of this kind will come to court. Which director of an online service or Internet service provider, in the face of such legal uncertainty, can face doing business in China where a large part of the content provided by him is available on the Internet, but is forbidden?

The administration of justice is also uncertain regarding digital products because they are based on laws which were made for completely different sets of circumstances. Sometimes minor variations in formulation of a law in different states leads to great differences in the effective legal position.

Copyright protection and control

At the beginning of this chapter we talked about digital guerrillas. They are all violating copyright in some way. The precise legal position is not always clear. On the Internet the first question is: what constitutes an illegal copy? Ultimately several copies are made of a web site every time it is viewed. The service provider takes copies (cache), the browser stores the latest pages, the local RAM memory has a copy and sometimes the user protects against a system crash with automatic backup copies. There are judgements that have declared these types of storage as violations of copyright. Furthermore it is not clear whether breaching copyright is done by sending your friend a file in private or allowing him online access to your own files. If not, what is the situation with a circle of friends? Or a closed user-group? And what happens if this last group includes all of AOL's 19 million members?

One thing is certain, and that is that the way in which libraries work today is not sustainable in a digital world. Even in the scientific field, no publication can survive if it can sell only one copy, for example to a generally accessible digital 'Library of Congress'. But in a digital world who needs extra copies in local libraries?

The following are ground rules for protection from copying:

◆ *Let honourable people remain honourable*
Absolutely secure protection is pointless. The system should have a certain threshold to allow 'trifling offences'.
◆ *Keep protection simple*
A complex system destroys its consumer appeal. Steer clear of hardware solutions. These are certainly secure, but expensive, and make innovations difficult.
◆ *Use self-protecting formats*
Digital watermarks are a good example that can be identified at any time.
◆ *Separate content and licences*
A separate user key allows simple distribution but with simultaneous control for all users.

Ultimately, these rules cannot obscure the fact that we have yet to define the protection that is really needed and a workable legal framework to achieve this.

Many of the questions we raise in this section will remain unanswered for the foreseeable future. No-one has yet devised a workable set of rules, and the institutions covering this area will need years to implement a single solution. Furthermore, any country in the world which does not sign up to regulations can help sidestep justice in any other country because of the globality of the Internet. Only in areas where everyone is in agreement (e.g. in the suppression of child pornography), will real progress be seen.

In most digital content areas, for the near future at least, you had better prepare yourself for a *legal no-man's-land*. You will realise how dramatic this is in the next chapter when we explain that all information and services will become largely digitised. The digital economy will shake the very foundations of our legal and tax systems. Federal and state governments are already beginning to worry about the potential loss of sales taxes as e-shopping takes hold.

Exploit the opportunities in digital products

Digital goods create the possibility of completely new business systems being developed. In this section we look at what characterises opportunistic strategies.

An example of how to benefit from what at first appears highly threatening comes from the *film industry*. The industry was horrified by what it saw as a threat from television and later the video recorder. As far as video recorders are concerned, *Universal* and *Disney* began a famous law suit against *Sony* in 1976 in which each side thought that it was fighting for the survival of their industry. In 1984 the film studios finally lost in the US Supreme Court. Five years later, sales of videos overtook cinema receipts and completely changed Hollywood's business system. Today this business system focuses on a tiered marketing model: large cinemas, small cinemas, video, pay-TV, free TV; together with toys, t-shirts, books of the film and much more. Without this new business system and its tiered marketing not one studio would have survived. At the end of the day, video grew the market and with it studios' income streams.

In the same way, there are a number of profound changes which the Internet will drive.

Old distribution structures will disappear ...

The majority of physical video shops, music shops and book shops will not remain long-term. You can make the shopping experience much more interesting on the Internet than in shops today. Music publishing concerns will be challenged as far as their current structures are concerned. Established stars like George Michael or Prince do not need music companies any more and are already offering their songs for sale on the Internet. This means that control of distribution is no longer a powerful instrument. Distribution push becomes replaced by a need for 'pull' which must be achieved with a strong brand. This is a completely new world for many media players.

... New intermediaries are cropping up

New companies will appear to deal with digital distribution of content, transactions and licensing. Licences will replace the sale of digital goods today, because ownership of a digital product is an old-fashioned idea and, strictly speaking, cannot be precisely defined. Fees will be charged depending on the amount used. Digital-product intermediaries will offer a complex, more-strongly linked system than for physical goods. They need to be designed to be strictly user-friendly, otherwise they will quickly fail. Industry experts experienced the demise of *DIVX*, a cleverly devised licensing system for DVDs early in the summer of 1999, which failed in this respect.

Mass-produced goods are out ...

There is no acceptable protection against copying that can save today's mass-production. It offers too strong an incentive to copy. Buying legally at low prices, which would be acceptable even in China, is too costly.

... Personalisation is in

As with physical products, customer-specific digital goods will become standard, only it is much simpler with digital goods. For example, CDnow provides a selection of hundreds of thousands of titles so that you can make up your own individual CD order. Alternatively, *Musicmaker* offers machines which will make up an individual collection of music from today's CDs from online orders. It should be clear that today's practice of collecting together a few hits with boring filling material on a sampler CD will not last much longer. With online newspapers the 'unbundling' of articles is already an accepted practice. If properly done, personalisation increases profitability because the costs of personalising digital goods are low but the value for the customer is high.

Static goods have outlived their usefulness ...

Static digital goods are not going to be the basis for a promising business system in the future because they can only be sold once. For example, CD-ROMs with no hyperlinks to web-sites or software with no updates provided.

... Versioning and combined services are making their entrance

Versioning in electronic games can take a number of forms. At its simplest versioning is represented by the release of 'Part 2' to a successful game – i.e. the game developers themselves write further episodes or screens for the game. More sophisticated is orchestrated user versioning, where enthusiastic and knowledgeable players can get access to the source code needed to develop their own episodes to the game. These new episodes are then released over the web to other players. We described earlier how the same principles might be applied to keeping travel guide books up to the minute in terms of information currency.

Versioning will also make its entrance into other digital product categories. A combination of product and service, made possible by the ease with which digital products can be modified, shows promise. For example, with digital photography, not just developing is now offered, but innovative creative services (removing unwanted third parties from picture background, recomposing pictures, etc.). Even digital books offer a large number of starting points for new ideas. Often the limited functions of an access device are the biggest hurdle to offering unusual services.

With the remarks above we hope to have illustrated the elements of a successful business model in the digital world. The infrastructure is ripe to launch a challenge to established companies. Even in the oligopolistic media industry there are great opportunities for innovative companies. Creative talent will always be sought after and the talent will have the potential to earn good rewards. For example, in the music industry, a supplier like *MTV* could become a strong studio if it builds up its brand and uses its fan community for a direct music business on the web. The first 'Internet hit' is certainly not far off.

Many developments in digital goods industries are still in their infancy. Just as a few years ago Amazon had a chance in electronic shopping with physical goods, at the moment there are many opportunities with digital goods to those not fearing the lack of regulation.

E-tail searchlight on web-sites for Chapter 10

- Microsoft   www.microsoft.com
- Linux   www.linux.com
- Opensource   www.opensource.org
- Shareware.com   www.shareware.com
- RedHat   www.redhat.com
- Spinner.com   www.spinner.com
- Diamond   www.diamondtechnologies.com
- Pontis Electronic   www.pontis.de
- mp3.com   www.mp3.com
- Beyond   www.beyond.com
- IBM   www.ibm.com
- Sony   www.sony.com
- Intertrust   www.intertrust.com
- Universal   www.universal.com
- Real Networks   www.real.com
- Film.com   www.film.com
- Sightsound.com   www.sightsound.com
- Cyberstar   www.cyberstar.com
- Roadrunner   www.roadrunner.com
- Sundance Institute www.sundance.com
- Wall Street Journal www.wsj.com
- NuvoMedia   www.nuvomedia.com
- Librius   www.librius.com
- Softbook   www.softbook.com
- Reciprocal   www.reciprocal.com
- DIVX   www.divx.com
- Musicmaker   www.musicmaker.com
- MTV   www.mtv.com

Chapter 11

Brave New World
of Services

The twenty-first century heralds the creation of new information- and service-based businesses. These are a growing part of the digital economy. The e-tailing of services will assume a position of central importance in the future. Many attributes of the e-tailing of physical goods are directly transferable to selling service on the net. In this chapter we concentrate on what is unique about e-services. We observe that the dividing line between business-to-consumer and business-to-business services often blur.

The developments we foresee will massively reduce direct human interaction in the provision of services. In many areas service without a face may at first take people aback. But, whether we like it or not, we are confronted with a 'brave new world of services'.

E-tail searchlight illuminates Chapter 11

◆ *E-tailing of services*
Services require confidence, since they can only be de-scribed rather than experienced prior to being con-sumed. The Internet as an information medium is highly suitable for this, and will ultimately revolutionise serv-ices even more than product businesses. We present a framework that shows which services can be consumed or substituted online.

◆ *The ultimate self-service medium*
Just as the vacuum cleaner and the washing machine displaced domestic servants, the Internet will simplify many services and convert them to self-service models, most dramatically perhaps in public-sector and finan-cial institutions. Truly successful suppliers must develop personal customer relationships and entertain the cus-tomer too.

◆ *The sex industry – a well-shaped model?*
For services that cannot actually be provided online, virtual substitutes are on the increase. The online sex industry – the controversial nature of its content not-withstanding – is the most innovative area in the e-tail-ing of services.

◆ *The yin and yang of product and service*
Each product is a service and each service is a product. Being aware of this duality stimulates business innova-tion.

E-tailing of services

If you ask anyone on the street if they can imagine shopping electronically for services, you will be surprised by the strong polarity of their answers. If you delve deeper, you will find that those responding 'no' are thinking of haircuts and hospital op-

Service \ Recipient	People	Objects
Tangible actions	– *Search, reservation, transaction, and substitutes are digital* (travel, healthcare, fitness centres, restaurants, sex)	– *People's critical interactions are digital* (freight transport, repair, retail distribution, laundry, gardening)
Intangible actions	– *Significant part of consumption is digital* (information services, communication, consulting, education, religion)	– *Service consumption is digital* (accounting, banking, insurance, legal services, security investment)

Fig. 11.1 Digitalisation matrix for services.

erations, whereas those saying 'yes' are thinking of bank transfers and cinema tickets.

Service business cover such a wide field that in order to discuss them sensibly we should first classify them. Professor Chris Lovelock's structure is helpful (see Fig. 11.1).

The most important difference to recognise is between tangible and intangible services. The latter become digitally consumable. The former is relevant because it determines whether you have to reach out directly to a person to provide the service.

Intangible actions for ownership of an object will be completely digitally consumable

The e-tail service pioneers are all in the software industry. Bringing out new software releases and maintaining upgrades is already being done on a wide scale online today. Netscape showed how the Internet can fundamentally change business systems. Digitisation in this service group will gradually reach all areas, from online banking and online broking to legal work and accounting services. We believe that the electronic delivery of these services will become standard as Internet use increasingly becomes as natural as reading, writing and as integrated into our business and personal lives as the telephone. Personal contact will only be necessary for complex matters. The industries concerned will undergo a massive restructuring. For an early example in this area, relating to accounting services, for small businesses, look at the 'online accountant' offered by UK startup *Ascot Drummond*.

Intangible actions for people will become largely digitally consumable

According to the level of interaction, digitisation is already established as standard today in this class of services (e.g. in customer support, information services). It is creeping into segments in some areas (education, consultancy). In other sectors it is still hard to imagine the service being provided digitally (religion, psychotherapy).

Let us take a specific look at a rather controversial example: religion. Even if you think that TV evangelists and 'Dial-a-prayer' are commercial exploitations of religion, you will perhaps not think it unusual that the Pope's *Urbi et Orbi* blessing reaches the international Catholic community through the television. There is an online market for a significant number of religious services, and it is not only for an isolated single-user audience: the Internet can gather a group and they can consume the service together. We go into this further in the next section on self-service. Many religious communities are already actively using the Internet today.

PrayerWheel offers a computerised service of prayers in seven denominations for stressed believers. You can name up to three people for whom you would like a prayer said. The prayers are posted onto the web. Three catholic prayers sent three times a day every day for a year cost $19.90. Twelve Islamic prayers cost $29.95. The company has sensibly protected itself legally;

Screenshot: Digitalthink.

in the small print it says that there is no guarantee that the prayers will be answered!

Areas such as the law, management consultancy and education are showing interesting development. The area of tension here is between digitally delivered content, which is often better and cheaper, and the personal relationship or social component of the service, which is also part of the value derived. This is an area that is ripe for innovation.

In education, correspondence courses are increasingly losing their niche as Internet video based interactive schemes are developed, particularly in the area of IT training and testing from companies like *Digitalthink*.

Tangible actions on objects: total e-shopping

Online consumption of these services is very like e-shopping for physical goods. The absence of 'look and feel' and the increased requirement for information, however, make these services even more suitable for the web. The Internet is an outstanding medium in terms of ability to provide a constant stream of information to support a service that is being delivered.

A well known, but still excellent example is parcel transport. In many cases all the information components needed to send a package, and subsequently the exact information on the current status of the consignment, is a critical customer-benefit. It is now part of most carriers' standard service offer. Federal Express was an early leader in this 'tracking & tracing'. The service costs the supplier relatively little – he has only to access information drawn from internal tracking systems and make it accessible externally on the web.

Tangible actions for people: search, reserve, order and substitutions will be digital

The best example in this category is the travel industry which is restructuring at breathtaking speed. There are so many individual sites offering travel services and guides that a global guide to them all such as *Planetrider* is a useful starting point for any web user planning travel. Travel and holiday planning will soon be most effectively done over the Internet. As well as simple information on countries, personalised catalogues, context-related virtual communities and feedback on the areas visited will all be included in travel service sites. This is much more than a single agent can offer. *TheTrip.com* is an example of one of a number of players trying to establish a position in this market. The international leader in Internet travel services is *Travelocity*, part of American Airlines.

A further essential aspect of these tangible services for people is that 'doing it yourself' often triggers a great interest in information about the quality of the service provided. In today's world, this information is only provided in very limited form. An example of this is the health service, where the points of contact one has as an actual or potential patient are able to give you relatively little information. Doctors are the key infor-

Case study – Healtheon/WebMD

You don't need much imagination to see how the Internet could completely alter the whole health sector. In the US Healtheon and WebMD (merged in May 1999) were both set up as Internet companies. They are financed by Kleiner-Perkins (Healtheon) and Microsoft (MD-Web) and have start-up capital of several hundred million dollars.

Healtheon/WebMD want to create an information platform for the whole health industry, that allows participants to communicate with each other, to obtain fast access to clinical and administrative information and to conclude transactions efficiently. The 'participants' here are the patients, the doctors and hospitals, the insurers, the employers and state contributions programmes as well as laboratories and pharmaceutical companies. Online dispensing of drugs will be dealt with by partners like *Drugstore.com*.

A few key statistics for 1999:

♦ 150,000 registered doctors
♦ over 450 insurers
♦ 1 million online transactions a month
♦ over 50 million administrative and clinical procedures
♦ over 1.5 million registered 'consumers'.

A complete description of the massive plans that Healtheon/WebMD have would be too much to go into here. But let's take a look at the range of services they provide from the consumer's point of view. The company allows access to medical and insurance databases, offers advice on health and diet and provides news on important legal issues and changes in the health service. There will be detailed background information on doctors and hospitals. It has great potential to become a successful 'health portal'. Ultimately they will be able to record a complete medical history for patients, list emergency services at home and abroad and create forums for communicating about rare illnesses. Most people will find some utility in the site.

It remains to be seen how Healtheon/WebMD will develop. One thing is certain, that the health sector in every country will sooner or later undergo fundamental change enabled by the Internet.

mation-point, but their time is in significant demand and highly valuable. And who provides systematic information about the performance of doctors? (See Healtheon/WebMD insert.)

The fact is that acting on the body is actually often only an intermediate step towards reaching the brain. This creates a potential for virtual substitutes that we go into later.

A self-service medium par excellence

An essential economic aspect of e-tailing services is that a major part of the work done is transferred to the customer – the concept of self-service. The retail trade can use much of its experience of self-service in the new medium of the Internet, but on the web self-service goes much further than in traditional businesses. It is massively more scaleable than in physical retailing because a single digital service model is sufficient for many millions of customers.

One significant self-service area is *public services*. It is now standard practice that information and forms are available online (e.g. income tax self-assessment advice from the UK *Inland Revenue*). The particular nature of the public sector means that this will not automatically lead to a reduction in fees, but many citizens would already be grateful if queues for physically delivered services could be reduced.

The sector that has both made the greatest progress in web-based service (and is subject to the greatest change) is the fi-

Case study – Charles Schwab

In 1974 Charles Schwab revolutionised the US securities business by starting up as a 'discount broker'.

In spite of his phenomenal success, he decided in 1985 to offer online broking, still on a proprietary platform. In 1993 he moved to a Windows platform and finally in 1996, onto the Internet. Schwab is building its online business aggressively, although the company has to accept a 60 per cent lower margin for each transaction. This is only possible because the customer executes a significant amount of the work himself. He manages his portfolios, looks up share prices, enters orders and much more.

Schwab is also an outstanding example of how to combine an online and offline offering. Almost all customers are acquired in real-world branches, whereas more than 80 per cent of transactions are done online, in both cases optimising efficiency and costs.

But the self-service concept can go even further. At $30 per transaction, Schwab is up to three times as expensive as, for example, *Datek*, or *E*Trade*, leading cut-price suppliers. The difference is that Schwab still has 300 physical branches and has developed its advisory business, whereas Datek offers no advice and only offers technical help by phone. Even though it has fewer customers, Datek performs well because it attracts a transaction-intense customer base, fuelling a business model built for high-volume, low-price processing.

nancial sector. Here, once again, we find US stockbroker *Charles Schwab* one of the most interesting examples. It is the only case we know where a company that was a market leader in the physical world also conquered the market in the online world and has successfully defended its leading position.

But even online brokers have their problems. Delays between online ordering and execution when demand for shares is heavy can mean a great risk for the small investor if they fail to specify an upper limit for the order. All online brokers have experienced systems crashes at least once through sheer volume of traffic. Events such as these led *Merill Lynch*, America's leading investment house, to say in 1998 that 'Internet trading should be regarded as a serious threat to Americans' financial lives'. However, a few months later Merill Lynch gave up the fight against the online trend and announced its own online broking service – at the same price as Charles Schwab.

Something interesting followed: within a few days all the large US investment banks announced their own online initiatives – and shares fell. This was a novelty: generally the announcement of an Internet strategy had always led to an upturn in a company's shares. But in this case Wall Street realised that pressure on margins in the whole industry would increase and it reacted accordingly. There will be similar developments in other industries too, if the market leader announces that it is embracing the Internet. Only market leaders and innovators can generate value.

Perfecting 'PC-enabled self-service' requires resolving issues around lack of personal contact and the buyer's purchasing experience.

Personal contact

Business users already appreciate that electronic tools can significantly help in identifying people to do business with and, once made, maintain contact. Initiating, building and deepening a relationship, however, relies heavily on personal contact. It is no different for e-tailing many services. Personal contact is an important first step. This can be done on the telephone or even online, but most people quite rightly like someone specific to contact, especially if a long-term business relationship is envisaged. Even fictitious online characters work (remember 'Jenny' from Chapter 7) as long as they are specific to the user. For e-service providers the issue is one of balance between cold 'process efficiency' and 'the personal touch'.

Schwab has demonstrated good balance here, and emphasises the interplay between physical and electronic components of service. A significant number of accounts are still opened in branches, even if they are then conducted online. For larger transactions, many online customers come into the branches, where staff can concentrate completely on potentially important moments in their customers' lives.

At the other end of the spectrum, some people don't want personal contact. Notable cases are 'Tereza' and 'Tonyd'. These are the cover names of two of the biggest customers of InterCasino, an online gambling site. In 1998 'Tonyd' had placed at least 400,000 bets (approximately 1100 bets a day) while 'Tereza' had spent 1090 hours (around 136 working days) in the online casino. Both were personally invited to spend a week in Las Vegas. Both declined.

The customer's buying experience

'Entertainment' is already one of the most important new themes in consumer-focused businesses. Look for example at the incredible success of '*Mall of America*' in Minneapolis, which combines a shopping centre and an amusement park. Its 40 million visitors a year make it even more popular than Disneyland.

An online store should be no different. The possibilities for combining self-service and entertainment mean that the online store should have many possibilities to engage its shoppers. We described some in Chapter 6. But let's consider this area further, particularly with respect to the crossover between physical and electronic experiences. Consider the very elderly. For this group, shopping can be physically strenuous, which often limits it to their immediate vicinity. At the same time, the elderly often find (the generally young) sales people in stores non-communicative and lacking in rapport. In addition, electronic shopping is of limited interest for the very elderly for one major reason: shopping or going to the post office provides essential variety and routine in their daily life.

Imagine how different things might be if they could meet friends for coffee and a snack and then shop in an e-shopping centre with large-format screens, people on hand to help and advise, and other features tailored to this group. For many older citizens, this might be the concept to ignite their interest in e-tailing.

Today's Internet cafés are an early first step towards combining online activities with a broader social experience than one might get sitting at home in front of the PC. There is still a long way to go and lot of room for innovation around entertainment.

The sex industry – a well-shaped model?

Sex has been part of the web from its early days. Many people getting online for the first time try a sex site for want of a better idea of what to look at. Early on, when there was little recreational online content, sex was a significant motivator for surfing the web. Even with all the discussions and regulations on the Internet, sex still plays an important role in the life of the web. At least one adult site still regularly features in rankings of the top 50 most visited web properties.

Although its importance on the Internet is significantly reduced, sex is still the most commonly searched keyword on all search engines and, as the saying goes 'sex sells', especially on the net. The 1998 Internet publication of the Starr report and associated indictment of President Bill Clinton attracted millions of readers for one reason only: the details contained in the report about the president's sexual activities in his office could not have been more explicit. In spite of its controversial content we should not ignore the Internet sex industry. It is both a 'model case' of the virtual substitution of services and one of the most innovative industries on the net, introducing and perfecting many new ideas and technologies.

Internet sex is a big business, grossly underestimated in our view, in Internet statistics. It skilfully exploits the anonymity of the web to remove one significant barrier to use: fear of being seen as a consumer of these services. Let's be clear, physical outlets for videos still represent the largest channel for the retail of this kind of adult material. But technological change will alter this rapidly as broad-band access becomes more widely and cheaply available.

What is most interesting is that the sex industry has managed to reach a segment of users who previously were relatively unreachable: those who belong to the 'I wouldn't be seen dead in an Adult shop' school of thought. The interest has enabled a new pool of demand to be served.

The industry needs to take care not to overstep the mark here, targetting those who should not be reached, e.g. minors, or governments may intervene more actively.

Statistics and controls

Internet sex is well documented, and some statistics make curious reading: 50 per cent of international visitors to American sex sites come from Germany, and 70 per cent of US traffic runs during the normal working day between 9 and 5.

We talked in Chapter 7 of the power of recommendation. In this particular industry, statistics on the number of visitors to a site are highly valued as a key to generating visitor frequency. As a consequence, false statistics flourish in the sex industry and so do attempts to weed out this false reporting, creating what are leading-edge recording systems. If you want reliable information on the frequency of visits to sex web-sites, go to *SexTracker*. It offers the most cleverly devised procedure on the whole Internet to ascertain the real visitor frequency on a website. It also exposes – and follows up – any attempts at manipulation. SexTracker also records all other relevant statistical data for its sites, differentiates between various definitions of visitor frequency and gives monthly and hourly breakdowns. Top-performing sites generate about five million visitors per month on pay sites and fifty million a month on free sites.

Self-regulation of the industry is reasonably well developed. Several industry organisations, such as United Adult Services and YNOT, check web-sites, develop ground rules for the trade and simplify discussion in the business. They expose and pursue web-sites which steal content and those that do not pay bills on time. Copyright protectors, such as WebPosse, pursue copyright violators. Overall, co-operation among Internet players in the sex industry is well developed and effective.

Co-operative networks

Co-operation within the industry goes beyond self-regulation. As well as the top web lists, industry organisations and copyright patrols, there are co-operative indexes, banner-exchange agreements, collective offers and a range of other partnerships. Co-operation in attracting customers to pay sites is particularly well developed. A visitor is first attracted to a free sex-site (known as a 'farm') and then gently led to a pay site. There are few sites which are not networked to others, in what are known as 'web rings'. These lead the visitor from one web-site to the next. Co-operation is worthwhile. If a visitor is ready to pay, the web-site which fed the receiving site can get up to 50 per cent of any subscription proceeds.

Amazon's successful partner programme which was started under the 'Affiliate Program' title, and which has been copied by thousands of e-tailers, itself emulated the sex industry's approach to co-operation on the web.

One practice closely linked with the co-operative network idea is 'interstitial challenging' and the closely related trade in 'exit traffic'. 'Challenging' describes what happens when a visitor who leaves the site is presented with a new offer, opened in a new window. The surfer has to close several windows to clear the screen before he can finally leave. In the same way a visitor can be transferred automatically at exit to another site. The real world analogy is this: you walk out of the store, straight into another store rather than into the street that you were expecting. Even involuntary 'exit traffic' generates a few cents per 'hit' in referral fees. Finally there are interesting attempts by sites to generate packaged offers from multiple suppliers.

These 'adult verification systems', allowing access to web-sites of various suppliers for a single fee, are an attempt by sex e-tailers to broaden their range offered. To make it clear by analogy, similar models adopted in mainstream publishing would mean that, if you subscribe to a major magazine title you may get others bundled into the same subscription for free. Whether these combinations lead to success is still to be seen. One thing is certain though: in the sex industry there is hardly any (business) coupling that has not been tried!

Some may argue that the sex industry represents more of the Internet's wild frontier and that these practices would not be accepted in other sectors. One has only to look at the use of intestitials by mainstream players such as AOL to realise that if these tools make commercial sense they will be adopted, whatever their origin.

Outsourcing

The Internet sex industry is one of the most focused that we know of. Anything that cannot be created efficiently is contracted out to someone else. This is how a large part of the content generated by companies such as Babenet or iBroadcast is created. Many suppliers donate content in exchange for links or cross-selling opportunities. Operating infrastructure and technical services are most commonly outsourced, coming almost exclusively from leading web-hosting companies like Exodus, Digex and Frontier Global Centre. In some cases even these services are bartered for advertising.

The purchasing decision

The greatest challenge for the sex industry, which mirrors one for mainstream e-tailers, is the purchase decision. The methods used to persuade the visitor to 'buy' are so refined that other e-tailers appear laggards. Arousing interest with partial content or samples is relatively obvious. More sophisticated is the creation and maintenance of 'chat rooms' and virtual communities which are then systematically researched for useful buying incentives. The most important methods, however, are 'up-selling' and 'cross-selling'. For example still images are offered at a low standing charge, but live scenes only at an additional charge ('up-selling'). Especially effective is the offer of free participation in the chat on the live scenes (without pictures). The comments of 'chatters' arouse a stronger desire to buy than the best salesman could. 'Cross selling' operates in the same way but with different offers. The surprising thing about the online sex industry is the amount of analysis of customer behaviour that has been done and the number of experiments that have been carried out around customer purchase decision making.

The Internet sex industry is a highly developed example of a virtual substitute for a real world service. Video shops, sex cinemas and peep shows will disappear.

The yin and yang of product and service

In the last section of this chapter we want to examine the relationship between product and service more closely. To do this we first need to introduce an analogy from science:

In quantum theory, the basis of modern physics, one of the most important findings was the duality of particles and waves. The leading physicists realised at the beginning of the twentieth century that light is ambiguous in its nature. It shows characteristics that can be ascribed to particles, but also behaves as you would expect a wave to behave. This led to heated debate among theoretical physicists as to how these dual natures should be interpreted. The practical physicists cared very little about resolving the issue, instead analysing things from both sides and pragmatically asking: how do I interpret this in a particle paradigm – and in a wave paradigm? From this 'dual perspective' modern physics created a deep understanding of our world and its natural phenomena.

We see a similar duality in e-tailing: *each product is a service and each service is a product*. You have to look at the provision of a service from both viewpoints, as a product and as a service, in order to understand the full range of possible opportunities for profit. Let us compare the sale of a PC and an equity share. Usually a PC is seen as a product business and the latter as a financial service. Now let's change the perspective:

♦ When *selling a PC* we first offer the customer an analysis of his needs. This begins with the applications for which the computer is to be used, and related considerations (e.g. web-surfing, word-processing, spreadsheeting, at home, in the office, networked, standalone, etc.). Then, using build-to-order process, the PC is put together and delivered. Up-selling of service contracts (hotlines, repairs) and software programmes is attempted. Possibly subjects like networking, security/firewalls and backups and other possible solutions are discussed. Without going any further it should be clear that this is all about delivery of a service.

♦ With *equity-share buying* it used to be the case that a broker carried out such an enormous amount of service (recom-

EXAMPLE

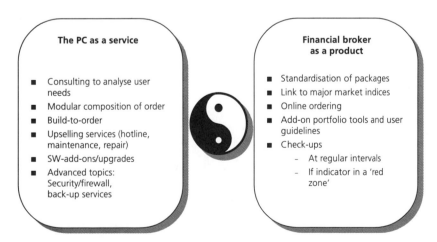

Fig. 11.2 The duality of products and services.

mending, observing stock performance, buying, selling, conducting portfolio reviews) around the acquisition of the product (the equity) that this was truly a financial service. Now that the electronic brokers have put these activities back into the hands of the investor, they have effectively 'productised' what was previously a service. Online brokers now have a set of Internet-based products which they sell.

The duality of product and service should inspire you to look for a new angle to traditional business. The Internet is 'productising' health, online banking, online brokering and insurance services. Personalisation, built-to-order ranges and personal licensing are creating services out of traditionally product-based industries. Much of the innovation in online businesses today is based on this duality of product and service.

Summary

As the power available at the desktop continues to rise, as broad-band access becomes cheaper, as compression technologies get better and better, we will move to a wholly new environment in which the virtual service comes to be more effectively, amusingly or excitingly delivered than in the real world. We are in the infancy of what will be a 'brave new world of services'.

E-tail searchlight on web-sites for Chapter 11

- Ascot Drummond   www.ascotdrummond.co.uk
- Digitalthink   www.digitalthink.com
- PrayerWheel   www.prayerwheel.com
- Federal Express   www.fedex.com
- Planetrider   www.planetrider.com
- The Trip   www.thetrip.com
- Travelocity   www.travelocity.com
- Healtheon   www.healtheon.com
- WebMD   www.webmd.com
- Drugstore.com   www.drugstore.com
- Inland Revenue   www.inlandrevenue.gov.uk
- Charles Schwab   www.schwab.com
- Datek   www.datek.com
- E*Trade   www.etrade.com
- Merrill Lynch   www.merilllynch.com
- Intercasino   www.intercasino.com
- Mall of America   www.mallofamerica.com
- SexTracker   www.sextracker.com

Chapter 12

The Capital Market –

a Survival Kit

The capital markets are enormously important to e-tailers. E-tailers need to grow rapidly while creating primarily intangible assets, such as powerful brands. Debt financing would inevitably lead to bankruptcy. Every aspiring entrepreneur must learn how to use the capital markets to set up a successful Internet business. In this chapter we also address investors who are interested in understanding valuation and value creation of Internet companies. This is no temporary period of 'odd' stock market behaviour. The Digital Economy and its leading companies with primarily intangible asset bases will permanently and significantly increase the volatility of stock markets.

E-tail searchlight illuminates Chapter 12

◆ *If you can't beat them, join them*
Mastering capital markets is part of operating an entrepreneurial Internet business. You should find ways to use them to your advantage.

◆ *Voilà, the value of Internet companies*
'Eyeballs', 'Stickiness' and 'Switching Costs' determine the value of Internet companies. Underlying business models are secondary – for now. The predominance of 'intangible' assets will permanently increase volatility in the capital markets.

◆ *Venture capitalists are the 'keiretsus'*
Venture capital firms are the new masters of the universe, exerting a massive influence on the Internet industry. They are well positioned to drive the creation of new markets and are critical in helping companies achieve success. Their investment portfolios make interesting forecasting tools.

◆ *'Equity is the new cash' for Internet companies*
Mergers and acquisitions are a key part of Internet business life. Paper transactions are often the only practicable mechanism to avoid deadly goodwill depreciation. Looking after the share price is a key task for every e-tailer – as a currency for one's own acquisitions and as a poison pill against take-overs.

If you can't beat them, join them!

Did you think that, if you were looking after operating the business, the accountants should be worrying about financing it? Is debt your primary source of financing? Do you think that Internet valuations are meaningless and only important for speculators? Then think again or your e-tailing initiative risks failure.

The phenomenal growth in Internet businesses would not be possible without venture capital and the capital markets. This is because the digital economy creates primarily intangible assets, which worry traditional financiers enormously. We discuss this in the next section. First of all, let us summarise the most important things to remember about the capital markets.

Debt financing is not an option ...

Internet companies have to conquer global markets and invest heavily for growth. These investments help build assets which are predominantly intangible, and cannot generally be entered on balance sheets. Classic accounting and balance sheets are not designed for Internet companies. Debt financing is not an option. The company would very soon be over-indebted on traditional measures. Amazon would not have survived its first few months had it been debt financed.

... Equity capital is what's needed

An Internet company needs investors to take equity capital. Venture capitalists fund the younger companies while investment banks and the stock market provide equity financing for maturing businesses.

Financing rounds are a part of operating the business ...

Internet companies should grow at 50–100 per cent a year early on – often without any income to speak of. 'Cash flow' is replaced with a 'burn rate' of cash and can be benchmarked against other companies in the industry, the focus being on whether they are spending enough. For the entrepreneur, this means that financing rounds are part of business as usual. 'Operating' cash flow effectively becomes the average increase in equity capital less the 'burn rate', a stark contrast to traditional companies.

... Right from the start-up

The unusual aspect of financing Internet businesses is that they are very often required to continue making losses after the company has gone public. Generating profits in an Internet company during its 'growth phase' can be taken as cause for alarm indicating under-investment. A few years ago Compuserve was the only profitable online service – and soon lost its position completely.

Equity capital counts as payroll ...

The link between equity financing and operating the business is underlined by the practice of allowing employee share options to be an essential part of the payroll. An Internet company's wage bill is not just represented in the profit and loss account; share options have to be included, as they are an essential part of the incentive system. Even the most successful companies can lose their best staff to insignificant start-ups if they do not offer attractive options packages.

... It also finances acquisitions

Internet businesses are usually acquired via share exchange rather than payment in hard cash. There are two reasons for this. First, current valuations are so high that very few purchasers have enough cash for a takeover. Second, and more important, is the fact that the intangible value of the firm acquired has to be written off as 'goodwill' after the sale, which is a heavy burden on results in following years. As a result, Internet acquisitions are effected by share exchange and high valuations allow leading companies to make multiple acquisitions, protecting themselves from would-be predators.

Starting a successful e-tailing initiative without understanding the mechanisms of the capital market and how to use them is extremely difficult. So don't try to run against the tide, use the capital markets to strengthen your own business!

Voilà, the value of Internet companies

Let's state the obvious: the value of an Internet company has nothing to do with its physical assets. Traditional asset-based valuations would be as meaningless as wanting to determine the value of an industrial company's land in an agricultural economy. Modern-day bookkeeping, which originated in the Middle Ages, introduced depreciation. It was an essential innovation to allow the recording of major business purchases to be matched with a charge in the accounts appropriate to the life of the assets purchased.

If a company's essential assets are *intangible* and difficult to value, they are difficult to record *in the accounts*. Although Yahoo creates real value, which is appreciated by the capital market, and reflected in the stock price, all investments to create this value are handled as current expenses in their books. An Internet company's results are comparable to those of an industrial company which has to grow quickly but can't put any of its investments on the books. Early in its development it would show very significant losses and could not be financed with bank debt as it would soon be over-indebted.

A direct, and somewhat uncomfortable, consequence is that the *balance sheets* of most Internet companies are an irrelevant piece of paper so far as a valuation is concerned. This is not really new: the software industry is not overly influenced by balance-sheet assets. Microsoft has been building up massive cash reserves as their largest asset items for a long time. The new thing about the digital economy is that this phenomenon is no longer limited to the software industry.

Hardly more informative than valuations driven by balance sheets are *price–earnings ratios*. In the growth phase of an Internet companies there is no profit to show so P/Es have no meaning. Taken together, this means that there are no simple 'formal' financial criteria with which to evaluate an Internet company. Traditional business-lending banks are particularly hard hit, often being referred to by the Internet industry in rather derogatory terms as 'dumb capital'.

The next problem with valuing an Internet company is *historical data*. What happened last year is hardly relevant in a market where annual growth rates are 100 per cent or more. The business environment is changing to such a degree that soon it won't make sense to compare future markets with to-day's.

So we arrive at *discounting future cash-flow*, considered the basis for assessing 'shareholder value' and the 'correct' method for all valuation. The difficult thing here is that, although this method is formally correct, it is not very practical. Given the uncertainty of the Internet environment, how does one estimate future cash flows other than very roughly?

So, how do we value an Internet company? It is important to remember that *Moore's Law* and the *exponential growth of the Internet* will apply for many years. They will underpin large increases in value for successful Internet businesses. Even the smallest investor has now realised that entering e-tailing can potentially unlock huge market growth for a company, so announcement of e-tailing initiatives in traditional retailers can lead to huge leaps in share prices. Macy's parent company share price took a leap in 1998 when the company announced that it was to invest in electronic shopping.

How does the Stock Market value Internet companies?

The most important answer is: *eyeballs*, i.e. visitor frequency. Let's just pause a minute here to understand this. Many people have wondered how Yahoo, a search engine, which does not charge any fees for its services can be valued at over $40 billion. Disregard for a moment the absolute level of its stock market value: what makes Yahoo valuable at all? *Eyeballs!* In nearly every country Yahoo heads the list of the most visited web-sites. Eyeballs reflect traffic, which influences potential revenue.

There are two more criteria which are fundamentally more difficult to quantify and are used to a more limited extent in current valuations. The first is *Stickiness*. By this we mean the ability of a web-site to retain the visitor for an extended period of time, for example with interesting content. Stickiness leads to a large number of return visits as well as creating a large number of opportunities to advertise to the same user. The second is *switching costs*, i.e. whether a company makes it hard for the visitors to change to a near alternative. In previous chapters we have talked about the tools for doing this.

But how does good performance against these criteria make money for the company? The honest Wall Street answer is 'No idea', because it is by no means certain that investors are clear how exactly one makes money out of visitors. Obviously there is an advertising income steam from banners, and potential sponsorship deals to do, but these alone cannot justify today's valuation. The 'gap' is potential profit from e-commerce.

Valuing an e-tailing company has to go beyond the traditional models. Free TV broadcasters are valued on their viewing figures. For these one knows almost exactly where the money comes from: advertising, no more, no less. Knowing the viewing figures enables a relatively objective valuation.

The thinking behind Internet company valuations runs like this: if anyone has a business which regularly has millions of visitors (*eyeballs*), who spend a significant amount of time there (*stickiness*) and have a good reason not to go anywhere else tomorrow (*switching costs*), this is an outstanding base for any type of business. You can decide later which type of valuation method is the most suitable. Any attentive observer has seen how Amazon has made huge inroads into the CD market in a few months simply by offering its millions of visitors CDs. It began to 'fill the valuation gap' by entering a new category.

Overall, current valuation techniques do not work well when applied to Internet companies, although comparative value is much more readily available than absolute value. The Internet is so varied and changes so quickly that valuation techniques are still evolving rapidly, as can the business model which the company intends to follow. With a few million dollars in your pocket this change can happen very quickly. One budding Internet business, PogoPet, openly admitted to not knowing where precisely their profit would be generated from in terms of product category sales. In some extreme cases companies start with nothing to sell.

All this may seem completely absurd to a traditional entrepreneur. However, the stock markets are probably right in how they think about valuation, the real problem being that nobody has yet built really high switching costs. Compare the ease with which you can change portals with the trouble you would have changing your PC operating system, and you will understand what real *switching-costs* are. This means that all Internet valuations are extremely volatile!

Anyone entering the e-tail arena must first clear the hurdles of *eyeballs, stickiness* and *switching-costs* before thinking of selling product. In many of their online initiatives, traditional retailers have failed to understand this point. Traditional retailers and analysts could argue until they are blue in the face that Amazon was overvalued as a bookstore. But they had to look on as the company took America by storm, expanding into the fields of music, video, auctions, gifts, electronics and more.

How should the investor behave?

We know now what is valuable. For the investor there is a much more important question: how much is it worth? And which companies should they invest in?

First of all a few basic rules: the simplest investment strategy is to back the *market leader*. In the last few years this would have been enormously successful – it's a pity that the past is no longer relevant. But market leadership is important. A market leader has the best chances of success in the future, given all we have argued so far.

Market leadership is most important when there is a *clear network effect* in the customer base. Auctions are an excellent example here. On the Internet the benefits for the individual increase exponentially with the number of participants. So, when it solves its platform problems, eBay could quickly achieve self-reinforcing market domination.

The essential argument for investing in market followers is that these may be suitable takeover candidates for established companies. Even better, for Internet market leaders from related areas, where acquisition would extend their service or product range. Investors can earn a great deal from waiting for large takeover premiums. But we are straying too far into the field of speculation.

Many investors have realised how the rules of the digital economy favour early entrants, so market leaders are becoming increasingly expensive. Consider the example of AOL.

Case study – AOL

AOL is undisputed leader in online services and a powerful portal. It is a true blue chip in the Internet world. Investors who recognised AOL's potential drove its shares up to ten times their original value in a 12-month period in 1998.

In mid-April 1999 at its peak, AOL's market value was more than 190 billion dollars, putting it among America's top ten companies. On a sales ranking it was in 415th place and on results 311th. On balance-sheet value, however, it didn't even make the top 500. If AOL was assessed on results or sales, its value on the basis of comparables in the US market would be around $5 billion. At a value of 190 billion dollars its stock traded at 350 times net profit.

If you look at AOL's basic business model, its 17 million subscribers worldwide are the most important part of the equation. Each subscriber pays about $240 a year, but is valued at more than $11,000. Even if AOL's customer base in the USA were to double overnight, it would not be sufficient to justify its valuation on the basis of subscriber revenue alone.

Now look at a different way. If AOL were a 'mature firm' trading at a high price–earnings ratio of 30, it would have to make an annual profit of more than $6 billion to justify its market capitalisation. Even if in the long term it could achieve margins of 15 per cent, it would still need annual revenues of $40 billion. In comparison IBM, which in the 1960s and 1970s controlled almost 80 per cent of the computer market, reached the spectacular levels of a price–earnings ratio of 65 in 1961. Although for more than 15 years IBM grew by more than 18 per cent per annum and was almost a monopoly, the company was overvalued and IBM's stock growth subsequently underperformed that of the Stock Market index.

The *Wall Street Journal* sounded this type of warning to AOL investors in April 1999. After this, AOL's stock fell to around 50 per cent of its peak. It has since recovered to within around 20 per cent of its peak. Is this the end of the story? No, you have to consider a few things.

First of all, *eyeballs*: AOL controls Compuserve, now a shadow of its former self, though still with two million subscribers. It also owns ICQ with 32 million and Netscape with 15 million registered users apiece. These groups only overlap AOL members to a small degree. The imminent introduction of AOL TV holds further possibilities to reach new users. Nearly all US companies are standing in line to discuss partnership with AOL because of its incredible customer reach.

Winning large numbers of paying subscribers sets AOL apart from most other portals. But success can be a double-edged sword. For one thing, fees slow down growth. For another, free services like Dixon's 'Freeserve' can become market leaders rapidly. By the middle of 1999 Freeserve had almost twice as many members as AOL. AOL has now launched its 'Netscape online' free ISP to combat Freeserve's success. In the US a similar attack from Altavista has not yet triggered a reaction – except from AOL's worried shareholders.

Consider *stickiness* and *switching costs* at AOL. Traditionally AOL has been weak on the former, many people just use it for Internet access, but it is relatively strong on the latter, particularly so far as its e-mail base is concerned. But AOL is beginning to suffer increasing customer defections or *churn*. This is particularly acute in the UK against Freeserve (and around 200 other free ISPs)!

Another *switching cost* that AOL, particularly in Europe, has managed well is the quality and speed of its infrastructure. Sites load fast, connection failings are minimal. Whether this advantage can be sustained is an open question. In the US the next generation of technology, attractive broad-band access via cable TV is being denied to AOL because AT&T and the local cable companies have so far successfully managed to prevent it having access to the channel. Instead AOL is switching to broad-band telephone lines (ADSL) and satellite access – technologies that are less widespread and technically more complicated to implement. As always, the Internet future is uncertain.

The case study above goes to show what an investor has to think about before valuing AOL objectively. You are always seeing articles which make a great show of advising investors on which Internet firms will survive. This list is usually headed by companies like AOL, because so far AOL has proved that it has an outstanding business model. But, between 'surviving' and sustaining a P/E ratio of 350, there is lot of room for investors to lose a large part of their capital. Private investors must take note that Internet values can easily fall by 70–80 per cent if the company begins to falter. So 'cheap' purchases after individual companies' prices have 'come off the top' by a few tens of percentage points are dangerous. Most banks are poor advisers on Internet values; many of them approach us, wringing their hands, asking us to help them find their way round the Internet market and its valuations.

So do today's stellar valuations reflect the fact that institutional investors have carefully weighed up all the relevant criteria and the fact that most Internet stocks are relatively illiquid, with only 15–20% of the company in free float at best and come to a considered answer on value? The answer is clearly 'No'. Many Internet share price peaks are being driven by a small number of private investors wanting to take part in the Internet boom. As the number of leading companies becomes relatively more limited, their scarcity has an influence on prices which pushes them well beyond reflecting their real value. In our opinion, the present workings of truly efficient capital markets are not yet much in evidence.

Interestingly enough, lack of fundamental underpinning to prices does not mean that they cannot go any higher, nor that today's shareholders will at some point be the victims of a major correction. The large volume turnover in actively traded Internet stocks suggests that new investors are always trying their luck with Internet shares. So current high prices may continue for some time – so long as there are more speculative buyers than sellers. A further underpinning of stock prices comes from the mergers between Internet companies currently in vogue. Buying other companies can dampen volatility in the underlying stock.

Take *eBay* as an example. At the end of April 1999 the company was valued at $26 billion (a price–earnings ratio of about 3000)! For 260 million dollars in shares it acquired one of the largest and oldest auction houses in the USA. The target company, Butterfield & Butterfield, had many times the turnover of eBay, but only one per cent of the market capitalisation.

Spreading investors' equity risk in a single share helps reduce the possibility of a dramatic drop in individual prices. Ultimately, however, buying even well-known Internet shares is risky. Their share price has to be 'earned' by the company one day. Companies can carry this 'future obligation to profit' around for a long time, but at some time or other they have to start generating real profits. Exactly when is, partially, down to investors to decide.

Will the capital markets return to their old ways after an Internet boom?

The answer is *no*! The digital economy will continue to create very valuable intangible assets as the Internet allows new ideas and offers to be rapidly developed, tested and brought to market. These will continue to be hard to value, so the volatility of the market will not decrease. What once applied only to high-tech companies will begin to affect the whole economy as the Internet becomes a mass-market medium.

Mechanisms used to eliminate inefficiency in the market cannot resolve fundamental difficulties in valuation. However, with the growing transparency and availability of information, increasing globalisation and electronic share-dealing, stock markets around the world will converge to similar valuation points for these stocks. The intangibility of assets in the digital economy will, however, prevent it from moving to a 'perfect' market.

What does this mean for the entrepreneur?

Entrepreneurs need to use the capital markets and understand how they work, but avoid worrying about an exact valuation of their company. Perhaps a successful e-tailing initiative will only return 10–15 times the invested capital instead of 100–1000 times – but it is still a worthwhile investment. As some in Silicon Valley say: 'The fools are dancing – but the bigger fools are watching.' We may seem mad to participate, but those who remain spectators only are madder still.

Venture capitalists are the new 'keiretsus'

If bank funding is out, how do young Internet companies get access to capital before they reach the size to float on the Stock Exchange? *Venture capitalists* are the answer. Originally an American invention, venture capitalists are now widespread in

Europe. One interesting point worth noting for European readers who have entrepreneurial dreams is that European investors in this area have tended to be much more risk averse than their US counterparts. Venture capital is systematically more expensive in Europe than in the US today. So make sure you talk to a US-based firm as well as European players if you are looking for venture funding. The scale of US venture capitalists' appetite for risk-investment in e-tailing, e-shopping and Internet-related ventures is extremely impressive. In 1998 venture capitalists invested $4.5 billion in young companies in Silicon Valley alone, a billion more than in the previous year. This represented about a third of all venture capital investment in the US. 786 Silicon Valley firms attracted financing with an average investment of 5.8 million dollars.

The Internet was a major target investment, attracting $1.6 billion: a 57 per cent growth on the previous year. Earlier investment was largely for technologically orientated concerns but, in the last quarter of 1998, 72 per cent of investment went into e-tail and e-commerce ventures. At the moment there is continuing investment in e-tailing.

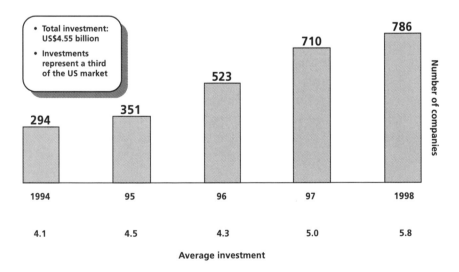

Fig. 12.1 Venture capital investment in Silicon Valley between 1994 and 1998. (Source: *San Jose Mercury News.*)

*Two years ago we thought that most money would be made
in business-to-business e-commerce. In 1998 it became clear
that opportunities [for venture capitalists] in business-to-consumer could be even bigger.*

Promod Haque (Partner, Norwest Partners, Palo Alto)

This consumer focus has now made Silicon Valley one of
the most important centres for e-tailing initiatives in the world.
Most venture capital firms are partnerships that obtain their
investment money from institutional investors (e.g. pension
funds, mutual funds). They invest against a set of criteria that
clearly sets them apart from those institutions whose money
they are themselves investing.

It is worth understanding how venture capitalists access
investment opportunities. Even if you do not plan to fall back
on venture capital, you can measure your own e-tailing initiative using their criteria and should watch the way your competitors deal with financing.

Unlike debt funding, venture capital ultimately withdraws
from the company at a given time, providing the venture investors their 'exit'. Their money is made by the company's increase in value up to their 'exit'. As a rule most venture capital
funds have an investment horizon up to ten years. The most
talked-about exit for a company is *listing on a stock exchange*. As
soon as the company is traded on the capital market, the initial
investors can, over time, sell their shares and realise their profits.

As most of our readers will be aware, the leading international exchange for young, growth-orientated and technology-
related companies is the Nasdaq, based in New York. The *Neuer
Markt* in Frankfurt has a similar set-up but is comparatively small,
while the Easdaq is a rival exchange based in Luxembourg. The
Neuer Markt is perhaps the most successful in Europe, accounting for around 80 per cent of European capitalisation for such
new stocks. The Neuer Markt is currently mostly traded by private investors. For many institutional investors, there is still not
enough liquidity in the market, i.e. purchases or sales of large

Venture capitalists' criteria

◆ *A potential 'mega-market' opportunity must exist*
The company should have an addressable market potential of several billion dollars. This is no problem for many e-tailing companies.

◆ *The venture should have a clear 'unique selling point' (USP)*
The proposition to customers must be new and superior, and a demonstrable competitive edge must be defensible. This is by far the greatest obstacle with e-tailing ventures. For first movers there is often a first-to-market advantage which needs defending by raising switching costs and building customer loyalty. In some instances the USP rule is relaxed because the option of a sale to a wealthy competitor is seen as a critical 'exit' route.

◆ *The company should be a market leader in its sector*
As there are now no limits to expansion, but there are also low entry barriers to a sector, aggressive growth is critical for success. Growth is needed in demonstrating leadership, bottom-line results are less important. Paradoxically, good bottom-line results too early make people suspicious that the company is not investing enough in expansion. Market-leaders aim to get into a self-reinforcing cycle rapidly and outgrow their competition.

◆ *The company should be a springboard for other business ideas*
Venture capitalists look for entrepreneurs with more than just one isolated idea; they want a lever for getting into additional businesses. Hotmail, now owned by Microsoft, is a good example here. At its outset, many venture capitalists saw it as simply a web application that mirrored functionality available to corporate users on their office networks. As such it was a potentially valuable idea on its own. To Microsoft, and to those venture capitalists with heightened insight, it was a springboard for delivery of a whole range of additional services and functions.

◆ *The company must have a strong management team*
The management team must include a good mixture of fresh idea generators and people experienced in the industry. For example, Amazon systematically reinforced its young team by poaching from Wal-Mart, the world's largest retailer. (After Amazon had poached 15 of their management team, Wal-Mart reacted with a lawsuit that has only recently been settled.)

◆ *The company has to show flexibility and pragmatism*
Internet companies need to be able to evolve rapidly. Markets, technology, competition, customer preferences and business frameworks will constantly change. The company and its management need to exhibit capacity for flexibility and demonstrate that they can pragmatically deal with change.

amounts of shares are either not possible or lead to heavy falls in prices.

An alternative 'exit' is a 'trade sale' of shares to another company. Venture capitalists have tended to see this as a second-best option, because the valuations obtained have been lower than those on the capital markets. There are signs that this is changing as the Nasdaq, in particular, is quite crowded with new IPOs (initial public offerings) on the one hand and established Internet players pay huge acquisition premiums on the other. On a trade sale, venture capitalists usually sell all their shares in one go and withdraw from the company immediately.

Established venture capital funds in the US are now so large that they often no longer participate in the early stages of founding a company. The amounts to be invested are simply too small to be worthwhile. A 'foundation' role has been taken over by the so-called *business angels*, often entrepreneurs who have already made money from the Internet boom and want to offer it as start-up capital to young entrepreneurs. Large funds now tend to concentrate on investing capital in the later stages of a company. Some start-ups require very large capital input early on, so that they can conquer a mega-market quickly. *Healtheon/WebMD*, which have the whole health market in their sights, are such an example.

Venture capitalists will sit on the board of the company and take an active part in business strategy. Through their contacts, they can set up alliances with key business partners. They often headhunt management. The participation of a leading

Venture capital case study – Kleiner Perkins

The list of successful investments of Kleiner Perkins (KP) is so long that it reads like a *Who's who?* of the Internet. Figure 12.2 shows their most important investments in Internet companies, and underlines the fluid nature of how and where investments 'make it' for their backers. For example, Netscape, in spite of its importance today as a portal, is still listed under software investments. Kleiner Perkins has so often been compared to a Japanese 'keiretsu' that it now describes itself as such. The most important similarity with a keiretsu is its activity in initiating partnerships among its investments. This is an important plus-point for young entrepreneurs. Jeff Bezos, founder of Amazon, chose Kleiner Perkins as its 'lead investor' for this reason, although it valued his company much lower than other investors. The acquisition of Drugstore.com by Amazon was KP senior partner John Doerr's idea – he was the lead investor in both companies. A catalyst for such deals is the twice-yearly meeting of the current CEOs of the companies in which KP has invested – one of the most important events in Silicon Valley.

Kleiner Perkins' power to lead a company to success is now so great that a call to ask whether you would like to be CEO of one of their investments is treated like a win on the lottery.

One impressive demonstration of KP's power was the deal between AOL, Netscape and Sun at the end of 1998.

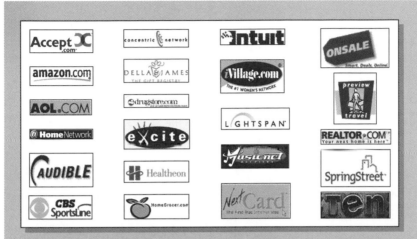

Fig. 12.2   Kleiner Perkins Caufield & Byers' Internet portfolio.

All three companies are financed by KP. AOL acquired Netscape, known for its Internet browser. But AOL's real interest in Netscape was for its Internet portal and its e-commerce platforms. Still more significant was the simultaneous alliance with Sun, which gave access to Java technology but also an entry into AOL TV. Without KP the alliance would not have taken place.

Interestingly, all this is perhaps only one piece of a larger jigsaw which maps a fight between KP and Microsoft, although publicly KP denies going up against them. Ultimately, for some of their investments (e.g. Compaq) KP needs good relations with them. In other areas (e.g. Healtheon/WebMD), KP and Microsoft are even investment partners post-merger. There is at least one other large initiative in which KP is participating. John Doerr is a close friend of Al Gore and is supporting his campaign for the US presidency. There are clear indications that Al Gore was the driving force behind the US Justice Department instigating cartel proceedings against Microsoft.

In Silicon Valley many people see Kleiner Perkins' dabbling in politics as a step too far.

venture capital firm is a strong endorsement of quality for a start-up and is of enormous value beyond the number of dollars invested. Venture capitalists need to make things happen rapidly to protect their investment in a fast-moving marketplace. One good example, and a mould-breaker for the industry is *Idealab!* In this incubator ideas are originated, founded and then the company that results is actually supported with management and office infrastructure until it reaches 40, 50 or more staff. This active support of growth effectively reduces the risk of investment.

Venture capital firms expend a great deal of energy searching for markets with great opportunities. Often, but not always, these opportunities arise through new technology developments. As soon as interesting markets have been identified, companies in the relevant field are systematically sought out and financed. In this way venture capitalists aggressively 'filter out' those business plans which interest them from the hundreds (if not thousands) that they receive each year. Sometimes they go so far as finding the right management team for their own ideas and initiate the start up themselves. This is the space in which David Gross' *Idealab!* operates.

As an example, take another look at eBay. *Benchmark Partners*, the lead investor, gave founder, Pierre Omidyar, the start-capital in 1995. They maintain that they had already identified the idea of an Internet auction house as a promising business model. Given this, the deal went through very quickly and Benchmark took an active part in completing the management team, laying the foundation stone for its current success.

The large venture capital firms exercise a strong influence on the whole of Internet business and that means e-tailing too. The most powerful among them is *Kleiner Perkins Caufield & Byers*, Kleiner Perkins or KP for short. Within Kleiner Perkins, John Doerr is the undisputed star of the scene.

All large venture capitalists in the US adopt similar 'investment networking' strategies with their investment portfolios, even if not at the same level as Kleiner Perkins. Softbank, lead investor with Yahoo, is perhaps the most closely connected to this 'Kereitsu strategy' as it has a Japanese parent company, but Mayfield, Sequoia Capital, Benchmark Partners and many others are similar in approach.

We hope our brief excursion into the world of venture capitalists gives some perspective on what they can do for a company. For young entrepreneurs, having an influential venture capitalist on side is one of the keys to success.

Keeping up with e-tailing trends

If you are interested in the prospects for e-tailing, watch who is putting large sums of money into it! Examine the portfolios of the large venture capital firms regularly. These are usually published as public relations material. An informative web-site in this area is operated by *San Jose Mercury News. The Red Herring* magazine is a good source of information too. For anyone entering e-tailing, understanding the next generation of competitors and who is backing them is a must.

'Equity is the new cash' for Internet companies

Success on the capital market is important for the entrepreneur for many reasons, as we explained at the beginning of the chapter. In this section we look more closely at mergers and acquisitions and why a buoyant share price can be a distinct advantage.

Mergers and acquisitions are a core element of any successful e-tailing strategy, and highly rated shares make them a cheap way of achieving success in two areas:

Innovation

First one has to be innovative to survive. Even leading companies in Silicon Valley have seen that the majority of innovations happen outside their companies, often by entrepreneurs who leave to fund their own start-ups. So there are regular acquisitions in the Internet industry, buying innovation 'back in'.

One company that has perfected the principle of 'Innovation through acquisition' is *Cisco*, the world market leader in routers, which provide much of the infrastructure of the Internet. Cisco systematically buys technologies and entrepreneurs and has been very successful doing so. In the last five years they have made more than 30 acquisitions, mostly around $100–200 million. But these price tags are rising too. Recently Cisco has stunned the world by acquiring Cerent Corp., a technology company with only $10 million in sales, for more than $7 billion. Many of Cisco's purchases have been of firms which have not yet managed to generate any sales. Where others have failed, Cisco stands out. Even as a large company it can successfully form alliances with entrepreneurs and integrate small acquisitions. The key to this success is that CEO, John Chambers, personally looks after the wellbeing of acquired companies. Many of Cisco's business units today can be traced back to an acquisition of a specific idea or technology.

Cisco's success story is worth a book of its own, exploring how it has always known where to lead the technologies of those companies it acquired, using both experience and market muscle.

Speed

Fighting for market leadership demands speed. Often acquisition is the best way to do things quickly. When *Amazon* realised that it had to expand into Europe as quickly as possible, it bought into England and Germany. To expand into new business areas it acquired *Drugstore.com* and took shares in *Sotheby's*, the auctioneer. Their technology platform was strengthened by acquiring *Junglee* and *Accept*. You need only look at the acquisitions history of Amazon to get a feel for how important they are as part of any development strategy.

The currency for these acquisitions is shares in the acquiror. For one thing, Internet buyers are short of cash, so they can only finance acquisitions with shares. For another, there are tax-efficient ways of exchanging shares, which at the same time solve the problem of large goodwill write-downs. Usually buyers and sellers are 'growth stocks', i.e. they pay no dividends and the shareholders expect their compensation when the shares go up in value.

As we have said already, share exchange is also another way in which very highly valued companies can 'invest' part of their value in other businesses. But it would be risky for an Internet company to acquire a large traditional player in this way. For example, what if *AOL* were to try to take over a media giant like *Disney*? It would probably cause AOL's share price to collapse. For one thing it would lose its clear positioning as a stock (growth or dividend?), for another, Disney is so much bigger that it would ultimately become the dominant business and the original value of AOL could be destroyed.

These examples make it clear how important it is to look after the share price as part of the strategy of a young company. A high share price gives many degrees of freedom with acquisitions. The press like reporting on acquisitions, and customers sit up and take notice while investors, sensing growth, feel reassured that they have bought into the right company.

We have already advised many large companies who have asked us how to be successful in their e-tailing without access to equity capital markets. Our answer is always the same: 'If you can't beat them, join them'. Hive off your e-tailing initiatives and bring them to the stock market yourself. If you don't want to take all the risks, find venture capitalists as co-funders. Our profound hope is that if you follow the advice in this book, you will have the chance to create more wealth than you ever could with your established business.

E-tail searchlight on web-sites for Chapter 12

- ◆ AOL   www.aol.com
- ◆ Compuserve   www.compuserve.com
- ◆ Netscape   www.netscape.com
- ◆ ICQ   www.icq.com
- ◆ eBay   www.ebay.com
- ◆ Interstoxx   www.interstoxx.de
- ◆ Benchmark Partners   www.benchmark.com
- ◆ Kleiner Perkins   www.kpcb.com
- ◆ Idealab   www.idealab.com
- ◆ Sun   www.sun.com
- ◆ San Jose Mercury News   www.mercurycenter.com
- ◆ The Red Herring   www.redherring.com
- ◆ Cisco   www.cisco.com
- ◆ Mobilcom   www.mobilcom.de

Epilogue

E-Tailing is driving a fascinating transformation of the relationship between companies and their end-customers. What does it mean for the future? Where will it end?

Jeff Bezos, founder of Amazon.com, sketched this picture of the future in an interview with the Wall Street Journal: 'The Internet today is like the Cambrian explosion 550 million years ago. That was when single-celled life exploded into multicellular life. Nobody knows what caused that. It's a mystery. That was the greatest rate of speciation ever seen on the Earth – but many people don't know that it was also the period with the greatest rate of extinction. There were a lot of dead ends.' (WSJ Special Report E-Commerce, 12 July 1999).

Unlike biological evolution, entrepreneurs do not have to depend on help from arbitrary mutations to develop their businesses. The present climate contains many risks, but you can learn what promising initiatives in the new, unfamiliar environment look like. A pure copy of supposedly successful concepts elsewhere, however, will not help you. You have to be innovative, creative, and become the market leader in your own segment if you want to master the *challenges of the next stage of e-tail evolution*:

◆ rapid globalisation via acquisition or strong partnerships
◆ installation of anytime, anywhere access for an attractive customer group
◆ complementary online/offline concepts for future brand ubiquity
◆ new forms of customer relationship management for an increasingly discerning client base
◆ redefinition and re-invigoration of markets with built-to-order concepts
◆ innovative business models for digital products and services
◆ mastery of the capital markets – rather then being mastered by them.

Like Columbus you have to embrace the risks of setting off in new directions, but you do not have to set the sails blindly. This book is intended as your constant travelling companion.

We would like to conclude with the words of Thomas Middelhoff, the Internet-savvy CEO of media giant Bertelsmann, warning his operations-minded contemporaries:

'Strategy matters in these fast changing times!'

Acknowledgements

We would like to thank our wives Farhah, Steffica and Sue for their loving support and our children Edward, Emily, Jack, Jennifer, Myriam, Tamara and William for accommodating their fathers.

We are grateful to our colleagues at OC&C Strategy Consultants and The McKenna Group, in particular Vijay Bobba, Hans-Dieter Kleinhückelskoten, Peter Menk, Marc André Micha and Markus Thill for their valuable contributions and support during our work on this book.

Our fellow partners at OC&C and The McKenna Group Joachim Bähre, Luke Jensen, Hans-Christian Limmer, Regis McKenna, Pam Kline, Amiel Kornel, Hiroshi Menjo, Riccardo Monti, Geoff Mott, Chris Outram, Gerd Schnetkamp, Amy

Shuen and Narry Singh have encouraged us throughout the writing of this book and made valuable contributions.

Finally we would like to express our indebtedness to our clients on both sides of the Atlantic. Developing their strategies and meeting their challenges provided an intense stimulus, without which this book would not have been possible.

Index